The Army in Texas
During Reconstruction,
1865–1870

The Army in Texas During Reconstruction

1865–1870

WILLIAM L. RICHTER

TEXAS A&M UNIVERSITY PRESS
College Station

Library of Congress Cataloging-in-Publication Data

Richter, William L. (William Lee), 1942–
    The Army in Texas during Reconstruction, 1865–1870.
    (Texas A&M University military history series; no. 3)
    Bibliography: p.
    Includes index.
    1. Reconstruction—Texas.   2. Texas—History—
1846–1950.   3. United States.   Army—History—19th
century.   I. Title.
F391.R54   1987   976.4   86-30056
ISBN 0-89096-282-0

To my father and mother

Contents

List of Maps and Tables

Preface

In any volume dealing with a past era, certain terms may confuse the reader. In this book, such terms include the complicated and bewildering series of political labels used in Texas during Reconstruction. During and after the Civil War, two broad groups dominated the state's political climate. One of these factions was known as the Secessionists and included a majority of the state's white population. The Secessionists had favored Texas' adherence to the Confederate cause and had little desire to recant their principles during Reconstruction. The Secessionists were opposed by an active minority faction labeled the Unionists, or Loyalists. This antisecession group comprised Texans who had actively or passively resisted Confederate authority during the war. These two factions were joined after the war by a third group generally called Conservatives. Although opposed to Reconstruction, the Conservatives wished Texas to rejoin the Union as quickly as possible. They included some Loyalists who desired to forget the war's hatreds and a large group of former Secessionists who were willing to make some concessions to the victorious North and who tended to comply with President Andrew Johnson's Reconstruction policies.

By 1867, these groups had shifted their positions somewhat and had assumed new labels. Conservatives now were those who opposed the new Military Reconstruction measures. Within the Conservative party a few die-hard Secessionists preferred to be known as Democrats. But most Texans, believing that the specter of a revitalized Democratic party would be disturbing to the Republican majority in Congress, eschewed the name "Democratic." Opposed to the Conservatives, who counted most white voters in their ranks, was the infant state Republican party. The Republicans included former Unionists and converted Secessionists, who were collectively and derisively referred to as scalawags; a few newly arrived Northern immigrants, called carpetbaggers; and the recently enfranchised black population.

Texas Republicans enjoyed the backing of a select group of the registered voters. The party could not capitalize on this support, however, for it suffered from a severe philosophical split that became obvious during the 1868–69 state constitutional convention and that greatly weakened the party's already shaky minority position in the state. One faction was known as the Radicals. These men wanted to disfranchise the former Confederates in order to maintain Republican numerical and moral dominance in Texas and favored rejecting all laws passed and legal actions pursued by the Confederate state government during the war. The other faction was called the Moderates. These men, who saw themselves as the thinking element of the Republican party, believed that the party had to compromise with the Conservatives to attract the needed white majority to the Republican ranks. Hence they called for no political proscription of former Confederates and for the acceptance of most laws enacted and governmental actions taken during the Civil War.

In addition to political designations, military rank may be puzzling to readers. During the Civil War, the Union army expanded rapidly to meet emergency war needs. To facilitate this growth, an officer could receive a commission in either the United States Army (USA) or the United States Volunteers (USV) or sometimes in both. While USA commissions were fairly permanent, the USV commissions were understood to be effective merely for the duration of the conflict. Professional soldiers often had a USA and a USV designation, since the latter service, because it included a majority of enlistments, offered the potential of faster, although temporary, advancement. The citizen-turned-soldier always received a USV rank initially, but some of the more enterprising men managed later to obtain permanent USA ranks. Furthermore, within the USA and USV categories, each officer had the possibility of actual rank and brevet rank. The latter, a holdover from the old British army of the colonial era, was an honorary rank bestowed upon an officer for meritorious conduct in the field or given to allow him to serve on a staff or special assignment at appropriate rank without an actual promotion. The brevet officer usually had none of the pay and few of the other privileges of actual USA or USV rank, but he did command those who might otherwise outrank him.

During Texas Reconstruction, all general officers except Philip H. Sheridan and Winfield Scott Hancock served in USV or brevet capacities while commanding either the state or the regional department that included Texas. Controversies over seniority that developed were compounded when one officer had senior brevet rank while another in the same chain of command had the senior actual rank. These controversies may seem picayune and confusing today; they often were bewildering at the time, as well. Those interested in the technicalities of brevet rank should consult James B. Fry, *The History and Legal Effects of Brevets* . . . (New York, 1877); Mark M. Boatner III, *The Civil War Dictionary* (New York, 1959), pp. 84, 328–29; and Don Russell, "Introduction," in Percival G. Lowe, *Five Years a Dragoon and Other Adventures on the Great Plains* (Norman, 1965), pp. xvi–xxii.

Finally, in quoting documents of the period, I have retained the original spelling and punctuation. Rather than intersperse the quotations with [*sic*], I indicate any disagreement with the author's grammar or spelling in the note.

I am indebted to a great many people for their help in writiing this book. I appreciate the advice and criticism given by the late T. Harry Williams of Louisiana State University, as well as the personal support of Burl Noggle, Charles B. Dew, and John L. Loos. I am particularly grateful to James E. Sefton of the California State University at Northridge for his continued friendship and assistance. Bob T. Quinten and David Miller of Cameron University graciously cooperated in solving numerous research problems.

The directors and staffs of the following departments and institutions provided able assistance: the National Archives; the Federal Records Center, Fort Worth, Texas; the Manuscripts Division of the Library of Congress; the Barker Historical Center, the Archives, the Newspaper Collection, and the Library of the University of Texas; the Archives of the Texas State Library; the Archives of the Austin Public Library; the Library and the Department of Archives and Manuscripts of the Louisiana State University; the Morris Sweatt Library, Field Artillery Training School, Fort Sill, Oklahoma; the Library of the Museum of the Great Plains, Lawton, Oklahoma; the Library of Cameron University, Lawton, Oklahoma; and the Library of the University of Arizona. Part of my research was made possible by a grant from the Warrick Memorial Fund of Louisiana State University.

A final word of appreciation goes to Paul G. Hubbard, Otis E. Young, and Ron Smith, all of Arizona State University, for opening up the fascinating world of history to me; to Margaret Maxwell, Harwood Hinton, Bruce Dinges, Cecil Wellborn, and Robert Hershoff

of the University of Arizona, who gave me timely encouragement; to
Dr. James Rybski, of the Department of Family and Community Medi-
cine, Arizona Health Sciences Center, Tucson; and to Don Bufkin,
whose excellent maps illustrate this study. Most of all, I am indebted
to my wife, Lynne, whose love and assistance made this book possible.

The Army in Texas
During Reconstruction,
1865–1870

Introduction:
The Military Supervision of Civil Government

Under the head of Military Necessity, . . .
a nation has well nigh parted with her liberties.

—*Brownsville Daily Ranchero,*
March 6, 1868

The fall of the Confederate States of America and the impact of defeat on Southerners as Americans are subjects that have fascinated students of United States history for over a century. Part of the reason lies in the fratricidal nature of the Civil War, which gives that conflict a unique closeness and familiarity for Americans. Some of the reason rests in the fact that, among a nation whose history is largely a tale of momentous successes, Southern whites alone have known defeat and occupation by a foreign power. Southerners, after all, underwent Reconstruction.[1]

As one of the states of the Confederacy, the experience of Texas offers in microcosm a view of the Civil War's losers. As in other states, the Reconstruction of Texas saw the culmination of many ante- and interbellum political tendencies. Particularly important were the continual centralization of state government in the hands of the executive and the meddling in government by military commanders who were enforcing policies that emanated from the national capital. Military supervision of local government, whether Confederate or Yankee in origin, came to be viewed as a tyranny.[2]

Texas has had a history of fighting real or supposed tyrannies. Her own war for independence began in part over the power that the Mexican government attempted to assert in its northern provinces. The Texas revolutionaries were especially angry with Generalissimo Antonio López de Santa Anna's imposition of military rule and his suspension of political guarantees set forth in the 1824 Mexican Constitution.[3]

3

Introduction

The idea of military supervision of civil government, regardless of its justification, has always been reprehensible, not only to Texans, but to all Americans.[4] This dislike is a part of our British heritage that stems from the Whig suspicion of the army as the potential guarantor of executive tyranny. Parliament met this threat during the Glorious Revolution by passing the Mutiny Act, which severely limited military independence from the legislature by providing for an annual appropriation and a review of the soldier's necessity to British society.[5]

The view that the military forces were not independent or superior to the civil power became ingrained in our consciousness during the colonial period. Americans so objected to the use of British troops to enforce parliamentary legislation in the 1760s that they instituted a mass protest that culminated in the Boston Massacre and the removal of soldiers from administering civil affairs.[6]

When the army, under the Intolerable Acts, again administered the Massachusetts colonial government, the Founding Fathers felt compelled to list in the Declaration of Independence the military supervision of government and the suspension of the local legislature as prime reasons for our own revolution. This suspicion of armed force was enshrined in the Articles of Confederation, which provided for no national defense beyond the citizen militia,[7] and the later Constitution of 1789, which allowed for a permanent national military establishment but subordinated it to the civilian leaders elected by the people.[8]

The South, particularly the Southwest including Texas, considered itself a bastion of this traditional democracy. In Texas and other states of the lower South, the power of the governor was subordinated to the will of the legislature. Texans thus saw the increased power of the executive, represented by some state governors, the Confederate military command, and then the U.S.-appointed provisional governors backed by the Federal army district commanders, as an imbalance in government.[9]

During the antebellum period Texas, more than any other state, was controlled by states' rights Democrats. Even those within the party who had opposed secession admitted to states' rights, so long as the states stayed within the Union. When the Civil War began, Louis T. Wigfall, a Texas senator, helped lead the opposition to Jefferson Davis's centralization of Confederate power in Richmond, while state politicians back home guarded Texas from possible encroachments by Lieutenant General E. Kirby-Smith's military government, headquartered nearby in Shreveport.[10]

The demands of war caused Texas governors to act more aggressively and independently than at any time since the days of the Republic. Lieutenant Governor Edward Clark assumed control after Sam Houston refused to take the oath to the Confederacy and worked closely with Confederate authorities to raise and supply troops for the national war effort. He opened relations with Mexican officials as well. Clark lost a close race for reelection in August, 1861, probably because of his willingness to send state troops to defend Richmond.[11]

His elected successor, Francis R. Lubbock, prosecuted the war by centralizing as much control as possible in the governorship. Lubbock actively supported the Confederate war effort, openly prodding the legislature to accede to his proposed measures, which made Clark appear vacillating at best.

Lubbock guaranteed the state's credit, provided for the needs of indigent and soldier families, organized frontier defense, and carried on an active campaign against Union Loyalists and draft dodgers in which he supported the suspension of the writ of habeas corpus and the introduction of martial rule in disaffected areas. Lubbock also called a conference of the trans-Mississippi Confederate governors to show their support of the central government and to voice mutual concerns over the tendency of Richmond to ignore the far-flung areas of the Confederacy. For various reasons, some of which revolved around his support of the central government's interests rather than those of the state and his vigorous support of martial law, Lubbock did not run for reelection in the summer of 1863.[12]

At the time of the 1863 gubernatorial election, the Trans-Mississippi Department, of which Texas was a part, occupied a unique position. The Vicksburg–Port Hudson campaigns had separated the rebel state governments of Missouri, Arkansas, Louisiana, and Texas from the rest of the Confederacy. Officials west of the river realized that their isolated condition would make it virtually impossible to communicate rapidly with the Davis government. Accordingly, representatives from the four western Confederate states met in Marshall, Texas, on August 15, to discuss the situation and formulate a joint plan of action. The delegates concluded that the Trans-Mississippi Department was so disconnected from the rest of the South as to make it a separate nation within the Confederacy, and as such, it should have the right to act independently of the Richmond government.

Although President Davis did not like this departure from the Confederate Constitution, he quietly sanctioned the assumption of additional powers of government by General Edmund Kirby-Smith, the commander of the department. Kirby-Smith was permitted to handle the military functions of the secretary of war, to establish army bureaus similar to those in Richmond, and to discharge all military functions except the right to promote officers permanently. He was also given command of all areas in the department that had been previously outside his jurisdiction. In addition, Kirby-Smith was told to form a civil government, but no details were sent on its possible composition.

In December, 1863, the Confederate Congress extended Kirby-Smith's powers, making them more formal and official. The Trans-Mississippi Department was to duplicate all of the functions of the executive branch, and the region was recognized as completely separate from the eastern Confederacy. Although Kirby-Smith was not allowed to reproduce the entire Confederate government on a smaller scale, the Confederate Congress acquiesced in his personal assumption of wider powers of civil government as the situation demanded.[13]

In the meanwhile, Lubbock's successor as Texas governor, Pendleton Murrah, had assumed power in Austin. Murrah's position on the national and state issues of the day was vague. He considered himself a "strict constructionist" and a "conservative," but his electoral support came from those who would call him a "Confederate nationalist." He was as much in favor of final Southern victory as Lubbock (who had supported his campaign) but was uncertain as to how to prosecute the war. He did not like the use of Confederate military power in the civilian realm.[14]

Murrah and other trans-Mississippi state governors supported Kirby-Smith's administration until the spring of 1864, when the general tried to enforce the conscript law, impress cotton and slaves, and control transportation and trade to enhance the war effort. Immediately Murrah opposed the general's actions resisting particularly the impressment of slaves, the transfer of state troops to Confederate command, and the impressment of cotton.[15]

Although many newspaper editors criticized Murrah's actions as devious at best, he actually gave in on most issues at an August, 1864, conference in Hempstead with Kirby-Smith's Texas subordinate, Major General John B. Magruder. But for some in Texas, states' rights were more than mere talk, and they saw Murrah's stand—while it lasted—as heroic and principled and his critics as "sycophantic toadying creatures bought by the Military."[16] The rallying point for the states' righters was the suspension of the writ of habeas corpus by the Confederate Congress in February, 1864. A holdover from the Lubbock administration, this popular issue united Texans of all political hues, including Secessionists (states' righters), "Texas Firsters," and Unionists (anti-Confederates).[17]

The cutting edge of the attack against the suspension came from the state supreme court and the state legislature, not the governor. The court ruled on a series of habeas corpus cases during the war. The most important were ex parte *Frank H. Coupland* and ex parte *Richard Peebles.* Both were rebukes of military government, mild as these criticisms were in their effect.

In the *Coupland* case the court upheld the Confederate conscription laws. In a stinging dissent, however, Judge James H. Bell challenged government authority to use troops to enforce measures of doubtful constitutionality. He referred to the "necessary and proper" clause of the Confederate Constitution and declared that it was not an open grant of power but a means of guaranteeing the execution of specifically granted powers enumerated in the document.[18]

In the *Peebles* case, the state supreme court denied the suspension of the writ of habeas corpus and compelled the release of five men arrested under military authority for treason and conspiracy against the Confederacy. They fined the defendant, General Magruder, only the amount of court costs. In a series of resolutions, the state legislature supported the court, noting Bell's earlier stance.[19]

As Lieutenant Governor Fletcher S. Stockdale stated, "The military's tendency 'to absorb all power and to make the will of the Commander the rule of law' endangered the experiment in nation-making and the 'old English' and American 'principles of civil liberty.'" Stockdale greatly feared any officer, especially career professionals, who continually expressed doubts about the ability of republican forms of government to handle properly the demands of wartime emergencies.[20]

Although the opponents of Confederate policy probably did not intend it, the public conflicts with the military men who carried out that policy did intensify public dislike of the army. Just as Texans ardently opposed Kirby-Smith's control of civil government, so they had no inclination to allow any outside power to run local politics, no matter how noble the cause in question. They would even oppose their own elected Reconstruction government—the James W. Throckmorton administration—when that government had the temerity to suggest mild cooperation with U.S. Army Reconstruction efforts to prevent further coercion of the state by the conquering North. The fight to rid Texas of Confederate military despots ironically resulted only in rule by Yankee satraps.[21]

Historians have commonly traced the collapse of Reconstruction to the race problem.[22] And yet, had there been no racial conflict to solve, Reconstruction would have had to surpass another great barrier, namely, the onus of relying upon the army to enforce "proper" behavior in the South.[23] The use of troops as part of a fervent commitment to achieve a noble good blinded its adherents to important secondary consequences. In effect, it subverted centuries of British-American legal traditions.

The Yankees were not alone. White Southerners would deny due process of the laws to blacks yet guarantee it for themselves. The victorious North would deny it to white Southerners in an attempt to guarantee it to black Southerners. The U.S. Congress would then enjoin the states to provide due process by forcing them to approve the Fourteenth Amendment or suffer continued military rule. The sad result was the denial of basic rights to black Americans for one hundred years after freedom and a notion, which has survived to this day, that blatant military authority could be used against American civilians.[24]

Modern historians declare that states' rights, or an overdose of democracy, was instrumental in defeating the Confederacy.[25] In the words of one Texas historian, the "Confederacy at the end was centralized to the degree that state sovereignty had almost lost its meaning." Texans and all Southerners had "absolutely nothing left to fight for."[26]

But there was a resiliency to the issue that would surprise the reconstructing authorities. In the last analysis, states' rights may not have killed only the Confederacy; it also assumed a large role in defeating Reconstruction.[27]

PART ONE
Presidential Reconstruction: The Sheridan Era, 1865–66

The condition of civil affairs in Texas is anomalous, singular, and unsatisfactory.

Maj. Gen. Philip H. Sheridan to Bvt. Maj. Gen. John A. Rawlins, November 14, 1866

1

The Occupation of Texas

MAJOR GENERAL PHILIP H. SHERIDAN disliked obstacles. He frowned upon any opposition to his own stubborn will and possessed a nervous, driving spirit that sought to crush all foes. After all, one did not become a full major general in the United States Army at the modest age of thirty-three without having produced results. And like most persons who rise quickly to the heights of their profession, Sheridan was the center of continual controversy. His role in Texas after the Civil War would be no different.

Phil Sheridan was born in 1831, but his place of birth was contested, with Massachusetts, New York, and Ohio all claiming him as a native son. Born to Irish immigrant parents, the third of six children, Sheridan grew up in Zanesville, Ohio. At the age of seventeen, through some political influence wielded by an older brother, young Phil was admitted to the United States Military Academy at West Point.

Standing only five feet six inches tall, he was a barrel-chested, muscular youth whom contemporaries described simultaneously as the best natured and most belligerent person they ever met. During his third year of study, Sheridan demonstrated his bellicose nature when he started to attack a fellow cadet with a bayonet during a heated argument. Reason fortunately prevailed, and he only beat his opponent with his fists.

His defenders noted that he was a "natural boy, full of impulse, often uncontrolled," but the incident brought Sheridan a nine-month suspension, which delayed his graduation until 1853. According to legend, he graduated only because one of his instructors "employed the argument that a belligerent temperament was not a fault in a soldier." His superiors agreed, and Phil Sheridan became a brevet second lieutenant in the First Infantry.

The army utilized Sheridan's combativeness to the fullest in the following decades. Ironically his first duty station was Fort Duncan, Texas, to which he returned a dozen years later under more auspicious circumstances. In 1855, he was made a second lieutenant in the

Fourth Infantry and was sent to Oregon. There Sheridan spent several years fighting the Yakima Indians. In 1861, another promotion and transfer brought him to Jefferson Barracks, Missouri, as a captain. Here Sheridan acted as chief quartermaster and commissary officer for the Army of the Southwest.

Like many other career officers, Sheridan became a colonel of volunteers during the Civil War. He advanced to major general and division command in the Army of the Cumberland. He fought valiantly at Stones River, Chickamauga, and Chattanooga. Impressed with the dapper little Irishman, U. S. Grant took Sheridan east with him in 1864 as chief of cavalry in the Army of the Potomac. Sheridan whipped the lethargic horsemen of the eastern theater into shape by cutting away excess baggage, equipment, and do-nothing officers. Then he proceeded to eliminate the cavalry advantage held by J. E. B. Stuart's Southern cavaliers, killing Stuart in the process.

After Grant had bottled up the Confederates at Richmond and Petersburg, he sent Sheridan north to end Jubal Early's pressure behind Washington. The energetic Sheridan not only turned Early back but completely routed the Confederate army in a series of battles, during which the Yankees methodically destroyed the productive capacity of the rich Shenandoah Valley. Rejoining Grant for the Appomattox campaign, he led the attacks and pursuit that destroyed the Army of Northern Virginia and ended the bloody four-year conflict. At Five Forks the ever-controversial Sheridan sacked the commanding general of the V Corps, G. K. Warren, for not following orders. He replaced Warren with Brevet Major General Charles Griffin, whom he put in command of the District of Texas two years later.[1]

In 1865, Sheridan was easily the most popular Union general of the war, next to Grant and Sherman. Because of his close association with Grant in the eastern theater, it was natural for Grant to turn to him as a troubleshooter. In April of 1865, Grant had plenty of problems for Sheridan to solve. Jefferson Davis and the Confederate government were still at large and rumored to be heading for Texas. The Trans-Mississippi Department of the Confederacy had not yet surrendered, and there were ominous signs that it might fight on, possibly with support from the French imperial forces which had installed the Archduke Maximilian as emperor of Mexico in 1864.

Grant therefore ordered Sheridan to forgo the grand review of the victorious Union armies in Washington and to proceed to the Southwest immediately. In compliance with Grant's orders, Sheridan boarded a train and headed west to the Ohio River. He carried with him a letter from Grant that outlined his course of action.[2] Sheridan was to occupy the Red River as far north as Shreveport; the coastal areas of Galveston, Matagorda Bay, and Corpus Christi; and the Rio Grande valley. The Rio Grande area was to be occupied in force before the others in order to cut off Confederate retreat, should they decide to fight. If he needed more men, Sheridan was merely to ask for them.[3]

Sheridan steamed down the Ohio to Cairo and then up the Mississippi to Saint Louis for a conference with Major General John Pope, the commander of the Union Department of the West. On May 29, 1865, when he announced his assumption of command of the Military Division of the Southwest, Sheridan wrote Grant, "Texas has not yet suffered from the war and will require some intimidation." As he resumed his trip southward, Sheridan set out to accomplish just such intimidation.[4]

When he arrived at his new headquarters in New Orleans, however, Sheridan found that the situation had changed markedly since his leaving Saint Louis. Much of the bellicose sentiment in the trans-Mississippi had proved to be merely talk or confined to a few officers and men and the governors of the western Confederate states.

As the end of May approached, the non-Texans in Kirby-Smith's army began to break away from their units and drift home, which caused Kirby-Smith to open negotiations in New Orleans with Brevet Major General Edward R. S. Canby, commander of the Union Department of the Gulf. On May 26, Kirby-Smith surrendered the last organized army of the Confederate States of America.[5]

With Kirby-Smith's surrender, all authority inside Texas collapsed. The state was swept by chaos and anarchy. For the next three weeks, until the arrival of the first Union forces, dejected Texas troops roamed the countryside. The soldiers degenerated into disorganized mobs that broke into arsenals and took arms and ammunition, in violation of the surrender terms, before going home. Stores and whole towns were indiscriminately looted. The state treasury was rifled. Few people were injured; most stayed clear of the looting or agreed with the soldiers that Confederate property was due them for past services to the cause. Those who disagreed or suffered losses were too few to halt the raging mobs.[6]

The breakup of the Confederate army was so rapid and complete that Acting Rear Admiral Richard K. Thatcher found coastal installations already abandoned at Sabine Pass and Matagorda Bay. Brownsville surrendered on May 31, and on June 7 Thatcher arrived at Galveston and raised the United States flag. The navy encountered so little resistance that Thatcher reduced the number of fighting ships in his fleet, even though a blockade was still in effect. Only a lack of troop ships prevented the army from following up the navy's success.[7]

Sheridan, however, did not share Thatcher's estimate of the situation. He was troubled by the unavailability of transport shipping and by the stories about armed Texans roaming the countryside. Sheridan, more than ever, was determined to make the Texans cower by a strong show of force. He envisioned an Army of Observation of at least three corps for the invasion. "This may seem like the employment of a large force to you," he wrote Grant's chief of staff, "but it is always best to go in stronghanded."[8]

The first Union unit to advance into Texas was the XIII Corps. Originally part of the Union force that Grant had used to capture Vicksburg in 1863, this unit had been broken up for garrison duty in Louisiana and the Rio Grande valley in 1864. Reconstituted in 1865 under the command of Brevet Major General Gordon Granger, the corps had participated in the siege of Mobile. Now the unit was split into three segments and sent to Texas.

Outwardly Gordon Granger seemed an able man to trust with the chores of occupation. An 1845 graduate of West Point, he fought in Mexico with the Mounted Rifle Regiment and had twice been breveted for courage in action. After the Mexican campaigns, he had become a veteran Indian fighter during the 1850s. In 1861, he came east, served in the initial campaigns in western Virginia, went to Missouri, was present at Wilson's Creek, and commanded the cavalry of the Army of the Mississippi at Island No. 10 and the siege of Corinth. After holding various positions in Kentucky, Granger commanded the Reserve Corps of the Army of the Cumberland.

At Chickamauga he marched to the decisive point of the battle without orders and helped stall the Confederate attack. Granger then headed the IV Corps at Missionary Ridge and Nashville, winding up the war as chief of the XIII Corps at the capture of Mobile. He was "outspoken and rough in manner, kindly and sympathetic at heart," although his "independence came near insubordination, and at normal times he lacked energy."[9]

As he did whenever he thought a crisis existed, Granger moved quickly to carry out Sheridan's orders. On June 19, he occupied Galveston. As the troops came ashore Granger issued two proclamations. The first, General Orders No. 3, stated simply that "all slaves are free. This involves an absolute equality of personal rights and rights of property between former masters and slaves," said Granger, "and the

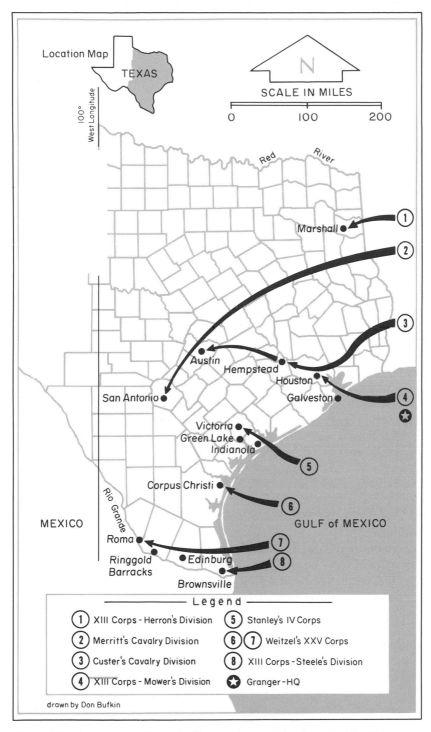

Map 1. The Occupation of Texas by Granger, June, 1865: Arrival of the Volunteers

connection heretofore existing between them becomes that between employer and hired laborer." Granger warned negroes not to congregate at army posts and not to be idle.[10]

The next, General Orders No. 4, declared all acts passed by the state authorities during the rebellion to be null and void. Confederate civil and military personnel were ordered to report to Houston, Galveston, Bonham, San Antonio, Marshall, or Brownsville to be paroled. All public property seized after the surrender was to be turned over to the Federal officials in these same towns. Those who failed to comply would be arrested and held as prisoners of war. Granger declared that those who violated the law by committing acts of homicide or theft were "outlaws and enemies of the human race who will be dealt with accordingly."[11]

Having accomplished his initial instructions, Granger then spread his forces across the vast Texas interior. The physical size of Texas was overwhelming to most soldiers stationed there and caused many mistaken notions about distances and travel time needed. More important, the size of Texas strained an already overtaxed supply and transportation system. Because the harbors were very shallow, men and matériel had to be off-loaded with lighters at all points except Galveston. Granger accordingly asked Sheridan for shallow-draft boats to use at Indianola, Corpus Christi, and Brazos Santiago.

Granger's first objective in the occupation of Texas was Houston, an important rail center for the eastern part of the state. On June 20, he sent two regiments to that city. Later, detachments from these units and four others were sent to Harrisburg, Liberty, Brenham, Hempstead, and Millican. Those towns that could not be permanently garrisoned were regularly visited by company-size patrols to promote "the cause of loyalty, safety, and industry." Usually these units searched residences and businesses alike for rebels and stolen Confederate public property.[12]

While Granger and the majority of the XIII Corps occupied Galveston and the surrounding area, another of Granger's divisions, under Brevet Major General Francis Herron, moved up the Red River to Shreveport. The townspeople welcomed Herron's men enthusiastically, glad to be rid of the looting Texans, who had fled westward.

Herron reported that the population was quiet. His greatest problem was wandering freedmen who tended to gather at military camps. By June 18, the Eighth Illinois Infantry had crossed the Texas border and occupied Marshall. Ten days later Federal forces, including two black regiments, were at Tyler and in the surrounding area.[13]

The third division of Granger's corps landed at the mouth of the

Rio Grande, under the command of Brevet Major General Frederick Steele. Brownsville had been occupied by the Yankees in late 1863, but a lack of manpower prevented them from establishing a good hold on the region. Then in July, 1864, Confederate forces wrested the city from Union control and prevented its recapture in the last battle of the Civil War, at Palmetto Ranch, May 13, 1865.

Expecting further trouble, Granger had detached Steele's command from the XIII Corps to secure the border with Mexico. Steele accepted the surrender of Brownsville on May 31 and received orders from Granger to advance up the river as far as Roma. He was also assigned command responsibilities in Indianola and Corpus Christi.

Steele occupied Roma on June 20. There he recommended further movement up the Rio Grande to Ringgold Barracks, Fort McIntosh, and Eagle Pass to seal off the Mexican border from refugees and bandits. But because of a lack of troops and transportation, Steele's men did not reach even Ringgold Barracks until August 1.[14]

Steele's ability to close off the Rio Grande depended on the arrival of the XXV (Colored) Corps from Virginia. Composed of some twenty thousand veteran soldiers, this unit had been organized in December, 1863. The corps had taken part in the Petersburg siege, was bloodied at the Battle of the Crater, and was the first unit to enter Richmond in 1865.

Commanded by Brevet Major General Godfrey Weitzel, the XXV Corps had the greatest distance to travel to reach Texas. To reduce the amount of shipping needed, Weitzel was ordered to take only one-half of his wagons and one-fourth of his mules to the Southwest, along with a "fair quantity of entrenching tools." The corps was to draw forty days' rations and embark from City Point, Virginia. By June, 1865, the XXV Corps had arrived at New Orleans, and Granger recommended that only one brigade be used to secure Indianola, another to land at Corpus Christi, while the rest of the corps would disembark at Brazos Santiago and be formed as a "movable column" to reinforce Steele.[15]

Sheridan meanwhile began to have doubts as to the necessity of expending the time and money needed to move the IV Corps from Tennessee to Texas. He already had thirty-two thousand men in Texas, a more than adequate force, judging by the lack of incidents with citizens or the French in Mexico. Before giving the IV Corps its marching orders, Sheridan made the first of his numerous trips to Texas to analyze the situation personally.

Leaving New Orleans June 20, he returned eight days later, angrier than ever. He told Grant that Kirby-Smith's surrender was a "swindle" because the Texas troops had gone home armed and unrepentant before United States authorities could parole them. He was also disturbed by the exodus of J. O. Shelby's Missouri Brigade to Mexico. Sheridan feared French complicity in encouraging more than two thousand Confederates to flee with "heavy equipment." [16]

The upshot of Sheridan's wrath was to send the IV Corps to occupy a line from Victoria to San Antonio in direct support of either Steele and Weitzel along the Rio Grande or Granger to the east. In spite of making great efforts to conclude its mission, the IV Corps found itself limited to coastal operation. One division commander in the corps said that he had enough troops "to smear all over the country, the only difficulty being the question of transportation." [17]

Finally on September 10, six regiments started marching on the road to San Antonio. Their orders were typical of the army's method of operations in Reconstruction Texas: they were to march in close order, at least one hundred yards separating each regiment, with a twenty-minute rest period each hour. The regimental officers were responsible for all straggling and illegal acts committed by the troops. No one was allowed to march separately from the column. [18]

While the infantry was struggling with its problems along the Texas coast, Sheridan was assembling an overland expedition of some nine thousand cavalrymen in the Red River valley of Louisiana to support the coastal operations. Under the command of Brevet Major General Wesley Merritt, the cavalry was divided into two columns. One, headed by Merritt, assembled at Shreveport; the other, under Brevet Major General George A. Custer, gathered at Alexandria.

Merritt's column was to travel to San Antonio via Marshall and Austin. Custer's was to march on a parallel course one hundred miles to the southeast, winding up in Houston. The cavalry would provide mounted support within marching distance of the Rio Grande, give mobility to the Union forces in east Texas, and counter the rebel sentiment in northeast Texas by a show of force. [19]

Merritt finished organizing his column several weeks before Custer, and because of the unsettled conditions along the Rio Grande, Sheridan ordered him to move without waiting for Custer's division. On July 9, "boots and saddles" was sounded and Merritt's column of 5,500 horsemen began its six-hundred-mile journey. Sheridan proudly reported that the division was "the finest which has marched during the war." The troopers suffered from the heat, which was "like the blast from a furnace," especially during the one hundred miles before Austin. Thirty days after leaving Shreveport, the column arrived in San Antonio. Merritt had allowed no straggling, and his provost marshals rode in the rear of each unit to keep the ranks closed up. It was a model march, with little to attract attention except the long column of horse soldiers that stretched back for miles in the summer sun.[20]

While Merritt's cavalry division sweated its way to San Antonio, General Custer was having a problem organizing his five regiments at Alexandria. Although Custer looked forward to the laurels he hoped to win in a campaign against either Maximilian or the unrepentant rebels, the men in the saddles behind him found their new orders to be a "sore disappointment" and expressed their "outspoken dissatisfaction" with them.[21]

The appointment of Custer was a bitter disappointment, not only for the lower ranks, but for Brevet Major General Benjamin H. Grierson, whom Canby had initially assigned to command the Alexandria column. Grierson took Sheridan's assignment of Custer as a personal affront, as he revealed ten years later when he unburdened himself to his wife on a more recent Sheridan slight. "It is in perfect keeping with the many orders I have received from Sheridan since I first came under his command in August 1865." Referring disapprovingly to the Irishman's reputation as a heavy drinker, the straitlaced Grierson wrote how "Sherry-dan" was merely "making a place for two of his *toadies*—Custer and Merritt." The usually mild-mannered Grierson vowed "sooner or later—I will get even with this man," a promise he never kept. Sheridan relegated him to a nondescript staff job and ultimately had him mustered out of the volunteer service and sent home to Illinois. Although Grierson never publicized his ire that summer of 1865, his was a sentiment the men in the ranks echoed.[22]

The dissatisfied troopers of Custer's division left Alexandria on August 8, crossed the Sabine River, and entered Newton County, Texas. The heat and dust that had plagued Merritt's march played havoc with this second column. At night the men camped amid rattlesnakes and swarms of insects, which prevented any real sleep. When the column neared Houston, General Granger diverted its march to Hempstead, where the grass and forage for the animals promised to be more adequate. On August 25, the weary troopers dismounted at Hempstead, where they stayed until the end of October, before moving west to Austin.[23]

With the arrival of the infantry and mounted units of the Army of Observation, Sheridan could now turn to solve two command problems that had plagued him since coming to the Southwest. The first of these "anomalies," as Sheridan called anything he found distasteful, was his relationship to Geneal Canby at New Orleans.

In the original orders setting up the southwestern command structure, Grant had appointed Canby as head of the Department of the Gulf, which included the Gulf states from the Florida Keys north and west to the Sabine River on the Texas-Louisiana border. Sheridan, on the other hand, was responsible for the Military Division of the Southwest, which began on the west bank of the Mississippi River and included all territory south of the Arkansas River to the Mexican border.[24]

In other words, Sheridan and Canby each had jurisdiction over the part of Louisiana west of the Mississippi. Even more embarrassing to Sheridan was the fact that he had to "*request*" [emphasis Sheridan's] cooperation from Canby in all matters, especially staff work and logistical support. Sheridan jealously resented this requirement because Canby was his junior in rank, whether in the volunteer service, regular army, or by brevet.[25]

Grant was responsive to Sheridan's complaint and created a new Military Division of the Gulf composed of three departments, including Florida, Mississippi, and Louisiana and Texas. Sheridan then subdivided the latter into five subdistricts, two for Louisiana under Canby, who became Sheridan's subordinate in the new system, and three in Texas.[26]

Sheridan did not place the Texas subdistricts under the supervision of General Granger at Galveston, because Granger was his second command problem. Granger was simply too friendly with former Confederate officials. As early as May 29, when he was still in charge of Mobile, he had recommended to President Andrew Johnson that Alabamans immediately be restored to the Union "with their vested rights."

Because of this letter, Grant held Granger suspect and asked Sheridan if he thought Granger's removal was advisable. Sheridan took the hint and said it would be best that Granger leave Texas. He, too, believed Granger was lackadaisical in his Reconstruction duties, for Granger had allowed the organization of citizen police units (contrary to Sheridan's orders), assisted former slaveholders in enforcing labor contracts rather than Negro rights, and refrained from aiding the recently arrived provisional state government unless the United States was directly involved in the dispute in question.[27]

On July 19, Sheridan ordered Granger to report to the War Department for reassignment. When the puzzled officer asked why he was being relieved after serving less than a month in Texas, Sheridan feigned ignorance. He told Granger that the impending consolidation of the XIII Corps into one division was "probably the principle reason."[28]

Granger's replacement was Brevet Major General Horatio G. Wright, a man with an excellent military record. Graduated second in the class of 1841 at West Point, Wright had entered the engineers, supervised harbor and fortification improvements, and taught French and engineering at West Point before the war. He was captured by the Confederates at Norfolk in 1861, released, and then became a volunteer aide-de-camp and chief engineer under Brevet Major General Samuel P. Heintzelman, who was later one of Wright's subordinates in Texas. The following year, Wright led a brigade during the amphibious operations off the coast of South Carolina and commanded the District of Western Kentucky and the Department of the Ohio. In 1863, he was a division commander with the Army of the Potomac, and fought at Gettysburg. In 1864, he became chief of the VI Corps, which he led in the Richmond campaign, Sheridan's Shenandoah campaign, and at Appomattox.[29]

Arriving in Texas about the same time as General Wright was his civilian counterpart, the provisional governor of the state, Andrew Jackson Hamilton. Known to friends as A. J. or Colossal Jack, Hamilton had migrated to Texas from his native Alabama in 1847. Eventually coming to Austin, he practiced law and entered politics, serving as state attorney general and as state legislator.

A Democrat, Hamilton broke with the party's southern wing in the late 1850s and successfully campaigned on Sam Houston's Independent ticket for a seat in Congress. After supporting Stephen A. Douglas in the 1860 presidential race, Hamilton returned to Texas shortly after its secession. By 1862, his outspoken unionism forced him to flee to Mexico. After the Federal capture of New Orleans, Hamilton moved to the Crescent City, where President Lincoln tendered him a commission as brigadier general of volunteers. Soon thereafter Lincoln also made him the military governor of Texas. The failure of the Red River campaign in 1864 prevented Hamilton from being more than an exiled official with no real authority.[30]

In the spring of 1865, President Johnson appointed Hamilton provisional governor, with instructions to reestablish civil government, administer loyalty oaths and pardons, and convene a constitutional convention to adjust the state document to reflect the results of the war. Texans received the news of Hamilton's appointment with some apprehension. They feared he would be vindictive about the hostility which forced him to leave the state.

The new provisional governor disembarked at Galveston on July 22 and was met by a welcoming delegation of local Unionists. Three days later he issued a "Proclamation to the People of Texas." In this document, Hamilton announced his arrival and appointment as provisional governor, said that laws passed since secession were null and void, and spoke of the need to draft a new constitution through the efforts of Union men. The new governor told of the presidential amnesty available, asked Texans to take the oath of allegiance, and ordered a registration of voters. Finally, Hamilton reminded Texans that slavery was ended and must be so recognized in the new constitution. He also invited all loyal Union men to come to Austin and consult with him on the problems of forming the provisional government.[31]

After issuing his proclamation, Hamilton began his journey to the state capital. At Houston, Unionists threw a gala banquet at which Hamilton was asked to speak. His address seemed to confirm Texans' fears that Hamilton would be vindictive. "I do not adopt the cant phrase 'The Union as it was and the Constitution as it is!'" proclaimed Hamilton, paraphrasing the 1864 Democratic campaign slogan. "I want the Union as it wasn't and the Constitution as it Isn't." The tone of Hamilton's remarks so disturbed the crowd that they asked Elisha M. Pease, an important Hamilton supporter and himself a former governor, to encourage the new governor to tone down his public statements, lest he unduly alienate Texans against a Union government.[32]

On August 2, a committee of thirty prominent citizens of Austin met Hamilton several miles outside the city. With a cavalry escort provided by General Wright from the Brenham railhead, the committee conducted the governor to the capitol. As the parade passed the fluttering United States flag at Hancock Corner, where it had been torn down by the Secessionists at the war's beginning, onlookers cheered.

At the capitol Elisha M. Pease introduced the provisional governor. Pease said that Texans looked to Hamilton for guidance and moderation in these difficult times. Ignoring Pease's hint for a temperate approach, Hamilton launched into a vigorous speech during which he smugly reminded the crowd that four years before he had predicted a Union victory. Although the listeners punctuated his remarks with applause, there were large numbers of more sullen men on the fringes of the crowd who believed that Hamilton had once again taken too harsh a position.[33]

One of the first problems faced by Hamilton and Wright was the securing of public property. At key towns throughout Texas, public property had been collected by surrendering Confederate authorities and turned over to Governor Hamilton's new civil officials, who oftentimes reached interior locations ahead of the occupation forces. When the soldiers arrived, they would frequently seize all public property from Hamilton's men, operating under General Orders No. 8, which had been issued in Galveston. To prevent confusion and the compromise of his civil officials' authority, Hamilton asked headquarters not to enforce General Orders No. 8 if his own provisional government representatives had already assumed responsibility for public property. Wright assented to this request in October, 1865.[34]

Hamilton's main task as governor was to organize a provisional administration to handle state affairs until a new government could be elected under a revised constitution. He believed it was best to move slowly in the reorganization because of the lack of civil control, the vast size of Texas, and the impracticability of expecting General Wright to be able to put troops everywhere. Time was needed to find loyal men to whom the machinery of state government could be entrusted. Time was necessary to organize the Unionists into a political party with enough power to win the postwar election. Time was also needed to reorganize the army to support the new government.[35]

The new administration had to solve the last of these problems. Without proper military support, Hamilton's efforts would be next to useless. Unfortunately for the governor, it took the army nearly a year and a half to deal with the question of the French occupation of Mexico and to solve the problem of stabilizing its own force inside Texas before it could handle civil affairs adequately.

The Mexican issue was resolved first. From the start, the United States sought to impress Maximilian with its renewed power. In his orders to Sheridan in May, 1865, Grant had emphasized the importance of placing a large contingent of troops on the Rio Grande immediately, whether Kirby Smith surrendered or not. Fully one-half of all the soldiers sent to Texas were stationed along the Rio Grande to intimidate Maximilian and the Mexican imperialists and to suppress continual raiding by bands of desperadoes on both sides of the river.[36]

In July Grant told Sheridan to avoid war with the imperialists if possible but nevertheless to render all necessary aid to the liberal cause. It would "be better to go to war now," he concluded, "when but little aid given to the Mexicans will settle the question," than to risk a bigger war against an entrenched monarchy at a later date.[37]

In spite of the regular reductions made in the strength of the Army of Observation, its presence on the border meant that at any moment the slightest incident could lead to a declaration of war by either side. The "very saucy and insulting" attitude of the haughty French officers, who often sent pointed, sarcastic letters to their American counterparts, led to hot verbal exchanges.[38] But Secretary of State William H. Seward was adamant that there should be no provocation from the American side at any time. To ensure against any local commander assuming undue initiative, Grant ordered that only he, the secretary of state, or General Sheridan could issue orders on the Mexican problem. Whenever field officers overstepped these orders they received immediate reprimands. Grant and Sheridan also sent continual reminders to Texas that strict neutrality was to be maintained along the Rio Grande.[39]

Impartiality, however, concerned only overt acts. In Galveston, *Flake's Daily Bulletin* reported that army officers had little trouble in securing temporary leaves of absence to join the *Juaristas*. In Brownsville men could receive up to fifty dollars a month to enlist as "bodyguards" for certain unnamed parties having "business" in Mexico.

Filibustering units regularly crossed the Rio Grande, even though Sheridan warned General Wright to break them up if United States' neutrality was affected. The blue-coated Negro soldiers stationed along the border were reportedly in great sympathy with the liberal cause, and discharged soldiers regularly crossed south of the line to join Benito Juárez.[40]

Although Napoleon III had refused to force Maximilian off the throne, the rapid exodus of the French army in the spring of 1867 left the emperor of Mexico at the mercy of the liberals. The emperor hurried an army northward to Querétaro, where Juárez finally cornered him and forced his surrender. Ignoring American appeals for mercy, the Juaristas executed Maximilian before a firing squad on June 19, 1867.[41]

Seward's game of bluff, as enacted by Sheridan, Wright, and the Army of Observation, had been eminently successful. They believed, as Sheridan later wrote, that "it is but the end of the rebellion which had its commencement in this country and its tragic termination in Mexico." Sheridan also rather immodestly asserted that his actions and the proximity of American troops to the Mexican border were the decisive factors in French withdrawal. This assessment ignored the more important realities of the European political scene, which Seward had manipulated masterfully.[42]

A second major problem that faced General Sheridan and his chief Texas subordinate, General Wright, at the same time as the Mexican question was the demobilization of the volunteer soldiers in Texas and their replacement by the professional regular army. After all, the Union troops sent to the Old Southwest were sullen and disappointed at their postwar assignment. Most of them were three-year veterans who believed that they had served their time, and they wanted to go home with the rest of the men in the Northern armies. (See table 1.)

Matters were not helped any by the inefficient muster-out system used by the army. The high command, in an effort to be fair, often discharged veterans who had served the longest time before shipping the remainder of the troops to Texas. To keep companies at full strength, the reduced regiments were combined, reorganized as battalions, or filled with new recruits. The loss of unit designation caused a severe morale problem; while half the company was permitted to go home, the remaining soldiers had to finish their enlistment with strangers.[43]

The staggered muster-out method was the cause of a mutiny in the Forty-eighth Ohio Infantry Battalion. Formerly a full regiment, this unit was reconstituted from elements of three veteran regiments. On March 20, 1866, the men stacked their arms and refused to serve another day. When officers told their superiors that the men wished to go home, Wright had the battalion commander arrested for insubordination. By March 22, the Galveston Unionist sheet, *Flake's Daily Bulletin*, reported that the problem had been solved and the battalion "thoroughly reconstructed." Before proceedings could be instituted against the mutineers, however, General Grant intervened, released their colonel from arrest, and sent everyone home with an honorable discharge.[44]

Like the white volunteers, the Negro soldiers sent to Texas had not looked forward to their new assignment. The cavalry brigade of the XXV Corps mutinied upon receiving its orders to embark for the Gulf coast. Prompt action by its white officers, aided by a Pennsylvania artillery battery, prevented the rebellion from spreading.

Most of the black soldiers in Texas served in the Rio Grande valley, along the coast, or in the area around Jefferson. But no matter where they were stationed, whites looked askance at the black soldier. By most accounts their discipline was admirable, "but the idea of a gallant and highminded people being ordered and pushed around by an inferior, ignorant race," said one newspaper, "is shocking to the senses."[45]

By early 1866, because of the muster-out of white volunteers and

Table 1. Volunteer Regiments Mustered Out in Texas, 1865–67

Month	Infantry Regiment White	Infantry Regiment Black	Cavalry Regiment White	Cavalry Regiment Black	Artillery Regiment White	Artillery Regiment Black
1865						
July	8	—	—	—	—	—
Aug.	4	1	—	—	1	—
Sept.	6	—	1	—	—	—
Oct.	3	4	2	—	3	—
Nov.	10	7	4½	—	3	—
Dec.	16	—	—	—	—	—
1866						
Jan.	—	2	—	—	—	—
Feb.	1	4	3	2	—	1
Mar.	3	2	—	—	—	—
Apr.	—	—	—	—	—	—
May	4½	1	4	—	—	—
June	—	1	—	—	1	—
July	—	—	—	—	—	—
Aug.	—	—	—	—	—	—
Sept.	—	1	—	—	—	—
Oct.	—	2	—	—	—	—
Nov.	—	1	—	—	—	—
Dec.	—	—	—	—	—	—
1867						
Jan.	—	2	—	—	—	—
Feb.	—	—	—	—	—	—
Mar.	—	—	—	—	—	—
Apr.	—	1	—	—	—	—
May	—	—	—	—	—	—
June	—	—	—	—	—	—
July	—	—	—	—	—	—
Aug.	—	1	—	—	—	—
Totals by race	55½	30	14½	2	8	1
Totals by regiment	85½		16½		9	

the delay in replenishing the ranks of white regulars, black soldiers were at their greatest proportional numbers for the whole Reconstruction period. Sheridan reported to Grant that the Department of Texas had three times as many black soldiers present for duty as white troops. Not until January, 1867, did Grant order Sheridan to demobilize the last of the Negro volunteers. Until that time, black troops had provided most of the Federal power along the Rio Grande and the Texas coast.[46]

While demobilization involved a long, anguishing process for the volunteers, it was too quick for Governor Hamilton, who wrote a protest to Sheridan. Hamilton felt that the muster-out would be disastrous to the interests of Unionists and the Federal government. If the Yankees left, "there would occur a scene of violence, and outrages upon the Union men of the State and upon the Freedmen, such as to shock the moral sense of the entire country."[47]

But Sheridan was more worried about the wrath of the disgruntled volunteers, who had already begun to destroy public property. The mutiny of the Forty-eighth Ohio clinched his desire to get rid of the volunteers and to rely on the steady regulars, a position with which Grant heartily concurred.[48] As for the volunteers, the *San Antonio Herald* correctly summed up their sentiments. It said the information on their final discharge "will be glorious news to the white volunteer troops on duty in this vicinity as it seems to be that they have long sighed and languished for."[49]

Before the volunteers could be mustered out, they had to be replaced at the inland duty stations by regulars. The demobilization of the various volunteer regiments, combined with the delayed arrival of the regulars and responsibilities inherent in the Mexican venture, resulted in a troop shortage in the Texas interior. Throughout 1865 and 1866, only two interior towns were consistently occupied by Union soldiers—San Antonio and Austin, where Merritt's and Custer's cavalry divisions were stationed. All other Federal influence was limited to an area around Marshall, Tyler, and Jefferson; a line from Indianola through Victoria to San Antonio; various outposts on the rail lines emanating from Houston out to Brenham and Millican; the coastal areas of Sabine Pass, Galveston, and Corpus Christi; and, of course, the Rio Grande valley from Brazos Santiago to Ringgold Barracks. Each area of control was augmented by patrols, but in reality there was little Federal presence beyond the fringes of Texas. The problem was aggravated by poor communication. It took until November, 1865, before suitable telegraphic systems linked Galveston with Austin and San Antonio.[50]

In an effort to maintain army control of the interior, Sheridan pestered Grant for as much regular cavalry as he could spare. Ultimately, Grant sent the Fourth and Sixth regiments to Texas. Both cavalry regiments arrived in New Orleans in November, 1865, a trip the Fourth Cavalry remembered because they crossed the Gulf in a river steamboat.[51]

Even though the regiments were understaffed, Sheridan immediately sent them on to Galveston, where they established a base camp at Pelican Island. General Wright then sent the Fourth Cavalry to San Antonio to relieve Merritt's volunteer division. The Fourth went by ship to Indianola and by rail to Victoria. Troopers remembered that the locomotive was so small for the load that they had to jump out of the cars and push it up each hill. At San Antonio, the unit was issued horses from Merritt's departing volunteers and was sent through the city at "advance carbine." None of the troopers knew why they needed to make such a show of force until they reached the far edge of town. There they rode into a camp of volunteers left behind for further duty and crushed a mutiny.[52]

Having stabilized the situation at San Antonio, Wright moved the Sixth Cavalry to Austin to replace Custer's units. Although there was no mutiny to quell in Austin, the departing volunteers did try to ambush Custer as he left town. The general somehow got wind of the plot, and according to one account, he escaped the night before, using a relay of horses.[53]

While the two cavalry regiments marched inland, the volunteers along the coast were being replaced by a regular infantry outfit. Assigned to Texas in March, 1866, the Seventeenth Infantry was one of nine new regiments authorized by President Lincoln in the spring of 1861, when the regular army was expanded to meet war needs. These "Lincoln regiments" had twenty-four companies each, or were the equivalent of two and one-half normal-sized regiments. Unlike normal ten-company regiments, the new outfits were organized into three battalions of eight companies each and were usually deployed in battalion size in the field.

The Seventeenth had seen much service during the war. Nearly wiped out by the summer of 1864, the regiment received a well-earned rest at Fort Lafayette in New York City. Here for the first time, the entire twenty-four companies were joined together under the leadership of Brevet Major General Samuel P. Heintzelman, the regiment's actual commander.[54]

Heintzelman found it difficult to recruit new men because most preferred the lax discipline and large bounties paid to those who joined volunteer regiments. Hence, by 1865 the Seventeenth Infantry was a mere skeleton of its former self. Worse than the lack of recruits was the quality of those who did join. They represented the dregs of society. "The army was in a bad way," admitted one officer, "with only the riff-raff of the war left among the enlisted men, and the officers quarrelling among themselves" over who had the highest brevet or regular rank and thus the most privileges.[55] In spite of such difficulties, the first one thousand men of the Seventeenth Infantry reached New Orleans on April 18, 1866. Sheridan forwarded them to Galveston a few days later. On April 24, a detail was sent into the city after days aboard the cramped ships in the harbor.

The soldiers made the most of their liberty by getting "rousing drunk" and starting numerous fights, including a small race riot. *Flake's Bulletin* recommended that the army restrict the sale of liquor to soldiers except through ordinary quartermaster channels and expressed the hope that "regular discipline" would be effected soon.

When the city's liquor supply was declared off limits, the ever-thirsty men broke into stores and saloons at gunpoint and ordered drinks for all present. "We have never had a garrison that so disgraced itself, and violated the public peace," commented *Flake's*. This pro-Union newspaper did not wish to end military rule in Texas, but anything seemed better than occupation by the Seventeenth Infantry. The article concluded that even black soldiers were preferable to the white military marauders now pillaging the town.

If Galveston could swallow its traditional hatred of the black soldier because of the pitiful conduct of the Seventeenth Infantry, the situation must indeed have been bad. General Wright ordered out a reinforced provost guard and told it to get tough and make arrests. When two drunken soldiers from the Seventeenth began smashing windows in the business section and became hard to handle, the guard bayoneted one man in the leg.

Wright's crackdown brought results. By June the local authorities noted a change in discipline among the regular infantrymen. Order was "rigidly enforced," and offenders received long sentences at hard labor in the Dry Tortugas.[56]

By midsummer of 1866, Wright had spread the Seventeenth Infantry throughout eastern Texas in company-sized units. In addition, two companies were stationed at San Antonio, two more at Galveston, and three "skeleton companies" of one battalion were at Galveston awaiting reinforcement and reassignment. Wright reported that only the Third Battalion had its full complement of eighty-three men per company.[57] Because of his complaint, the First and Second Battalions arrived late that summer, but not until November did the three companies near Detroit, Michigan, join the regiment.

By that time, Congress had divided all of the army's oversized units into three ten-company regiments by adding two new companies to each battalion. In Texas, this realignment meant that the First Battalion retained the title of the Seventeenth Infantry and was assigned to east Texas. It was still commanded by Heintzelman.[58] The Second Battalion was sent to Austin and became the Twenty-sixty Infantry, commanded by Brevet Major General Joseph Jones Reynolds. The Third Battalion at San Antonio was made the Thirty-fifth Infantry, under Brevet Major General Charles Griffin. All three officers were assigned to duty at their normal rank of colonel of infantry, and each later played a part in the course of Texas Reconstruction.[59]

The arrival of the regular regiments and the solution of the Mexican problem allowed the army at last to turn its full attention to the internal problems of restoring a properly elected government to Texas. In a summary report to Grant's chief of staff, Sheridan condemned the European intervention in Mexico as "only the history of the buccaneer Morgan on a more extended scale." Convinced that his movement of troops to the Rio Grande was the decisive element in Maximilian's defeat, Sheridan reiterated his belief "that the occupation of Mexico was a part of the Rebellion" and that the Juarista success, like the Northern triumph in the Civil War, was a victory for republicanism.

As for the demobilization of the volunteers and the arrival in Texas of the regular regiments, Sheridan considered that this too was a holdover from the recent rebellion. He pointed out in the same report that his staff had efficiently moved the equivalent of over ninety thousand men thousands of miles (he counted each man twice, coming to Texas and leaving). Sheridan was piqued at the attitude of the quartermaster's department, which had held up transportation funds for six months, but pointed out that forty-seven thousand of the fifty-two thousand volunteers in Texas had been mustered out and returned home.[60]

Sheridan did not mention that the Mexican question and the troop movements had seriously impaired General Wright's ability to occupy the Texas interior and to aid Hamilton's provisional government in reconstructing the state. Texas accordingly became the last of the former Confederate states to complete the requirements of President Johnson's Reconstruction program.

2

The Army and the Freedmen's Bureau

GENERAL PHIL SHERIDAN fumed as he leafed through the mass of papers on his desk. He thought a moment and then began to scribble furiously. "The condition of civil affairs in Texas is anomalous, singular, and unsatisfactory," he wrote.[1] Sheridan was especially appalled by race relations in Texas. The atrocities were too numerous to catalog, but one incident undoubtedly stuck in his mind.

Two privates from the Eightieth United States Colored Infantry had gone for a drink of water near Jefferson. Along the path they met the deputy town marshal, Jack Phillips. As they passed, Phillips swung his double-barreled shotgun into position and blasted the two soldiers at point-blank range. He then drew his revolver and, as the dying black infantrymen writhed in pain on the now bloody ground, calmly blew their brains out.[2]

Unbelievably, Marshal Phillips was still in office months after the murders, although it is doubtful whether his arrest and removal would have had any positive result. "My own opinion is that the trial of a white man for the murder of a freedman in Texas would be a farce," wrote Sheridan. In spite of continuing racial incidents of this nature, most Texans, including the loyal provisional governor, A. J. Hamilton, seemed more interested in suppressing Indian attacks on the frontier. "It is strange that over a white man killed by Indians on an extensive frontier, the greatest excitement will take place," complained Sheridan, "but over the killing of many freedmen in the settlements nothing is done."[3]

Sheridan's priorities here were valid, because, in the last analysis, the primary issue of Reconstruction was the Negro and his or her relationship to the white majority in American society. The blacks were no longer legally enslaved, for the Civil War, which had begun over secession, had culminated in freedom for the slaves. Reconstruction promised a revolution in the entire social structure of American society, and it was over the issue of equality that the South drew the final battle line—and won. Southerners won because, unlike Sheridan, the

North overall lacked the commitment necessary to force the issue to a successful end, as the history of the black in Texas after the Civil War graphically illustrates.[4]

During the Civil War, Texas had largely escaped the horrors of the battlefields. There were few engagements and no massive cavalry raids, and crops had not been affected. The nearby states of Missouri, Arkansas, and Louisiana, however, did not fare so well. When the Yankees invaded these states, their slaveholders saw Texas as a haven from the ravages of war. Slowly at first, then in droves, the residents of the trans-Mississippi area sent their bondservants to Texas for safekeeping. There were 275,000 slaves in Texas in 1861. By 1865, the black population had risen to 400,000.[5]

To solve the problems brought on by the end of the war and emancipation, Congress set up a new agency on March 3, 1865. Its name— Bureau of Refugees, Freedmen, and Abandoned Lands—expressed clearly the issues that faced the South. This agency was more commonly known as the Freedmen's Bureau and was to last the duration of the war and one year thereafter.[6]

The bureau was to introduce and promote productive industry through a system of compensated labor in the South; provide for the destitute, aged, and sick; protect loyal refugees; establish black schools; and adjudicate differences between blacks and whites whenever civil courts in the south failed to provide this service.[7] Even though it was a separate bureau administered by the War Department, its commissioner was Brevet Major General Oliver Otis Howard, and many subassistant commissioners and agents, especially in Texas, were army officers. In Texas, if a post area had no Freedmen's Bureau representative, the commanding officer of the nearest army detachment had to assume the duties of the bureau in addition to his troop assignment.[8]

There was plenty for the Freedmen's Bureau to do in Texas. Former slaveowners firmly believed that emancipation was an unconstitutional wartime expediency soon to be overruled by the Supreme Court and that, in spite of the Thirteenth Amendment, they would eventually be compensated for the slaves they held in 1865. Texans were therefore especially brutal in preventing the mobility of the newly freed slaves that was prevalent after the war. This movement was more than a mere testing of freedom. These blacks had been forcefully removed from homes and loved ones during the war. Now they wished to return to the nearby states whence they came. But in the eyes of the whites who had held them, each Negro who left Texas was one less slave to be compensated for.[9]

This belief led to unparalleled brutality in the treatment of blacks in postwar Texas. The existing racism was pushed to extremes by expected profits, which never materialized. From all over eastern Texas came letters complaining of continued slaveholding. Blacks who had the temerity to leave their former masters were hunted down like the runaways of old. One reporter told of how a Negro in Van Zandt County was staked out on the ground and given five hundred lashes for refusing to work for nothing. In Caldwell County blacks were so elated by their freedom that local whites "could not endure them." White vigilante groups took action, and it became common each morning to see blacks hanging from trees by their necks, thumbs, or toes.[10]

Whites formed secret societies in nearly every county with the avowed purpose of compelling blacks to return to their former masters. These planter societies allowed no one to employ blacks unless he or she had owned them prior to the war or had the former master's permission. People of both races who violated this unwritten law were beaten or killed. If soldiers temporarily prevented retaliation, violators were warned that the Yankees would not be there to shield them forever.[11]

More grating to Texans than the incessant wandering on the roads was the refusal of many blacks to continue working. This attitude seemed to confirm slaveholders' fears that, as freedmen, blacks were incapable of serving the labor needs of the state. Many white landowners shifted their crops from cotton to wheat, where their traditional dependence upon black labor would be much less. Some went so far as to move into the region near Dallas, where climate and soil were reported to produce better food crops.[12]

Others hoped that improved agricultural methods would eliminate the need for human labor or that the state government would be rapidly restored and institute some kind of substitute labor program. Although by the mid-1870s hired black labor proved more reliable than had slavery, white Texans in 1865 were so despondent over the labor situation that planters organized the Texas Land, Labor, and Immigration Company to induce settlers to come to the state from abroad. A Brenham planter, Thomas Affleck, toured Europe for the company, with little success.[13]

The blacks' reluctance to work came partly from the never-to-be realized hope that the Federal government would grant them small plots of their own land—the legendary "forty acres and a mule."[14] This land was available in much of the South where the havoc of war had caused the abandonment of large acreages by their original land-

owners. In Texas, however, the Freedmen's Bureau found little abandoned land, making the dream of black property ownership more elusive than ever. But blacks thought that some land would be granted
them around Christmas, 1865. It therefore seemed unnecessary to work
in the interior for some white farmer. Instead, blacks congregated in
towns near army posts and awaited the day of the land grants.[15]

Whites meanwhile grew terrified at the prospect of disappointed
blacks going on the rampage when they learned the truth. "Negro-
gogues" were promising the world to the blacks, complained an irate
Danville man, and if they obtained liquor he feared they would "run
amuck" at Christmas. Whites thought the angry freedmen would
forcefully divide up the white man's property "at a future date," and
numerous requests were sent to Governor Hamilton asking him to
raise militia companies to preserve peace during the holiday season.[16]

Others organized self-defense units without state or federal sanction, some of which were still in existence the following summer.
Blacks were reportedly becoming more and more confused at contra-
dictory white promises, said a La Grange citizen, and he called for the
interference of the Freedmen's Bureau quickly, for "Christmas is coming fast apace."[17]

With the assistance of Hamilton and General Wright, the Freedmen's Bureau was already doing its best to counteract the land distribution myth. But like all things in Reconstruction Texas, the bureau
had a late start. The bureau headquarters had been set up in the Galveston Customs House only on September 5, 1865, under the supervision of Brevet Major General Edgar M. Gregory, the assistant commissioner for the state of Texas.

Gregory had been a civilian before the war, volunteered for the
army in 1861, and served as colonel of the Ninety-first Pennsylvania
Infantry. A steady officer, he had received two brevets at the siege of
Petersburg and was noted for his "bravery and energy." He received his
appointment from the bureau chief, General Howard, who was impressed by Gregory's "well reputed . . . stand he always took in the
army in favor of clear-cut uprightness of conduct." Howard so liked
Gregory's fearlessness in the face of dangerous opposition that he "sent
him to Texas, which seemed at the time the post of greatest peril."

As assistant commissioner, Gregory typified the men that Howard
placed in charge of state Freedmen's Bureau departments. College
educated, native born, Yankee Protestant, and lacking "an amenity of
manner" and "savoir faire," Gregory believed that one found salvation
by working to perfect one's own world. Of all the assistant commis-

sioners in the ten bureau districts in the South, only Gregory was an avowed abolitionist before the war, which did not endear him to Texas whites.[18]

After taking some weeks to familiarize himself with the Texas situation, Gregory issued Circular No. 1, which listed his goals as assistant commissioner. Gregory served notice that he was aware that Texas Negroes had not been fully apprised of their emancipation and that they were being grossly intimidated and even murdered for assuming their freedom. He immediately announced, like Granger before him, that slavery was ended and enjoined bureau officials to make this decision clear to the population. Officers of the bureau were to adjudicate all differences between blacks and whites, should local courts fail to do justice. Blacks were admonished to work and enter into voluntary labor contracts with employers of their choice. Bureau agents were to supervise this process and to ensure that no one was forced to work for "obnoxious" employers. Finally, Gregory ordered all authorities to correct the false impression that the land of former slaveholders would be redistributed to blacks on December 25.[19]

In cooperation with Gregory, Governor Hamilton a month later issued "An Address to the Freedmen of Texas," which was sent to the county judges for distribution. In it and an earlier proclamation issued in September, the governor emphasized that slavery as an institution was forever destroyed. He expressed his friendship for freed blacks and his admiration of the manner in which they had handled themselves and extended his wishes for continued happiness and prosperity. But Hamilton cautioned them that no land would be given them under any circumstances. Hamilton wrote the president and informed him of continuing slavery in Texas, white abuse of black rights, and the need for more intensified military occupation to cure these evils.[20]

During the rest of 1865 and early 1866, Gregory busied himself with the organization of the bureau and the spreading of its control throughout the state. He began this arduous task with a series of trips into eastern Texas to feel the pulse of the people. In November, Gregory and the inspector general of the bureau, Brevet Major General William E. Strong, traveled through the region drained by the Neches and Trinity rivers. Gregory covered seven hundred miles and saw twenty-five thousand persons. He was impressed with the good crops but scoffed at rumors of Negro revolt. Instead Gregory found the blacks to be kind and courteous, with strong religious sentiments; he reported that "their morals are equal if not superior to those of a majority of the better informed and educated," a statement that shocked contemporaries and later historians.[21]

The assistant commissioner said that, contrary to white beliefs, blacks were not assertive of their rights and indeed that many seemed unable to comprehend what freedom actually meant. He hoped to find suitable whites to be local agents but was sorry to see that "few, comparably, feel and manifest that interest in the advancement of the freedmen that they should." Brutality toward blacks abounded in areas remote from military control.[22]

General Strong found conditions even worse than did his companion, Gregory. Strong praised the assistant commissioner's approach to problems in Texas and was impressed with Gregory's speeches to blacks and planters. Strong believed that there was "a fearful state of things" in areas not occupied by the army. One planter told him that the reason for killing blacks was merely to "thin out the niggers a little," which convinced Strong that the occasional cavalry patrols into the interior were nearly useless. Atrocities stopped when the army approached, only to be continued again on its departure.

"It is the same old story of cruelty," said the inspector general, "only there is more of it in Texas than any other southern State that I have visited." Strong thought that a "campaign of an army through the eastern part of the State, such as was made by General Sherman in South Carolina, would improve the temper and generosity of the people." He was amazed at the "most intense hatred" shown by Texans toward Yankees, soldiers, and the national government. Strong could not account for this dislike, "unless it may be for the reason that they know less about the war, and have seen less of our troops than any other people, and therefore cannot appreciate the power and strength of the government." The inspector general asserted that if whites treated blacks fairly, the freedmen would work hard. As it was, less than one-third of the Negroes received payment for their labor. Those whites who did pay did so only at the point of a bayonet. The so-called idle wandering of the blacks was actually very purposeful, Strong believed. He understood their desire to return home to other states from which they had been removed during the war.[23]

In December Gregory traveled alone along the lower Brazos and Colorado rivers. There he found conditions better than they had been earlier. Most of the blacks were under contract, and vagrancy, idleness, and theft were things of the past. Black laborers received from eight to fifteen dollars per month wages or a quarter to half of the crop raised. Gregory believed that assault and intimidation by whites were on the decline but observed that "wrongs increase in proportion to their distance from United States authorities." There were still un-counted cases of anti-Negro actions, "ranging from downright murder, savage beatings, merciless whippings, hunting men with trained blood-hounds" to lesser crimes.[24]

At this same time, Gregory's surgeon general, S. J. W. Mintzer, re-ported the health of the blacks to be good, considering "miasmatic influences" and the quality of water. The closer to large rivers and bayous the blacks lived, the more their health declined. Housing for freedmen generally consisted of small shacks, poorly ventilated and overcrowded. When Mintzer asked a group of planters to provide better accommodations, they replied that, if the shacks were good enough for fifteen-hundred-dollar slaves, they were good enough for free Negroes of no value. Mintzer erroneously concluded that Texas' prosperity owed much to Gregory's appeals and influence in the state, and he even thought the planters agreed, which he considered a great victory for the reconstructing forces.[25]

In his continuing efforts to extend the bureau's control down to the regional level, Gregory did his best to find suitable subassistant com-missioners, as the local agents were called. Gregory was pleased with the public response. He wrote Howard in the fall of 1865 that over one hundred planters had expressed willingness to help the bureau and pay fair wages. In some areas black schools had been set up. More im-portant, many men had said they were willing to serve as bureau agents; some of them even had letters of endorsement from Governor Hamilton or other state officials.[26]

In December, the assistant commissioner appointed his first dozen agents and a five-man Galveston staff. Other appointments followed shortly. Although a majority of the agents and all of the staff were sol-diers, about 40 percent of the subassistant commissioners were civil-ians, a ratio that remained constant throughout the bureau's existence in Texas.[27]

Even though General Wright provided a list of five officers in each local area "who could be depended upon for doing justice" to bureau duties, by the end of January, 1866, there were only twenty-five suit-able agents in the state. Inspector General Strong had estimated ear-lier that at least fifty agents, each with a detachment of soldiers, would be needed to perform a tolerable job in Texas.[28]

Nonetheless, the agents went ahead with their main task that win-ter: drawing up contracts between white landowners and black workers.

All labor agreements for longer than one month's duration had to be in writing, with a copy going to the bureau, the landowner, and the freedman. Contracts were to be negotiated with heads of families, stipulate goods and services rendered and received, detail quarters, rations, and wages or the share of the crop agreed upon. The contract was considered a lien on the crop and was in force until a subassistant commissioner or a local judge agreed that it had been fulfilled. Any violation of the contract by the laborer meant forfeiture of wages. Should the employer disobey the terms, the laborer could sue for damages. Those blacks who refused to work were to be dealt with in the same manner as white vagrants. Any contract laborer absent over twenty-four hours from the job or more than five days a month could be declared a vagrant and be put to work on the public roads by the local courts. Although Texans swore otherwise, there was no charge or tax levied for the contract mediation service provided by the bureau.[29]

Gregory's announced policy was not revolutionary, except perhaps in the sense that blacks were now free and, along with whites, had rights in the contract-making process, but Texans highly resented the bureau as a third force intruding into labor problems. "The agent of the bureau and the provost marshal commanding at Columbia are far more important functionaries practically to us than your Excellency and the President," wrote one hostile citizen to Governor Hamilton. he asked that the bureau agents—"strangers," he called them—be recalled.[30]

Another planter wished to draw up a five-year contract with his black employees but feared, correctly, that the bureau would not allow it. "Yankee-like, they will not give up their assured right (the right of might) to interfere between me & the negroes at all times," he complained, "and that, after a contract is made, I will not tolerate."[31] This attitude was so widespread that, when President Johnson vetoed the renewal of the Freedmen's Bureau Bill in early 1866, Gregory issued a cautionary circular to his agents to expect increasing resistance from planters.[32]

While Gregory did little more than encourage blacks to stay at home, sign a contract, and work for their former master, Gregory's reports to Washington and his assertions that blacks were equal, if not superior, to Texas whites in character caused him continual trouble. Gregory was also unpopular because he increased army patrols in plantation areas and enforced contract terms at the point of a bayonet. Gregory's greatest sin was trying to make the former slaves free in fact, not just on paper.

In short, he was much too conscientious, and complaints flooded headquarters at Galveston, New Orleans, and Washington. Howard asked General Wright to investigate. Wright remarked that Gregory was a good officer who worked hard at his job, but he felt that the assistant commissioner was clearly very unpopular and that someone with more tact might fare better in the position.[33]

Shortly thereafter, David G. Burnet, an important prewar Texas politician, accused Gregory of fomenting racial unrest with his anti-white speeches and of being too inclined to accept the freedmen's side of controversies.[34] Burnet's accusations reached President Johnson, who referred them to Howard. The commissioner of the bureau personally never doubted Gregory's integrity, but he succumbed to the political pressures brought against him and promoted Gregory to an inspector general's position, thus removing him from Texas. The joy of Texans at his removal can be seen in the one-sentence comment that appeared in the conservative *Galveston Daily News:* "Gen. Gregory left yesterday for New Orleans!"[35]

Gregory's replacement as assistant commissioner was Brevet Major General Joseph B. Kiddoo. Many saw his appointment as a concession to Texas plantation owners. Like Gregory, Kiddoo was a civilian at the start of the war. He rose rapidly through the ranks, serving as a private in a three-month regiment and as a noncommissioned officer in the Sixty-third Pennsylvania Infantry on the Peninsula, and finally gained a commission as lieutenant colonel of the 147th Pennsylvania Volunteers in the summer of 1862. A year later he resigned his commission and joined the new colored infantry service, where he gained great distinction at the siege of Petersburg. The price of his gallantry was gaping leg and spinal wounds which never healed properly and which caused him excruciating pain. Doctors of the day knew only one cure—amputation—but feared that the shock of the operation might kill Kiddoo.[36]

Initially Kiddo fully satisfied the planters. He issued new circular orders preventing any employer or person from "enticing a laborer away" from a contracted job. Contracts were to safeguard both sides, said Kiddoo, white as well as black. Whites who enticed away black laborers could be fined from one hundred to five hundred dollars by the local agents. The freedman involved could be fined up to twenty-five dollars, and the amount garnished from his wages.[37] Agents were reminded to enforce the law to the letter, especially during planting and harvest seasons.[38]

In addition to issuing tougher labor regulations, Kiddoo approached

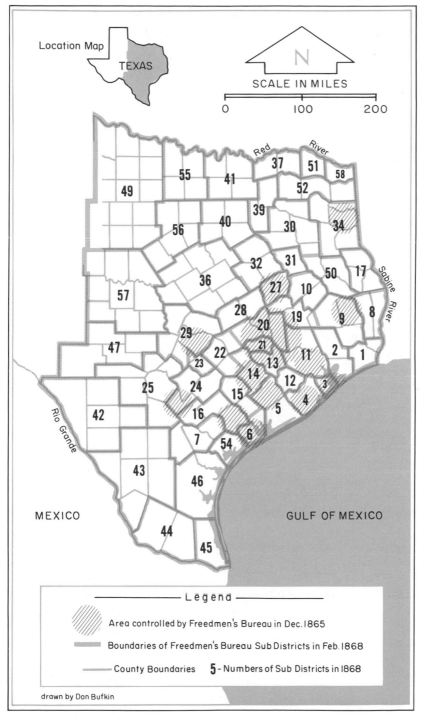

Map 2. The Freedmen's Bureau in Texas, 1865–68: Growth from Agencies to Subdistricts

two matters which Gregory had not previously emphasized and which cost Kiddoo much of his initial popularity. The first was the establishment of a school system for Texas blacks. In the beginning, bureau attempts to educate the freedmen and their children were spasmodic, but under Howard's guidance a full-fledged system of education was eventually established in all states.

The officer in charge of black education in Texas was First Lieutenant E. M. Wheelock of the Seventy-sixth U.S. Colored Infantry. Wheelock was an energetic soldier who made rapid advances in founding schools for blacks throughout Texas. Using his experience among the black troops as a guide, he recognized the desire of the freedmen for learning and used as many former soldiers as he could for instructors. To interest qualified teachers, Wheelock offered a salary through the bureau and sponsoring Northern missionary groups. By the summer of 1866, Wheelock had sixty-five teachers in one hundred schools, with over four thousand enrolled students of all ages—all from an initial start of one black normal school in downtown Galveston less than one year before.[39]

The bureau's program to educate the blacks met severe opposition in the state. Texans resented the evangelical fervor of the Yankee teachers, who acted as if they were God's chosen instruments to save the South. Texans claimed that Negroes were too subhuman to be educated successfully and disliked the Yankees for proving them wrong. The whites also believed that those who taught blacks placed themselves on the same social level as their students. A bureau inspector of schools told how "sometimes we were driven out of places on our mission becoming known. Frequently we had to do our business in secret and travel is disguise."[40]

To Texans, one of the most disgusting features of black education was the social relations established between the students and their teachers, usually white, unmarried women. This interracial contact also extended to the visits made after teaching hours between the instructor, the students, and their parents and led to fears of "amalgamation."[41]

Recognizing this hostility and the increasing intimidation suffered by teachers, the bureau recommended the employment of male instructors. Recruiters sent to Chicago had some success, but the growing demand for workers was never fully satisfied during the bureau's tenure in the state.[42]

State newspapers ridiculed the blacks' ignorance and attempted to show that the freedmen were no better than uneducable children. At the same time, schools were burned out, teachers threatened or killed, and the students intimidated.[43] One Houston woman told the federal district attorney that she would sooner put a bullet in a Negro than see him educated.[44]

In spite of the obstacles, when Kiddoo and Wheelock turned the school system over to the Reverend Joseph Welch in 1867, they were pleased with the progress. They estimated that ten thousand blacks had learned to read and write. As the educators persisted, white Texans themselves began to support schools for blacks. By 1870, when the bureau withdrew from the state, the schools remained behind as its only really successful program.[45]

The second area in which Kiddoo concentrated his efforts, to the dismay of Texas planters, was organizing and systematizing the bureau courts. Impartial justice is basic to an American's civil rights, but the freedmen after the war found this right to be elusive at best. For example, Captain Harlan P. Spaulding, the subassistant commissioner at Victoria, reported a case in which a white beat a discharged black soldier with an oxbow. In spite of the intercession of the mayor, black testimony was disallowed in court, and the defendant was fined ten dollars and costs for simple assault. In a later occurrence in the same area, a white man cut a black man's arm open to the bone from shoulder to elbow. Spaulding believed that trying the defendant in the too-lenient civil court would be unfair.[46]

In Lamar County, a black named Orange Bray fled from a white man who wished to whip him. When he was cornered, Bray raised an ax in self-defense. The white drew a pistol and shot him. When the case was tried, Bray was sentenced to the state penitentiary, but the white was freed.[47]

States tribunals regularly fined blacks more than whites for the same offense. Whites who committed an act of violence or fraud against a black usually had the advantage of an overly lenient white jury. A black's testimony against a white person was rarely admitted as evidence, even by Loyalist judges. Blacks believed guilty were sometimes executed by mobs before they even received a hearing. Freedmen were also more likely to draw the death penalty. Van Zandt County's only legal execution during Reconstruction was of a black man convicted upon slim circumstantial evidence.[48]

Themselves members of a culture in which discrimination was widespread, many county justices were sincerely puzzled as to how to handle cases involving freedmen. Judge Hiram Christian of Bell County asked Governor Hamilton to advise him on such cases. Christian actually preferred to have the state legislature act, but it would not meet for months. He therefore asked Hamilton's advice on a series of sticky questions. Was the county to care for black orphans who had no means of support or should it bind them out? Who had the right to the services of a minor, the parents or employer, if the child was formerly owned by a different master? Could Negroes use courts and give testimony against whites? Could Negroes claim from their former master's property that they had used during slavery? Could a local court draw up a labor contract without consulting the bureau?[49]

Few justices had the courage, even if they had the inclination, to do away with the former legal customs of the state as did Judge Colbert Caldwell. In a charge to a grand jury in Harrison County, Caldwell instructed the jurors to treat blacks with "perfect equality" in all matters before his bench.[50]

In answer to all these problems, General Kiddoo established a far-reaching court system supervised by the local bureau agents. Kiddoo had no intention of replacing local courts and government but only of supplementing them. Bureau agents were accordingly not to act unless civil courts were not organized or failed to admit a black person's testimony. No cases were to be handled by subassistant commissioners unless a freedman was a party. All instances involving whipping and maltreatment of blacks were to go solely to bureau courts. All murder cases were to be adjudicated first by civil courts.[51]

Kiddoo's definition of the jurisdiction of the bureau courts brought a new aspect to the administration of justice under the provisional government. Three court systems now operated in Texas. Within the limits set by Kiddoo, the Freedmen's Bureau courts had control of disputes involving blacks. There were also military commissions that handled cases involving civilians, but they were distinct from the courts-martial, which dealt with charges against soldiers. Finally, the ordinary civil courts existed, after a fashion, on both state and federal levels. The jurisdiction of each court system tended to overlap during all of Reconstruction. It was possible to obtain a ruling in one tribunal, only to have it overturned by another.[52]

Bureau courts often prescribed jail sentences to offenders who would have received only fines in state court; military commissions could hang offenders with a two-thirds vote of the panel of judges and approval from higher authorities; neither kind of military court provided for juries—all of which was highly controversial. Even before Kiddoo consolidated the bureau courts, General Wright had written Governor

Hamilton that "the subjects in which the civil and military are most likely to be at cross purposes are the relative jurisdiction of civil and military tribunals, and matters connected with freedmen."[53]

Just how far military jurisdiction through the military tribunal or the bureau court ought to extend was hotly debated during the period of the provisional government. The decisions of "military men who for the most part know but little of civil justice and law and not much more about its administration" bothered one citizen, who voiced his worries to Governor Hamilton. He called on the governor to remove state judges who refused to uphold equal justice for all citizens, be they black or white, former Confederates or Unionists. Otherwise the bureau would take over and lean unduly toward the Negro's side, because they were there for that reason, he said. "Would it not be better for the people to have their controversies and difficulties with the Freedmen settled by their own fellow citizens than by military strangers?" he asked. The writer concluded that it would also be best to have any court judgment enforced by "their fellow citizen sheriffs than by the bayonet in the hands of some military Tom, Dick, or Harry—by perhaps a white soldier—perhaps a black one!"[54]

In August, 1865, Governor Hamilton would have agreed with his correspondent. Hamilton had always believed that the civil government was paramount to the military authority. He saw the provisional administration as being only "*quasi* military; because it will be as it was intended to be, in contradistinction to purely Military Govt., *civil* in its character and functions." Hamilton thought it "strange if with the power delegated to create all necessary tribunals for the enforcement of the laws generally, I should still be regarded as unequal to the task" of establishing all necessary "offices and tribunals to enforce the laws . . . and protect all citizens."[55] While he allowed the army to make arrests of lawbreakers, the governor was adamant that the civil courts should try them. Hamilton's secretary of state, James H. Bell, took the same position. The provisional government was to aid the army and direct it in its Reconstruction efforts.[56]

But the massive chore of organizing a loyal government had caused Hamilton to modify his position by September. Appalled by the treatment of the freedmen and the general chaos in the state, he wrote General Wright a despondent note. "It must be obvious . . . that we cannot depend upon the Civil authority of our State for some time yet to deal out justice to evil doers." Hamilton asserted that "the appointment of Civil Officers was more for the purpose of affording remedies to the citizens for civil rights; than in the expectation, or hope of administering, with any efficiency, the criminal laws of the State." The governor realized that the army had no intention of interfering with the civil authority and that the federal government wished to "withdraw its Military hand" from the citizens of Texas, but he now saw the trial of civilians before military tribunals as a "necessity." He realized there was no organized resistance to the "General Government," but he was disturbed by the "sullen dissatisfaction, . . . manifesting itself in a total disregard of the rights of freedmen or the policy of the Government," which was displayed by the people. Military power was the only way to counteract this attitude.[57]

3

The Return to Rebel Rule

THE ARMY WAS LOATHE to assume the burden Hamilton passed its way. In response to a request from Wright, Sheridan advised him to "give way to civil authority" whenever the "legitimate rights" of the government or the Negroes were not affected. He added that "it is hard to enforce martial law, after war has ceased and a form even of civil government is in existence."[1] Wright notified Hamilton that all matters concerning whites were to be dealt with in the civil courts, all problems concerning Negroes were to be given to the Freedmen's Bureau, and all "military matters" would be handled by the army, which would support the civil government and bureau when necessary.

Wright hoped that Hamilton could live with this arrangement and that the governor's doubts regarding law enforcement were based on exaggerated rumors. Wright would not use bureau courts or military tribunals unless civil courts failed to find justice first. He urged Hamilton to get the state courts into operation quickly and asked Sheridan to have Washington do the same with the federal courts. When President Johnson confirmed his assessment and ordered all interference with the civil authorities stopped, Wright told Sheridan he was glad Johnson was so definite and timely. It is "just about what we have been aiming at."[2]

In early 1866, Wright, in compliance with instructions from Washington, warned all post commanders to protect officers, soldiers, and civilian contract employees from prosecution in state courts. They were also to safeguard Unionists and blacks charged with offenses for which former Confederates habitually received lighter punishment in state courts.[3]

Two months later President Johnson declared the rebellion ended and all of the Southern states readmitted to the Union. This decree caused considerable confusion in Texas because the state had not been mentioned in or excepted from the measure. Yet Texas had not completed the requirements of Presidential Reconstruction. Wright cautioned commanders not to discontinue the use of military courts or restrict the bureau courts in their operation, probably in response to secret instructions Grant circulated throughout the occupied South.[4]

A month later, however, in response to further instructions from Washington, Wright ordered military tribunals to consider cases involving civilians only if they concerned sutlers, military retainers, contractors, or fraudulent claims against the army. Not until fifty-four days after the president's proclamation was issued was the Department of Texas formally exempted from his declaration readmitting the South to the Union.[5]

To clear up any remaining confusion, Wright issued General Orders No. 21, which restated the military-civilian government relationship in strict terms. Commanders were told to deal with "regular military duties," suppress all disloyal acts "promptly and vigorously," render proper aid to the bureau, and watch all cases in any court in which the United States or its authorities were represented. The army was not to interfere with cases and crimes committed prior to the occupation or to intervene in any situation until local authorities had a chance to act. Criminal or civil cases involving whites and blacks were to be left to the provisional government and its agents unless justice was in doubt. Although General Grant issued an order in July authorizing commanders on all levels to arrest and hold any person charged with crimes against officers, agents, citizens, or inhabitants of the United States, the commanding general of the army indicated that a cautious approach like Wright's would be wisest.[6]

Wright's position distinctly subordinated the army to civil government in most cases but actually lost little military effectiveness, for Hamilton's loyal provisional government would always be willing to call for army assistance, should it be needed. But if the people of Texas installed a government of more dubious loyalty than the provisional administration, Wright's deference to civil authority could be disastrous to blacks and Loyalists.

As Hamilton increased his influence in the state through his appointments, he was able to concentrate on one of his chief duties, that of registering loyal voters and providing for the meeting of a constitutional convention. The same three-man board that administered the loyalty oath also registered voters. On September 11, 1865, in an "Address to the People of Texas," the governor cautioned Texans that only loyal men could vote or serve as convention delegates.[7]

The process of registration was so lengthy that Hamilton did not issue the orders for an election until November 15. He defended his course in a letter to an impatient President Johnson, stating that Tex-

ans had balked at taking the oath because it involved accepting wartime proclamations, including the one on emancipation. Many believed that this decision was an unconstitutional military act and still
hoped for gradual compensated emancipation at a later date. The convention election was finally held January 8, 1866, and the elected
delegates met on February 7.[8]

When the convention convened, it quickly became apparent that
the Loyalists were in a minority. While the majority was not secessionist (in spite of reports that the convention's secretary wore a Confederate uniform), it was definitely conservative and composed of men
who had followed Texas into the war, regardless of how they felt about
secession. Hamilton, in a disappointed letter to President Johnson,
described the members as "violent and impracticable" men.[9]

The convention delayed a full month before getting down to work
because the month of February promised to be a busy one in the nation's capital. President Johnson and Congress were sparring over the
renewal of the Freedmen's Bureau and a bill granting civil rights to the
former slaves. Texans paused to await the result of these debates. The
president's veto of these bills and his attack on key congressional leaders in his Washington's Birthday speech gave Texas conservatives new
hope. No matter that Congress would eventually override Johnson's
vetoes; the state convention now moved to support him and defy
Congress.[10]

Following the procedure prescribed in President Johnson's Reconstruction proclamations,[11] the convention took up the problems of
emancipation, the Confederate debt, and the repudiation of secession. It recognized the freedom of the black race as a fact established
by force of arms. Since slavery's revival was prohibited by the Thirteenth Amendment, the convention declared the peculiar institution
to be at an end, although it refused to ratify the amendment. The convention next asked the federal government to withdraw the Freedmen's Bureau from the state. It also granted blacks the basic rights of
person and property, the right to sue and be sued, to be punished in
the same manner as whites, and to testify in court in all cases involving their race. The convention left it to the state legislature to grant
blacks the right to testify in any other cases. Texans not only repudiated the war debt but nullified the entire state debt contracted between January 28, 1861, and August 5, 1865.[12]

Having disposed of slavery and the debt, the convention turned to
the secession ordinance. Here the longest, most volatile debate occurred. The question was whether to declare the secession ordinance

null and void ab initio (that is, from the date of its inception) or to repudiate it simply as a result of the war. The staunch Unionists favored the first position but failed to convince the majority, who voted for the milder provision. Hamilton and the army had at first declared all Confederate laws null and void ab initio but by now had reversed their position and accepted all Texas laws not in conflict with the results of the war; the convention decided to do the same.[13]

After the convention adjourned, unionists and Conservatives quickly plunged into the campaign preceding the June 4 elections. Because less than two months remained in which to canvass the state, both factions bypassed nominating conventions and selected their candidates by the old caucus method. The Conservatives put forth a ticket headed by James W. Throckmorton, the convention president.

The Unionists turned to Hamilton, who was forced to decline because of personal monetary problems. They then nominated Elisha M. Pease, a firm Loyalist, but one who held a circumspect position on Reconstruction. Pease had been instrumental in moderating Hamilton's invective when the latter assumed the provisional governor's chair in August, 1865.

Originally from Connecticut, Pease had lived in Texas since the first days of the Republic. A lawyer by training, he had handled numerous state clerical positions and served as comptroller of public accounts. Prior to the war, he was a state legislator and held the governorship for two terms. Refusing to support the Confederacy, Pease had sat out the war in Austin.[14]

Pease's inaction during the war and the very name of his Union party doomed him and the party to failure, and he knew it. There was but one question in the June elections—loyalty to the South. Regardless of what a candidate believed about secession, he must have supported his state and section. Throckmorton's backers wisely adopted the Conservative Union party label, indicating that they accepted the results of the war but did so without enthusiasm. In this manner they also tempered the Loyalists' charge that they refused to abide by the war's outcome.[15]

"Secession rule," as Pease called it, became an established fact on June 4, 1866, when the Conservatives soundly trounced the Unionists throughout Texas. Throckmorton garnered 49,000 votes, while Pease gained slightly over 12,000. (See table 2 for a record of Texas governors and military commanders during Reconstruction.) The same election saw approval of the amended state constitution, although by a mere 5,000 votes.[16] The election results stunned the Union party.

One disheartened Loyalist predicted Throckmorton's Conservative Union party would rule the state for years to come. Pease observed that the Union party carried the same proportion of the vote as they had in the 1861 vote on secession.[17] There had been no "reconstruction" at all. The provisional government seemed a total failure.

One hope was left to the Loyalists. President Johnson might refuse to accept the convention and the election results. After all, Johnson was now faced with the prospect of accepting a government composed of men not of his own choosing. But should the president reject the newly elected civil government, he would be siding with men who had just proved themselves unable to control state politics after a year's effort. He would also be denying the practicality and validity of his Reconstruction program.[18]

Rather than admit defeat to his congressional critics, Johnson made the best of a poor situation. After deliberating for a month and a half, he backed the results of the June election. The Texas election and the quirks of national politics had forced the president and the Conservatives into an unforeseen alliance.[19]

Johnson's former supporters in Texas—Hamilton, Pease, and the Unionists—now had to find a new sponsor or become politically impotent, a reality which Edmund J. Davis, an early Pease supporter and later Radical Republican state governor, well understood. He said that a home guard was needed to protect Union voters and to help organize candidates and votes.

Since Union men made up less than one-third of the white male population of the state, Davis recommended that the party call a state convention of all males, black and white, twenty-one years of age or over. Universal male suffrage and a party name change to Republican were essential for future victory, he said. "By *all means let us save ourselves, if in our power, from Rebel rule,*" he pleaded.[20]

As Davis was astutely analyzing the Unionists' weaknesses, Throckmorton arrived in Austin. He immediately warned President Johnson to be on guard against malicious attempts to discredit the new Texas government. Their purpose was to set aside the election results and continue the rule of the provisional administration, asserted Throckmorton. On August 13, 1866, Throckmorton was inaugurated as governor.[21]

A Tennessean by birth, the new state executive had come to Texas in 1841. He was elected to the state legislature several times during the 1850s and was a member of the secession convention, where he had the distinction of being one of eight to vote against leaving the

Table 2. Commanding Officers and Governors of Texas, 1865–70

Governors of Texas (GOV)

Andrew Jackson Hamilton (Appointed by the President)	June 17, 1865–Aug. 13, 1866
James Webb Throckmorton (Elected)	Aug. 13, 1866–July 30, 1867
Elisha Marshall Pease (Appointed by Maj. Gen. P. H. Sheridan)	July 30, 1867–Sept. 30, 1869
Vacant (Functions of the office handled by Bvt. Maj. J. J. Reynolds)	Sept. 30, 1869–Jan. 18, 1870
Edmund J. Davis (Elected, and appointed by Bvt. Maj. Gen. J. J. Reynolds)	Jan. 18, 1870–Jan. 13, 1874

Fifth Military District Commanders (FMD)

Maj. Gen. Philip H. Sheridan	May 30, 1865–Sept. 5, 1867
Bvt. Maj. Gen. Charles Griffin	Sept. 6, 1867–Sept. 15, 1867
Bvt. Maj. Gen. Joseph A. Mower	Sept. 16, 1867–Nov. 29, 1867
Maj. Gen. Winfield Scott Hancock	Nov. 29, 1867–Mar. 17, 1868
Bvt. Maj. Gen. Joseph J. Reynolds	Mar. 18, 1868–Mar. 24, 1868
Bvt. Maj. Gen. Robert C. Buchanan	Mar. 25, 1868–July 28, 1868
Bvt. Maj. Gen. Joseph J. Reynolds	July 28, 1868–Nov. 4, 1868
Bvt. Maj. Gen. Edward R. S. Canby	Nov. 4, 1868–Mar. 5, 1869
Bvt. Maj. Gen. Joseph J. Reynolds	Mar. 5, 1869–Mar. 31, 1870

The Fifth Military District was, at various times, Military Division of the Southwest, the Division of the Gulf, and the Department of the Gulf.

District of Texas Commanders (DT)

Bvt. Maj. Gen. Gordon Granger	June 13, 1865–Aug. 21, 1865
Bvt. Maj. Gen. Horatio G. Wright	Aug. 21, 1865–Sept. 24, 1866
Bvt. Maj. Gen. George W. Getty	Sept. 24, 1866–Oct. 24, 1866
Bvt. Maj. Gen. Samuel P. Heintzelman	Oct. 24, 1866–Nov. 28, 1866
Bvt. Maj. Gen. Charles Griffin	Nov. 28, 1866–Sept. 15, 1867
Bvt. Maj. Gen. Joseph J. Reynolds	Sept. 16, 1867–July 28, 1868

On July 28, 1868, Louisiana was readmitted to the Union, leaving only Texas in the Fifth Military District, and eliminating the need for the subdivision of the District of Texas.

Texas Freedmen's Bureau Commanders (TFB)

Bvt. Maj. Gen. Edgar M. Gregory	July 10, 1865–Mar. 30, 1866
Bvt. Maj. Gen. Joseph B. Kiddoo	April 2, 1866–Jan. 24, 1867
Bvt. Maj. Gen. Charles Griffin	Jan. 24, 1867–Sept. 15, 1867
(Functions of the office handled by 2 Lt. Charles Garretson)	Sept. 15, 1867–Oct. 23, 1867
Bvt. Maj. Gen. Joseph J. Reynolds	Sept. 21, 1867–Dec. 30, 1868
Bvt. Maj. Gen. Edward R. S. Canby	Jan. 18, 1869–April 8, 1869
Bvt. Maj. Gen. Joseph J. Reynolds	April 8, 1869–April 28, 1869

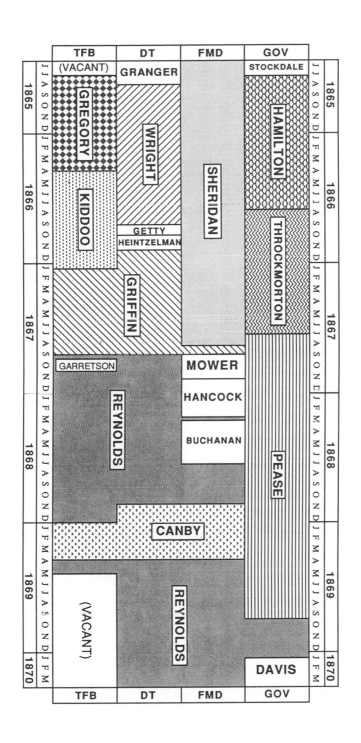

Union. He served in the state forces during the war and as a state senator. When Texas surrendered in 1865, Throckmorton was in Indian Territory treating with the Comanches. In electing him as governor in a landslide, Texans endorsed his type of wartime Unionism as the limit past which they would not go in placing a "loyal" man in office.[22]

On August 20, shortly after Throckmorton assumed office, President Johnson issued his proclamation declaring the rebellion in Texas to be ended.[23] Throckmorton and the Eleventh Legislature thought correctly that the proclamation reestablished the supremacy of the civil government over any military authority, and they acted to secure this power.[24]

In his message to the legislature, the governor recommended that laws be passed safeguarding Negro rights, that Federal troops be petitioned to withdraw from the interior, and that the frontier be more fully protected. Throckmorton also suggested that the part of Texas extending north of the Red River might be sold to the United States for Indian reservations. All in all, the governor's message was very moderate. It also revealed him to be a provincial man more interested in local issues than in national concerns.[25]

Within a week of his inauguration, the governor wrote to General Wright. Throckmorton enclosed several petitions from frontier counties requesting military protection from Indian attack. Throckmorton supported their plea and stated that he believed the interior posts could now be safely discontinued and their garrisons shifted to the west. The governor had not liked earlier army refusals to acquiesce in this need, but he understood how uncertain the mandate of the provisional government had been. Throckmorton, however, did not suffer from lack of public support, and he could no longer agree to continued occupation of an area declared loyal by the president.[26]

Because of Wright's tendency to defer to all civil government, Throckmorton expected quick agreement to his appeal. After all, in August Wright had indicated his willingness to send more soldiers to the frontier. But Sheridan had not approved the transfer then, and he did not do so now.[27] Wright's desire to cooperate with any civil government, whether Hamilton's loyal provisional administration or the new rebel regime, worried Sheridan, especially when he saw that Wright sympathized with the removal of the occupation forces.

Sheridan could not afford to be distracted by Texas matters now, because Louisiana alone was a full-time problem in itself. New Orleans had recently suffered a massive race riot that had outraged Northern

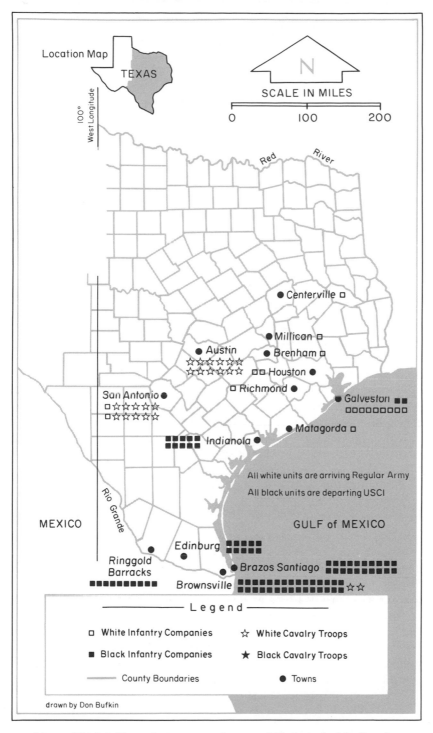

Location Map

TEXAS

100° West Longitude

N

SCALE IN MILES

0   100   200

Red River

● Centerville □

● Millican □

● Austin
☆☆☆☆☆☆
☆☆☆☆☆☆

● Brenham □

□□ Houston ●

□ Richmond ●

San Antonio ●
□☆☆☆☆☆
□☆☆☆☆☆

● Galveston ■■
□□□□□□□□□

● Matagorda □

■■■■■ Indianola ●

All white units are arriving Regular Army

All black units are departing USCI

Rio Grande

MEXICO

GULF of MEXICO

Edinburg ■■■■■

Ringgold
Barracks ●

● Brazos Santiago ■■■■■■■■■■

■■■■■■■■■

● Brownsville ■■■■■■■■■■■■■■■ ☆☆

─── Legend ───

□ White Infantry Companies   ☆ White Cavalry Troops

■ Black Infantry Companies   ★ Black Cavalry Troops

─── County Boundaries   ● Towns

drawn by Don Bufkin

Map 3. Wright's Troop Assignments, August, 1866: Arrival of the Regulars

public opinion and caused many to question Sheridan's ability to control his command. Sheridan was in fact overworked by the size of the Military Division of the Gulf, which stretched from Florida to the Rio Grande. To assist its beleaguered commander, the army reduced it to three states (Florida, Louisiana, and Texas) and renamed the new geographical unit the Department of the Gulf.[28]

Before Sheridan could adjust to the reduced load, the army expanded his authority again by appointing him the coordinator of all Freedmen's Bureau activities in the Department of the Gulf. This new assignment was too much for Sheridan. In a personal letter to General Grant, he objected strenuously to the command assignment. Sheridan wanted Florida to be put in a different department and offered to take Mississippi in exchange, and he could not comprehend why he was being charged with bureau responsibilities. He sarcastically asked Grant when he could expect to be made commissioner of Indian affairs in Texas. Speaking of Texas, Sheridan continued, it should be made a separate department in itself. He was desperately needed there to supervise civil affairs, the Rio Grande border problem, and the opening of the road to California. Yet he was "handcuffed" to his desk in New Orleans and overwhelmed by the new assignments.[29]

To reduce part of his load, Sheridan needed a man in the Texas command who could act independently in closely supervising Throckmorton and the legislature. Wright was not that officer. Without Sheridan's tutelage, Wright might well make the serious mistake of surrendering military control of the interior to Throckmorton. Hence when Sheridan's command was reshuffled, he had Grant muster Wright out of the volunteer service. The effect on Wright was to reduce him to his regular army rank of lieutenant colonel of engineers, and he was accordingly recalled to Washington for reassignment.[30]

Wright was replaced by Brevet Major General George W. Getty, an artilleryman who had served in the Seminole War and in Mexico and who possessed a fine Civil War record. A battery officer until 1863, Getty then became a division commander under Wright in the VI Corps of the Army of the Potomac. He was severely wounded at the Wilderness and had not yet fully recovered his health. He had finished the war as a corps leader and was present at Appomattox. Prior to assuming command in Texas, he served as head of the Subdistrict of the Rio Grande.[31]

Getty's illness and the army's consequent uncertainty over his assumption of command led to months of confusion in the Texas headquarters, and into the hiatus stepped the Eleventh Legislature. Although historians generally label Throckmorton an unreconstructed Rebel, as his opponents branded him, in August, 1866, the governor was still a Conservative of the Union variety. He understood what was expected of his state in Reconstruction, particularly in giving equal legal rights to the black population.

Conservatives like Throckmorton had controlled the state convention, where their prominent role had helped elect some of them to various local and state offices. Most of the Conservative Unionists, however, chose not to run for public office, which allowed the legislature to be dominated by Secessionists. Although Throckmorton was willing to compromise with the national administration, the Secessionists determined to obstruct Reconstruction as much as possible.[32]

In the legislative session the Secessionists began their quarrel with the Conservative Unionists over the election of the United States senators. According to prior agreement, the legislature was to choose one senator from the western part of the state and one from the eastern section. The Conservative Unionists expected at least one of the senators to reflect their political persuasion, and they supported John Hancock and Benjamin H. Epperson, both of whom had opposed leaving the Union. The Secessionists, however, banded together and elected outspoken Rebels David G. Burnet and Oran M. Roberts.[33]

The Secessionists then proceeded to deal with the racial problem, the main focus of which was the hated Freedmen's Bureau. The state convention had earlier begun the movement against the bureau when it sent the civil rights section of the 1866 Constitution to President Johnson. Although the Texas document did not provide blacks with as clear a declaration of rights as the president desired, it went further than most other Southern states.[34] At the same time, however, the convention had asked that the bureau be withdrawn from Texas, since it was "not only unnecessary to the protection, but absolutely prejudicial to the interests of the black race."[35]

Although the bureau was still in existence throughout the South, Texans believed that the examples of bureau prejudice, mismanagement, and interference with the elected government clearly supported their case for its removal. They resented in particular the local agents, most of whom seemed to side with blacks in legal quarrels.[36]

Bureau agents had interfered with local authorities ever since the beginning of the occupation. A Galveston man charged the bureau with expropriating a farm he bought in 1859 from a free woman of color who now claimed fraud. Sheriffs were denied military assistance in conveying black prisoners to jail. Other blacks who were convicted in civil court were forcibly removed from local authorities and exonerated of crimes in bureau courts. A seventy-year-old Webberville resident arrested on a "flimsy complaint" died in a local army stockade.[37]

Governor Throckmorton was especially disturbed when the bureau freed a black man accused of rape in Bosque County. The agent resided twenty miles from the scene of the crime and had no firsthand knowledge of the incident. The local sheriff was threatened with military arrest if he interfered. In Matagorda County, the bureau released a freedman charged with murderous assault. At Galveston, black sailors charged with mutiny were acquitted in a bureau court.

Complaints were so intense in Lockhart that, for his own safety, the local subassistant commissioner confiscated citizens' firearms with the aid of an infantry company. In nearby Prairie Lea, whites were disarmed while local blacks drilled in a militia company led by their nefarious leader, "the Doctor." Other black drill units were supposedly in existence in the state under bureau protection, and Governor Throckmorton asked General Kiddo to disarm these groups. On the other hand, Unionists complained that armed companies from the Black Brigade, a white terrorist organization, roamed the streets in one area threatening the freedmen. In this case, however, the governor failed to intercede.[38]

While whites grumbled about bureau "tyrannies," the subassistant commissioners had their own complaints. Agent William Longworth at Seguin reported that the civil authorities were so disposed against him that he needed a troop detachment for personal protection. Local citizens described Longworth as aribtrary, unjust, and vindictive and accused him of pocketing 10 percent of all fines collected and of demoralizing local black laborers.[39]

The Beaumont agent swore he would resign unless headquarters returned "his guard." The troops were not restored, and he carried out his threat a week later. Even agents who considered themselves well received requested armed assistance. Mired down by excessive troop requests, the adjutant in Galveston must have noted with surprise the report of James C. Devine, the agent at Huntsville, who saw no need for a military escort.[40]

Devine was not the only subassistant commissioner who did not need troop support. Some agents followed the easiest course and supported local planters rather than the freedmen. The Centerville bureau representative was courting an attractive widow and helped her discipline her black laborers. He tracked down runaways and hanged them by their thumbs.[41] The Austin agent, appointed on Governor Throckmorton's recommendation, required blacks to go through the civil courts in all equity cases before he would consider their pleas. In Victoria, the bureau agent often sided with white defendants in his court.[42]

Most clever planters learned to use the bureau to their own advantage. James M. Alexander at Huntsville regularly consulted with the bureau on how to work his laborers and how to divide his crop among his freedmen employees. Thomas Affleck of Brenham learned early in the occupation to rely on the bureau agent. A firm believer that blacks "*must* be kept in their places," Affleck still refused to run afoul of bureau regulations. When one of his employees admitted to theft, Affleck, "knowing the result of a white man resenting any indignity *now* from a negro," held his temper and reported the incident to the bureau.[43]

When several of his field hands "*grossly insulted*" his wife, Affleck reported, "[I am] under such a degree of excitement that I dare not trust myself to deal with them." He sent a loyal black man into town to bring out the local agent, "the officer in command of this class of people," to solve the problem. Such restraint saved Affleck from the three-hundred-dollar fine usually meted out to those who beat Negroes.[44]

The real problem, as the planters saw it, was that no civil law dealt with the blacks as freedmen. The Freedmen's Bureau was too temporary and irregular to rely upon forever, and Texans believed that some form of compulsory black labor was necessary.[45] The feeling resulted in the Black Codes, a series of controversial measures that sought to govern the use of former slaves as free laborers.

Thomas Affleck, the representative of the Texas Land, Labor, and Immigration Company, drew up the preliminary drafts for the bills passed. Although the laws were designed to regulate Negro labor, one important reason they were passed was to attract white immigrants to Texas by clarifying the negro's role in society.

Because Texas had been late in reorganizing its government after the war, she benefitted from Northern criticism leveled at Black codes passed by other Southern states. In many cases Texas used this knowledge to her own advantage by enacting army orders into state laws.[46] For example, the state act "to provide for the punishment of persons tampering with, persuading or enticing away . . . laborers or apprentices under contract" was quite similar to Freedmen's Bureau Circular No. 14 of May 15, 1866. The Texas law stated that anyone "who shall persuade, or entice away from the service of an employer, any person who is under contract of labor to such an employer" was liable to a fine or imprisonment in the county jail or both. Any person who employed a laborer still under contract to another employer would receive similar punishment. Employers who discharged an apprentice had to issue a written certificate of discharge to enable the apprentice to find a new position; failure to do so brought a fine. Circular No. 14 did not go into as much detail, but it did provide that those who enticed away a laborer or apprentice under contract would suffer a fine. In addition, the bureau circular provided that laborers who allowed themselves to be enticed away could be fined, with the amount to be withheld from their wages.[47]

The army also helped entrench the lien and sharecropping system in agriculture. In the fall of 1865, General Gregory had ordered any labor contract to constitute a lien on the crop. The state legislature passed a lien law one year later providing that any provisions, tools, stock, or cash that was advanced to make a crop constituted a lien on that crop. The lien had priority over all other debts that might be contracted except the rent of the land. Some time later, in December 1866, the bureau issued Circular No. 25, which ordered agents to recommend that negroes work for a share of the crop rather than wages. With the bureau's approval, the lien and sharecropping were well established in the state by 1869, and most black farmers were doomed to be tenants at the mercy of their economic betters.[48]

For similar reasons, the army acquiesced, passing a strict vagrancy law designed to make plantation work more attractive than idleness to the freedmen. The act defined a vagrant as any "idle person, living without any means of support, and making no exertions to obtain a livelihood, by honest employment." Included in this definition were gamblers, prostitutes, habitual drunkards, "or persons who stroll idly about in the streets of towns or cities, having no local habitation, and no honest business or employment." Such persons, when convicted, could be fined and put to labor on public works until their debts were paid off. Those who refused to work for the municipality could be lodged in the town jail and forced to live on bread and water until they changed their minds. Their sentences would not begin until they actually began to work them off.

The Freedmen's Bureau believed that vagrancy laws were a valid means of dealing with those who refused to sign labor contracts, as long as the laws were applied equally to whites and blacks. General Gregory had been very strict on this matter and had defined as a vagrant any black away from his employer more than one day "without a just cause."[49] The army, however, had grave doubts about the November 1 law, "An Act Regulating Contracts for Labor." Unlike the other laws, this measure obviously applied only to the freedmen.[50] Parts of the act followed earlier Freedmen's Bureau directives. Contracts binding on all family members were to be made with heads of families; they were to be written out in triplicate, with copies given to the employer, the laborer, and the county records; they constituted a lien on the crop; and the employees could not leave their place of work without their employer's permission.[51]

Other sections of the act, however, hinted at a reenslavement of the freedmen. If the laborer feigned sickness, an amount equal to double the wages could be deducted for the lost time. Any disobedience by the laborer incurred a fine. Losses due to theft were to be restored to the employer at double their value. Most important, the employer was allowed to assess these fines himself, although the laborer then had the right to appeal to the nearest justice of the peace. Another especially offensive demand was that laborers be on call twenty-four hours each day, with the stipulation that "it is the duty of this class of laborers to be especially civil and polite to their employer, his family and guests."[52]

The Black Codes have been attacked by recent historians, but they were an honest attempt by the legislature, blinded as it was by racial prejudice, to make what it thought was a workable system of free labor. To Northerners and Loyalists the codes were a disguised form of bondage.[53] John L. Haynes voiced the feelings of Texas Unionists when he listed six provisions of the acts as representing a form of pseudoslavery: (1) the section forcing freedmen to contract with the planter by January 10 of each year, (2) the clause declaring all blacks without contracts to be vagrants, (3) the part requiring the surrender of all guns upon signing a contract, (4) the article apprenticing young blacks to white guardians, (5) the paragraph preventing the enticement of laborers, and (6) the requirement preventing the entrance into plantation homes without the owner's permission. For the time being, however, the army did little except require Freedmen's Bureau agents hereafter to supervise all contract agreements between blacks and whites.[54]

4

Pride in Rebellion

ALTHOUGH GOVERNOR THROCKMORTON AGREED that laws were needed to define blacks' place in Texas society, he did not recommend the Black Codes. Neither did he desire the election of rebel senators. The governor found himself in the same predicament President Johnson had experienced in June; he had headed the ticket that helped elect the legislators, and he could not now repudiate his own state government. To do so would be an admission that Texas could no longer adequately govern itself, and Throckmorton was too much of a democrat to deny that the people were the wisest rulers of their own state. Like any good politician, the governor chose to lead his people and stay in power. Accordingly he moved over to the Secessionist side.[1]

Throckmorton's shift brought angry denunciations from both the army and the Unionists. Sheridan disgustedly asserted that the state executive had for his standard, "Pride in Rebellion; that it was a righteous but lost cause, being overpowered by the Federal forces." Sheridan was doing his best to support the elected government, "but it had been embarrassing in the extreme," he said. The general particularly marveled that, while Hamilton had constantly demanded more troops, Throckmorton seemed to deny that they were needed at all.[2]

The Unionists were equally dismayed about "rebel rule." A San Antonio man reported that the influence of Throckmorton was so strong that even the local federal garrison was on his side. Another Union man claimed that army supply contracts were let mostly to former rebels. Something obviously had to be done.

After his defeat in June, Elisha M. Pease had left for a Connecticut vacation, and now he and A. J. Hamilton were asked to explain the Texas situation to Congress. Unless Congress acted to save the Unionists, they warned, the loyal voice in Texas would die out. The office-holding clause of the Fourteenth Amendment was deemed insufficient to ensure Union control in Texas. Loyalists had even feared that Throckmorton's legislature would approve the amendment just to stay in power. More stringent measures to disfranchise all former Confederates were needed, wrote Judge T. H. Duval to Pease. Duval wanted to require all voters to take an oath that they had never voted for secession.[3]

The Union men need not have feared that the Texas legislature would approve the Fourteenth Amendment. Already confident that they had won final control of the state, the legislature rejected the amendment and began to attack those "experimenting, humbuging, rascally, fanatical hounds of hell," as Throckmorton characterized the Loyalists.[4]

The Conservative regime used the state's newspapers as its sounding board. The activities of Hamilton and Pease were denounced by the *Galveston Tri-Weekly News*. "It is not the practice in Texas to kill buzzards," began the piece on Hamilton. "We are there taught . . . to let the creatures alone; but if there is a buzzard in Texas that would condescend to puke upon Jack Hamilton," the *News* allowed as how "its life would not be worth the smallest fraction of the remotest possibility." As for Pease, the newspaper said that, since he was "too cowardly to rob, and too mean to beg," he had compromised and become "the swift and paid witness of those willing to pay for a lie."[5]

John L. Haynes wrote Pease to inform him of the hostile press. He doubted that Pease and Hamilton could safely return to the state. Haynes prayed that the national elections would "go right" and that President Johnson's supporters would be defeated. Only then would there be hope for Texas loyalism. Should the Johnsonites win nationally, continued Haynes, they would all have to say good-bye to Texas and "seek a clime more congenial."[6] Haynes's prayers in fact would be answered.

The immediate situation, however, was even worse than Haynes feared. In the fall of 1866, a series of notorious incidents of military misconduct caused the army much difficulty and critically affected its hold on the interior. One of these events occurred at Victoria, where two black soldiers accused of the murder of William Walker were shielded from local authorities by the Freedmen's Bureau. Throckmorton wrote Brevet Major General Samuel P. Heintzelman, commander of the Central district of Texas, to demand the alleged wrongdoers' arrest and trial by civil authorities. He protested the intercession of the Victoria subassistant commissioner in this case and others and, since the bureau agent was a soldier, called for his court-martial.[7]

The Walker case was part of Throckmorton's assault on military interference with civilian authority. The governor held that the president's proclamation of August 20, declaring the rebellion ended in

Texas, had restored all civil power. He now sought to have the army recognize this restoration, and General Heintzelman indeed agreed to allow a grand jury to investigate the incident. By early November, 1866, the panel returned a murder indictment which Throckmorton forwarded to Sheridan. The latter reluctantly concurred in the findings and agreed to turn the soldiers over to the civil authorities for trial, only to discover they had already left Texas and been discharged in Baltimore. Although he was angered with their getaway, Throckmorton considered the outcome of the Walker case to be a great victory for the restored civil government.[8]

Sheridan's foothold on Texas became more tenuous than ever because of two other incidents that had thoroughly undermined the army's position in eastern Texas. In a Bell County case known as the Lindley affair, the embarrassment was shared by Throckmorton and the army. Lindley was a horse thief who feared that two Bell County residents, Duncan and Davis, might have incriminating evidence against him. He cleverly accused Duncan and Davis of leading the mob that had hanged his son for pro-Union sentiment during the war. An army patrol led by a man variously described as "Sergeant" or "Major" Carpenter arrested the two suspects. Lindley traveled with the party and at one point shot and killed Duncan and Davis for "trying to escape." In a later military trial, the army denied Throckmorton's attorney general the right to be present and question witnesses. All parties involved were acquitted. Later, however, Lindley was arrested in Bell County. In spite of assurances to the governor concerning his safety, a mob took him from the jail and hanged him.[9]

The inability of authorities in Bell County to safeguard Lindley hurt Throckmorton's claim that his government could handle all civil affairs fairly. But Sheridan could not capitalize upon this incident because of one of the worst atrocities committed by soldiers during Reconstruction, namely, the Brenham fire in September, 1866, a holocaust involving both the army and the Freedmen's Bureau.[10]

Brenham had always been a rough place. Fights amused the toughs who idled along the sidewalks. Unionists, Yankee businessmen, and blue-coated soldiers alike were hated. The local newspaper editor, D. L. McGary, an unreconstructed Confederate who characterized his sheet as a "Red Hot Democratic Journal," contributed to the unrest by continually attacking federal authority.[11]

In the spring of 1866, garrison duties at Brenham had been assumed by a company of the Seventeenth Infantry, fresh from its infamous Galveston street fights. Along with the soldiers came the new bureau agent, Captain Samuel A. Craig. The subassistant commissioner zealously set to work guarding the hitherto ignored rights of the freedmen and establishing black schools. He was a proud, efficient man who was easily insulted, easy prey for McGary's biting editorials.

Craig endured as much as he could and then in August arrested the newspaperman for insulting comments on bureau education efforts. McGary refused to pay a two-hundred-dollar fine, triumphantly marched off to jail, and smuggled new editorials out of his cell—firsthand accounts of recent bureau "tyrannies."[12]

The editor became an instant martyr. Complaints poured into military headquarters on all levels. Inspired by McGary's example, the town harassed soldiers mercilessly in the streets. Tempers on both sides were high. On September 7, several drunken soldiers caused a disturbance by attending a Negro dance. When sponsors asked them to buy tickets, the soldiers broke up the party. White citizens who were holding a ball nearby tried to stop the trouble, but insults were traded and several infantrymen shot.

Later that night the soldiers returned, arrested two men, and looted a general store. The store was set afire and the conflagration spread to other buildings. A man identified as Brevet Major G. W. Smith, the post commander (or more accurately, some man on the major's horse), directed the whole operation. The threat of attack from townspeople caused the soldiers to fortify their camp. Ensuing investigations failed to cool the incident's impact. Ultimately, the army acknowledged that its men should have been punished, but there were so many conflicting stories that the matter was allowed to lapse, in spite of vociferous complaints from Governor Throckmorton, the state legislature, and local officials.[13]

The Brenham fire led other army detachments to capitalize on the terror it caused. Signs were posted around army camps located in hostile areas as warnings to local people: "If this camp is molested, every house in the community will be burned."[14] Both Captain Craig and Major Smith received transfers to other assignments. Craig reported to Seguin, where he continued his controversial actions. After freeing a soldier charged with gambling by civil authorities, he destroyed some court records, which led to his arrest by the town sheriff. Craig was released by another officer and spirited out of Texas posthaste, an action Throckmorton found "beyond my comprehension." Smith followed Craig at Seguin, oddly enough, and two and a half years later was court-martialed for embezzlement and misappropriation of Freedmen's Bureau funds.[15]

Several months after the Brenham fire, another event caused further public ire over the army's presence in eastern Texas. Two hundred Twenty-sixth Infantry recruits marching from Indianola to Austin had to endure jeers and threats from several armed mobs. Some bystanders even offered the soldiers whiskey in an attempt to make the men more responsive to the harassment. Especially rough treatment was reserved for the recruits' guards, a detachment of the Third United States Colored Infantry.[16] Finally the Negroes could stand no more and profanely told a Mrs. Oliver to keep quiet.

The woman's husband wrote a letter of protest to Governor Throckmorton, who forwarded the complaint to General Sturgis, asking that the troops' route of travel be altered. Sturgis admitted that the kind of treatment endured by the recruits and their guards had led to many unfortunate incidents, but he refused to order the men to change their course. Throckmorton immediately challenged Sturgis's contention, asserting that the soldiers had caused the ill-feeling by their own faulty conduct.[17]

All such incidents placed the United States soldiers under a dark shadow of suspicion during the fall of 1866. An elected government had assumed office, and the frontier was ablaze, yet soldiers were intimidating the populace and were burning and plundering throughout the interior of the state instead of defending Texas from Indian incursions. Accurately reflecting the opinion of those who elected him to office, the governor had already resolved to do something about this anomaly during his election campaign.

A week after his inauguration Throckmorton wrote to General Wright and asked him to send troops to the west. He also asked Wright to bring the matter to Sheridan's attention in New Orleans. On September 25, 1866, he wrote to General Heintzelman at San Antonio to complain about continued raids and to ask that a post be established at the mouth of the Big Wichita River. Evidently the governor believed that the army would not act, because he telegraphed detailed information on some recent attacks to President Johnson. Secretary of War Stanton replied for the president, saying that the matter was under consideration.[18]

Sheridan was not entirely unresponsive to the reported depredations. In early September, 1866, hoping to undercut Throckmorton's position, he ordered the Fourth Cavalry transferred from San Antonio to Camp Verde and Fort Martin Scott, near Fredericksburg. He did not send troops elsewhere, because he stated that there were no other official reports of raids.

Governor Throckmorton quickly informed the general that the Comanches to the north were the main cause for distress. He asked that posts be established to block the trails into Texas from Indian Territory. At the same time, he promised Sheridan that Negroes would receive justice and fair treatment, which would lessen the need for soldiers in the interior. Sheridan forwarded the letter to Washington, but in an endorsement stated that he thought Throckmorton had exaggerated the Indian problem and that he doubted that the governor could guarantee the impartiality of Texas officials toward the freedmen. Sheridan said he would set up more frontier posts the following spring.[19]

The governor's complaint to President Johnson had struck a sympathetic note, however, and Grant was asked to do something to solve the problem. Grant informed Sheridan that evidence amassed by Throckmorton made the problem look quite serious. Grant ordered an investigation and told Sheridan to break up the interior posts, if necessary, to ensure proper frontier defense. Grant wanted to make certain that the state government had no excuse for raising and employing state troops.[20]

Sheridan immediately informed Grant that he had ordered eleven companies of the Sixth Cavalry north to Jacksboro, which meant that his entire cavalry force of twenty-one companies was sent to the frontier, with the exception of two troops at Brownsville and one troop on orderly service at New Orleans.[21] Sheridan also indicated that the Second Battalion of the Seventeenth Infantry had been moved to Austin for possible frontier duty and that the Ninth Cavalry, a recently recruited Negro regiment, was coming to Texas. Sheridan hinted that, if the state behaved itself and did not protest Reconstruction unduly, this black unit would probably be sent to the west. The race-conscious Texans would then be spared the burden of occupation by Negro soldiers again. Sheridan also mentioned that he expected another black outfit, the Forty-first Infantry, to be placed along the frontier sometime in 1867.[22]

Although Throckmorton continued to flood military headquarters with accounts of Indian depredations, Sheridan never received official army reports of the Comanche raids and continued to suspect that they were exaggerated or false. The general believed that the freighting companies which held army contracts magnified and possibly invented stories of depredation to justify bigger contracts to supply additional frontier garrisons. He thought that the settlers also exaggerated actual attacks to secure posts in their area in order to build up the

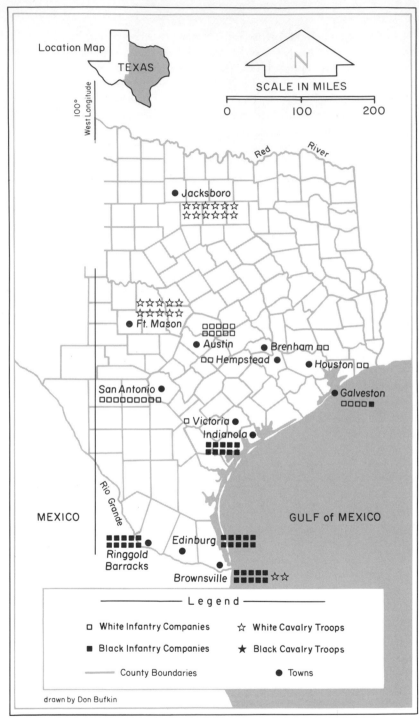

Map 4. Heintzelman's Troop Assignments, November, 1866: Troop Movement West

economy. The worst of Sheridan's suspicions seemed to be confirmed when a staff officer uncovered a false massacre story in the Camp Verde area.[23]

In addition, Throckmorton appeared to be using the supposed Indian raids as an excuse to raise a one-thousand-man force for "frontier defense." Throckmorton apparently was convinced that neither the Federal government nor the local army command would provide sufficient soldiers for West Texas.[24] Since Throckmorton did not give the army time to prove its intent on the frontier question, Sheridan suspected that these volunteers would be a threat to the national government's control of the state.

Even though state militia companies had been informally sanctioned by Governor Hamilton during the summer of 1865 and used ever since,[25] the new plan proposed by the state legislature and Throckmorton envisioned an official and more permanent force of state troops. When Sheridan received the governor's letter suggesting the possibility of raising Texas volunteers, he forwarded it to Washington, noting his disapproval of the plan. A week later Throckmorton sent President Johnson a similar report, but he never obtained an answer.

On September 29, 1866, the persistent state executive formally asked Sheridan's approval of the troops and mentioned that Indian attacks were increasing; he also sent a similar note to Secretary of War Stanton. Sheridan again referred the request to higher headquarters and later wrote Grant that he feared the state soldiers were being used as a guise to remove the army from the interior and to compromise the Reconstruction effort. Sheridan said he had already sent cavalry out to handle the Indian problem, and since "the troops raised in Texas would be of the element which fought against the government," he believed such units were not needed.[26]

Throckmorton quickly protested Sheridan's refusal to accept the Texas volunteers. The governor insisted that he had no ulterior motive in mind but merely wished to defend the state. Meanwhile Grant notified Sheridan that he agreed that there were enough regulars to handle the job in Texas. To appease Throckmorton, Sheridan promised that "as much protection as we possibly can give the frontier will be cheerfully given" but said he could not set up the western garrisons until the next spring.[27]

The wily Throckmorton was in no mood to wait and decided on a new course of action. The key to his plan was a command shift in the District of Texas. Because of his recurring illness, General Getty applied for and received a prolonged leave of absence. He was replaced as district commander by Brevet Major General Samuel P. Heintzelman, currently in charge of the Central District of Texas at San Antonio.[28]

Heintzelman was one of the oldest officers in the entire army, having graduated from West Point in 1826. He had fought Indians and served in the Mexican War, where he was brevetted for gallantry in action. In the 1850s, he had been stationed in Texas for several years and was well known and respected there. He became colonel of the Seventeenth Infantry in 1861 and was a division commander at Bull Run and a corps commander under McClellan. He was in charge of the defenses of Washington in 1863, commanded the Northern Department (New York and New England) in 1864, and served on various court-martial boards to the war's conclusion.

Heintzelman had a stern countenance and an unkempt appearance. He tended to magnify difficulties before him and was not an aggressive leader. Once again, Sheridan was saddled with an officer who, like Granger, Wright, and Getty, extended kindness, consideration, and sympathy to the former Confederates who made up the state's civil administration. When Heintzelman arrived in Galveston to assume command on October 24, he received a letter from Throckmorton. The governor said that he would not raise the controversial state troops if the army would send more men to West Texas immediately. He also, however, commanded state officers to organize their companies informally, in spite of Sheridan's orders to the contrary.[29]

Heintzelman may not have known about Sheridan's orders, but even if he had, he probably would not have protested the governor's action. Heintzelman had often allowed the use of ranger and militia companies before the war when he commanded at Brownsville. He even had encouraged them to raid across the border to counter similar Mexican threats, a tolerance that Throckmorton was counting on to assist the state in its current emergency.[30]

Unlike Heintzelman, Sheridan had assumed the whole matter was settled—until he obtained a copy of the *Waco Register* which contained a notice of a meeting of armed men interested in becoming part of Throckmorton's one thousand volunteers. Sheridan was incensed. He notified Grant that he would settle the problem and once again acridly and emphatically refused to allow Throckmorton to call up volunteers in any form.[31]

To satisfy Grant's earlier request for a complete inquiry, Sheridan sent his most trusted aide, Major George A. Forsyth, to the northwestern frontier to investigate the Indian forays. Forsyth arrived in

Galveston in November, 1866, where he spoke with General Heintzelman before proceeding to Austin to see the governor. Throckmorton received Forsyth cordially and gave him complete cooperation in his investigation.

As he left for Waco, the major informed Sheridan that he had no solid evidence yet, "but I am convinced that many of the people who are moving in from the frontier are doing it to better their economic condition, and not from any fear they may have of Indians." Ten days later, he wrote his superior again, this time noting that the newspapers in Texas were highly inaccurate in their reporting and tended to exaggerate their news items.[32] After traveling as far north as Weatherford, Forsyth returned and submitted a full report.[33] The major found several instances in which Indians had raided settlements and believed there had been others. The biggest problem, he discovered, was that those people living on the frontier were not the brave, hardy settlers depicted in the American myth. Instead the whole frontier was permeated with a fear beyond comprehension.

At Fort Belknap "the local settlement was pretty thoroughly stampeded, scarcely daring to venture away from the post."[34] The cavalry commander at Jacksboro told the major that those settlers who suffered raids were too afraid to leave their homes to report them. By the time he was informed of an attack, his patrols were already one or two days behind the Indians, and it was impossible to catch up to them on the "worthless horses" at his disposal.[35] Forsyth also reported that, even though the Indians did commit murder when the opportunity presented itself, their primary goal was to obtain horses and salable goods, not to kill. Local citizens believed the raiders came from Indian Territory, and they wanted the army to attack the villages there in reprisal, said Forsyth. In conclusion, the major recommended that a post be established near old Fort Belknap to extend army protection to the people there.[36]

Dissatisifed with Forsyth's report, Throckmorton sent out a printed form to all county judges, asking for a complete account of all Indian depredations within their judicial districts.[37] On the basis of the replies to this circular, the governor declared to Secretary of War Stanton in August, 1867, that since the Civil War, 162 persons had been killed by Indians, 43 captured, and 24 wounded. An estimated 31,000 cattle, 2,800 horses, and 2,400 sheep and goats had been stolen during the same period. Once again Throckmorton wrote to Galveston and urged that more forts be established.[38]

By now, the army was reeling in confusion from the Texas executive and legislative offensive.[39] Sheridan was repeatedly checked by Throck-morton's machinations, hampered by successive legislative acts (choosing rebel senators, rejecting the Fourteenth Amendment, passing the Black Codes, suggesting the enrollment of state defense troops to check the Indians), and embarrassed by the army's poor relations with the civilians in general, as evidenced by the Brenham fire and other incidents.

General Grant, Attorney General of the United States Henry Stanbery, and Governor Throckmorton all called on Sheridan to issue such orders "as will prevent the collision between military and civil jurisdiction in the State of Texas."[40] The army was clearly losing control of the state as civil government was strengthening its hand.[41] Throckmorton reportedly even had his own black adherents going among the freedmen to secure their support for his administration.[42]

The Unionists were deeply concerned abut Throckmorton's success. Defeated in the state election and with the army seemingly unable to counter Conservative plans, the loyal men in Texas needed congressional help to survive. One disheartened Loyalist predicted that he and others who believed as he did would have to flee the state by Christmas. Only Congress could save them by nullifying the actions of President Johnson and by countering the Conservative offensive, "if need be, by *real* military occupation."[43]

Then came the cheering news of the victory of Johnson's opponents in the 1866 national election. The Unionists realized that the ensuing months were critical. Congress was expected to act to deny control of the state to the Secessionists while Throckmorton's regime was still disorganized by the election results. Unionists quickly spoke to the issue. John L. Haynes wrote to Elisha M. Pease, angrily denouncing the actions of the Eleventh Legislature as a disgrace to the state. The legislature had degraded blacks, set up unfair monopolies, and gerry-mandered Unionists out of what little power they still possessed. He demanded that Congress reorganize the state government in harmony with that of the nation, as reflected by the 1866 congressional elections. The rebel government of Texas, he emphasized, must be "wiped out of existence."[44]

Sheridan also knew he had to act now to save the army's position in Texas. Fuming over the "increased indolence on the part of the functionaries of the civil law" in Texas, he wrote a comprehensive, biting report on his last year and a half as the area commander. He emphasized the duplicity of the Confederate surrender, the unrepentant rebel spirit which necessitated a massive invasion force, the logistic problems he had overcome, the neutralization of Maximilian in Mexico, the demobilization, Throckmorton's disloyalty, the injustice done the army at Brenham, and the harmless nature of the Indian problem. Sheridan's essay arrived in Washington immediately after the Republican victory in the national elections and the reconvening of Congress and consequently exerted great influence in the congressional decision to get tough with the South the following spring.[45]

Sheridan also decided to secure a different man to represent the army in Texas. After the wearing year he had just spent—going to Brownsville to stop filibustering raids, then to Galveston to oversee the elections for the new civil government, then to New Orleans for the July race-riot investigation, and back to Texas to cool the Brenham fire aftermath—he could take no more chances. He had to replace Heintzelman with a more reliable officer.

When Heintzelman returned some old cannons to the city of Galveston, Sheridan went into action.[46] With the connivance of Grant, Sheridan had Colonel Charles Griffin assigned to Galveston at his brevet rank of major general. Although Heintzelman's colonelcy predated Griffin's, Griffin had held his brevet rank longer than Heintzelman had held his. This technicality forced Heintzelman to step down and rejoin his regiment at the junior rank.[47]

When he heard of the change, Throckmorton wrote to the old general, thanking him for his courtesy while in charge and expressing sorrow at his leaving. He believed Griffin could alleviate the suffering on the frontier, but he especially would miss Heintzelman's hand at the helm of civil affairs. The letter was signed "your friend and humble servant," a rare show of affection from the usually very formal governor. Newspapers echoed Throckmorton's feelings, calling his note a "deserving compliment" and announcing Heintzelman's reduction in rank with regret.[48]

Throckmorton and the Conservatives had good reason to mourn the removal of General Heintzelman. In Charles Griffin, Heintzelman's replacement, Sheridan had found just the man he had been looking for. A ramrod-stiff regular, Griffin had been an artillery instructor at West Point before the war. He received a division in 1862 and served brilliantly with the Army of the Potomac in every major campaign in the East. He was considered a strict disciplinarian, and his solid qualities caused Sheridan to elevate Griffin to corps command on the battlefield at Five Forks.

Now, after the war, Sheridan again turned to Griffin, a soldier "seemingly of Sheridan's own volatile and arbitrary temperament"; in character, "bluff, bellicose, outspoken, and quick to take offense." More important, unlike his predecessors, Griffin understood the political purposes of Reconstruction. He would not hobnob with former Confederates. He would be suspicious of the intention of the state's civil government and would pursue the soon-to-be-announced congressional policy even more enthusiastically than had Sheridan.[49]

Griffin's accession to power marked the end of an era in Texas Reconstruction. Although it took three months yet for Congress to act, Presidential Reconstruction was over. Gone were the do-nothing generals with their outmoded ideas of an easy peace and the need to yield to any popularly elected official who ruled the state. Gone too was the all-pervasive influence of General Sheridan. Sheridan hereafter limited his Texas interests so that he might concentrate on the confusing turbulence of Louisiana politics. After Griffin's takeover, military and political power tended to rest in the hands of the District of Texas commander instead of the area commander in New Orleans or any provisional or elected state governor.

The Conservatives' offensive had spent its momentum. They had supported the wrong leader in Washington. Congress was about to emerge as the supreme political power and force the South to redo the whole readmission process. There had been continual warnings to Texans to take another course. Northern friends cautioned them to send loyal men to Congress.[50] The legislature responded with Secessionists. John Reagan admonished them to give up secession openly, to recognize the authority of the Federal government, and to give the black race at least a qualified right to vote.[51] The legislature answered with criticism of the occupation forces, rejection of the Fourteenth Amendment, and a proposal for a state defense force composed of former Confederate soldiers. President Johnson, in response to an inquiry from Governor Throckmorton, told the Texas legislature to pass laws guaranteeing civil rights and "equal and exact justice to all persons without regard to color."[52] The legislature answered with the Black Codes.

Years later John Reagan wrote of this era that the refusal to adopt the recommendations which he and others made "was giving a pretext to the more radical and violent members of Congress to adopt still harsher and more cruel measures of Reconstruction." Reagan admitted that "there is more chance of political success in appealing to the passions and prejudices of a people . . . than appealing to their reason and requesting them to make concessions necessary to their welfare." But he sorrowed that the leaders of Texas "refused to act and thus involved the State in all the horrors of military government, universal negro suffrage, and the cruel measures of Reconstruction." Politics had "worked a great evil—the leaders failed to act."[53]

Yet Throckmorton and particularly the legislature had done all they thought necessary. If they failed to act properly, it was because they did not know how. Texans' response to Reconstruction was sad, and yet it was typically American. Their response, and that of the other Southern states, was unique, for no part of the nation had ever lost a war before.[54]

PART TWO
Military Reconstruction: The Griffin Era, 1866–67

I trust so soon as the law will permit, there will be changes in the civil affairs of this state.

—Bvt. Maj. Gen. Charles Griffin to Maj. Gen. Philip H. Sheridan,
July 20, 1867

5

The Political General

DAVID J. BALDWIN had been one of former governor Hamilton's
original appointees to public office during the hectic days at
the end of the Civil War. Proud of his continual adherence to the
Union cause, Baldwin offered himself to the provisional government
in any capacity to assist Hamilton in reconstructing their wayward
home state. When the provisional governor asked him to serve as
United States attorney for the Eastern District of Texas, Baldwin
quickly accepted the post.[1]

As the Federal district attorney in Houston, Baldwin continued his
active loyalism. He especially enjoyed thwarting the efforts of rebel
judges who kept trying to prosecute military men or alleged criminal
behavior in their enforcement of army and Freedmen's Bureau edicts.
His most spectacular case in this respect occurred in December, 1866,
shortly after General Griffin assumed command of the District of Texas.

The litigation involved Griffin's predecessor, General Samuel P.
Heintzelman. General Heintzelman, in his former capacity as head of
the Central District of Texas, was accused of illegal interference with
state authorities. The specific charge related to his forceful release of
Captain Samuel Craig from the Seguin jail after the latter had been
indicted and arrested for destroying county court records that were
linked to arraignments concerning army personnel. In his legal advice
to Heintzelman, Baldwin vividly revealed the contempt that Unionists felt toward Throckmorton's elected government.[2]

Baldwin admitted to Heintzelman that in normal times the army
was distinctly subordinate to civil authority. The present state government, however, according to the district attorney, was "prostituted" in
such a fashion as to annoy military officers and oppose them in their
lawful duties. It was therefore necessary to cooperate with those who
acted loyally in legal affairs, postulated Baldwin, rather than worry
about civil versus military supremacy. He labeled Throckmorton and
his officials "mischievous and even bad men" whose disloyal "machinations" would never cease. "They have tried in succession nullifica-

tion, secession, and armed rebellion and failed in all." Such men have only brought grief to the nation, said Baldwin. "When war fails them, the forms of law are prostituted to cover their wicked designs," which included "acts of unblushing and murderous outrage."

It amused the district attorney that the ultimate defense for his and General Heintzelman's position rested upon the United States Supreme Court decision *Ableman* v. *Booth,* which had been decided by a unanimous rebel court led by the slaveholding states' rights advocate, Roger B. Taney.[3] Baldwin concluded that Heintzelman had acted loyally, hence legally, while the state's action in indicting the general was marked by "counterfeit values" which were absurd and illegal.[4]

Baldwin was not alone in his beliefs. W. C. Philips, an outspoken Loyalist, remarked that the only true remedy for the state's present problems was the reconstruction of Texas by loyal men alone. The temper of the population was more disloyal than before the war, claimed another Unionist. Throckmorton's influence was so pervasive that the population needed a prolonged education under a territorial government, asserted a San Antonio man.[5]

Unionists expressed their happiness that Elisha M. Pease and others were in Washington stimulating Congress to act properly toward the South. "We must have a change before we can have peace and quietness in the country." declared M. H. Beatty to Pease, adding that the "Modern Democracy," a reference to Throckmorton's regime, was a rebel plot to "rule or ruin" the country.[6]

The Unionists particularly called for an application of Federal strength in Texas. "*Power* alone" would hold the Throckmorton "rebels" back, said Judge Colbert Caldwell, and if it was not utilized soon the Unionists and the Republican party in the state would be finished. "Very little severity at the proper time could have settled matters," according to Morgan C. Hamilton, brother of the former provisional governor. He believed "even now it would work a wonderful change in our Chivalry." Morgan Hamilton thought the legal atmosphere under Throckmorton's administration so abominable that he believed one of Quantrill's raiders could escape indictment.[7]

The Unionists desired massive federal intervention because of Governor Throckmorton's continued pressure against the occupying forces. The conduct of the soldiers, to be sure, made it easy for the governor to criticize the army. The Seventeenth Infantry detachment at Galveston, for example, kept that region in an uproar. A half dozen soldiers demanded entrance at a show put on in the Galveston Theater. They refused to pay when asked to do so, produced an array of weapons, and implied they would force the entrance if necessary. When the proprietor asked for their orders, the bluecoats "replied insolently." Eventually the men were admitted to the performance and behaved quietly while inside. But the *Daily News* protested the appearance of these armed men inside the building. The newspaper admitted that soldiers had a perfect right to attend any show but called for restrictions on the carrying of arms by off-duty men.

The *Daily News*'s fears were well founded, for shortly after the theater incident, three white infantrymen severely beat and then knifed to death a discharged black soldier. The black man had screamed for mercy, run down the street, and collapsed on the porch of a house from which five terror-stricken white women watched him die. The ladies so distrusted blacks that they believed the whole episode was a ruse designed to trick them into opening their door. Again Galveston leaders demanded stricter discipline and the disarming of soldiers on leave.[8]

When General Griffin complained to the governor about whites who were robbing blacks, Throckmorton coolly replied that the only such crimes he was aware of were committed by white soldiers. The governor regularly wrote to Washington, hoping to get compensation for these and other property damages inflicted by occupation troops.[9] The governor's favorite target—like that of his constituents—was the Freedmen's Bureau. "While I am ready to acknowledge that many wanton wrongs are perpetuated [sic] upon black people," remonstrated Throckmorton as he stated his basic position to Griffin, "I cannot but mention it is a singular fact that while it is notorious that blacks themselves commit many wrongs and offer many provocations, still there is scarcely a mention of such occurrences."

Throckmorton was glad the bureau wanted justice for all people, but he decried the fact that the bureau courts trusted black testimony alone and assumed that the Negroes "are a guiltless, unoffending, and immaculate race." The governor repeated his charges against the bureau in a Wharton County case, where a bureau agent had prevented a white man from recovering a revolver supposedly stolen by a black man. Throckmorton dryly asked Griffin to order "the negro or officer in charge" to force the agent's appearance in a local court.[10]

A Galveston journal agreed with the governor's assessment of the situation. In its comment on the bureau's arrest of a white man in an altercation with a black over the possession of a turkey, the editor stated, "We are perfectly astonished at the conduct of [Lieut. Col. William H.] Sinclair. Had it been Gregory, we would have expected nothing else." Sinclair arrested the white party in the case when he refused to yield the bird to the claimant and wished the bureau to the devil. "We have borne patiently and silently, for some time, the arrogant assumption of arbitrary military power by the Freedmen's Bureau until we can no longer hold our peace," concluded the editorial. The newspaper was "determined to have our say, let the consequences be what they may."[11]

Another periodical expressed the fear that the only way the blacks could be truly elevated, actually free and equal, was through racial amalgamation, a disquieting thought to any "right thinking" white Southerner. "Then the kinky hair, the mellow eye, the artistic nose, the seductive lips, the 'emotional heart,' the gambril shins, the hollowness of foot, the ebony skin and bewildering odor will be all ours," moaned the editor, "all ours, ours, ours." The only alternative was to keep the negroes "in their places."[12]

The same newspaper deemed a Brownsville barbershop occurrence as "typical of the demands for equality and heightening of racial tensions" brought on by Reconstruction. A black soldier had gone into the barbershop for a haircut and was refused service. The incensed trooper drew his revolver and threatened the barber and two passersby. "G——d d——n you," he swore, "I'll blow the top of your head off, too." The soldier was reported to his superior, who had him bucked and gagged as punishment.[13]

White supremacy was often maintained in brutal ways. Phyllis Peebles, a freedwoman living near Cotton Gin, told a harrowing tale of how a certain Dr. Milner threatened to "give her bones to the buzzards" if she did not bind out her children to him. When she at first refused, he threw a water pitcher at her, hit her on the head with a loaded whip butt, and cut her in the throat several times until she assented.[14]

Such incidents understandably outraged military personnel. General Sheridan confined one Texan on Ship Island, Mississippi, for six months' hard labor because he had fired a shotgun at a black man. The general found the motive particularly appalling, "the object being not to kill, that was too much to ask, but to punish severely."[15]

In a similar outrage at Jefferson, a black man nicknamed "Rough Alexander" was shot and killed by a local tough, Hugh Freeman. The latter had a reputation for beating blacks, and over the years he had reputedly shot several soldiers. According to witnesses, Freeman had called Rough Alexander out of bed in the middle of the night and gunned him down as he emerged from his shack. A justice of the peace had ordered Freeman's arrest, but the deputy sheriff and the town constable had both refused to act, despite the offer of military assistance. When the garrison commander assembled a squad to make the arrest himself, an armed mob blocked the roads, and Freeman escaped.[16] In such cases, few whites would cooperate in the pursuit, and the army traditionally relied on black guides and informants to locate fugitives.[17]

As the protector of the Negro, the Freedmen's Bureau incurred the dislike of many whites. During the winter of 1866–67, one subassistant commissioner in particular was singled out to bear the brunt of Texan hatred—Jacob de Gress, a former Union brevet colonel. One citizen accused the controversial agent of forcing him to pay a debt by seizing and selling his property. Another complained that de Gress had fined him five hundred dollars for threatening a black woman with a pistol, after she said she would violate a labor contract to go to northern Texas. This plaintiff asserted that his bureau-approved contract with the woman allowed him "to use any means (except cruelty) to enforce it."[18]

More offensive to the critics of the bureau were de Gress's actions in two legal affairs involving indicted black defendants. A certain Dick Perkins escaped the Harris County jail and fled to de Gress, who was convinced of his innocence and the prejudice of the civil processes. So the agent held Perkins in the sanctuary of his office for a couple of months until public criticism died down; then he released Perkins, who escaped the area a free man.[19]

When Richard Harris was charged with assault with intent to kill in Grimes County, he also fled to de Gress's office in Houston and received the agent's protection. Governor Throckmorton invited de Gress to withdraw from the case, but the colonel replied in such a disrespectful manner that he caused the governor to ask for his courtmartial by the Adjutant General's Office in Washington. Throckmorton denied de Gress's charge that he did not have all the facts; he pledged to uphold all state and federal laws in the case but received no satisfaction.[20]

Shortly after these episodes, de Gress joined the Ninth (Colored) Cavalry in western Texas until 1870, when he resigned his commission and accepted the post of superintendent of public education under the Radical Republican government. He later served as mayor of Austin for one term and was a postmaster, an active Republican party member, and an official in the Grand Army of the Republic, a Republican veteran group. It is difficult to see de Gress as an "accepted, and even respected" person in Texas during Reconstruction,[21] given the fact that several attempts on his life were made, during or after the period had ended. His acceptance was conditional and limited to a small group of Loyalist and Republican friends because of his association with the bureau and his friendship toward blacks.

Another disagreement between the bureau and the state administration concerned the numerous black convicts serving time at the state penitentiary at Huntsville. The head of the Texas bureau, General Kiddoo, as early as October, 1866, had asked Governor Throckmorton to present information such as the number of prisoners, term of confinement, and prison conditions.[22] Bureau interest in the welfare of black inmates continued on an irregular basis thereafter.

Lieut. Col. William H. Sinclair, whom the Galveston press had accused of arbitrary acts, led the bureau investigation into the condition of Texas jails. Sinclair suspected that freedmen were denied comforts of life, chained, and frequently jailed for frivolous reasons. He believed better conditions could easily be made available.[23] By February, 1867, Sinclair had finished an exhaustive examination of prison conditions at Huntsville. He found that there were 411 convicts held, of whom 339 were black. He thought that the warden was capable and that all prisoners were well treated. Many inmates had jobs outside the walls and moved back and forth to their place of work without guards.

In spite of these good points, Sinclair was disturbed by the black prisoners' pleas of innocence. He realized fully that convicts routinely proclaim their innocence to all who will listen, but he nevertheless thought a majority of the Huntsville inmates were telling the truth. Most of their crimes would have been punishable only by a whipping under the slave regime, said Sinclair, and he believed that "their fate is indeed hard and unjust" for free persons. The bureau investigation maintained that, in their own way, these blacks were victims of Southern wrath and disappointment in losing the war.

Sinclair recommended that Texas follow the progressive example of Alabama, where the governor had pardoned nearly all of the black prisoners. He said that three-fourths of the Texas penitentiary inmates deserved executive clemency. Most had already served an average of six months in county jails plus three years at the state institution. Pardons would be just, claimed Sinclair, because the state law had since been amended, which showed the injustice of their original convictions.[24]

Although General Griffin was convinced enough to order the release of the black inmates, his message was ignored in Austin. All he received for his trouble was a refusal, coupled with an eight-page morality lecture from Governor Throckmorton. The governor was not opposed to the pardon of individual blacks, but he refused to issue reprieves in a wholesale manner.[25]

If Throckmorton was unwilling to compromise on the black prisoner issue, the army took a correspondingly hard line on the proposed funeral cortege of Confederate General Albert Sidney Johnston. Had Sheridan risen above principle and handled this incident in a compassionate manner, Throckmorton's stand against amnesty for black prisoners might have been more readily undercut.

In January, 1867, Johnston's body was removed from its New Orleans resting place and sent to Texas for reburial. Cognizant of Johnston's service to the Texas Republic, the mayor of Galveston asked Sheridan to permit a funeral procession through the city's streets. "I have too much respect for the memory of the brave men who died to preserve our government," replied the general indignantly, "to authorize Confederate demonstrations over the remains of anyone who attempted to destroy it."[26]

Following Sheridan's orders, Griffin forbade any funeral proceedings for the dead hero. "The order of General Griffin, forbidding the customary obsequies in honor of our distinguished dead, will no doubt cause a feeling of most painful disappointment in the hearts of thousands of our citizens," commented the *Daily News*. The newspaper said that, even if Johnston had fallen as a Federal soldier, rather than as a Confederate, he still would have been honored as an "old Texian."[27] At the journal's suggestion, the citizenry turned out quietly and marched bareheaded following the coffin anyway, a procedure Griffin had sense enough to allow, much to Sheridan's disgust. "I very much fear continued disturbances in that state," Sheridan stated in a letter to Grant defending his course of action.[28]

The only cheering news received by Texas Unionists during the winter of 1866–67 was the hardening attitude of higher ranking army officers like Sheridan toward Throckmorton's government. Many of these officers, especially in the Texas command, had been heretofore quite conciliatory to the elected state administration but now saw their kindness "as a waste."[29] Unfortunately, under the current laws and presidential proclamations, the army was unable to act, but some form of congressional action seemed imminent. There even was talk among loyal men as to whom they should recommend as the new provisional governor when the proper time came; Elisha M. Pease, James H. Bell, A. J. Hamilton, and William C. Philips were all mentioned as likely choices.[30]

85

The harsher view that ranking army officers took toward state government grew largely from the reassertion of military leadership by the new Texas commander, General Charles Griffin. Griffin was well aware that Throckmorton's complaints about army interference with his administration had enough substance to be damaging to the position of the military in Texas. Accordingly he sought to mollify the governor and public opinion whenever possible, skillfully holding the defensive until Congress acted to make his authority more certain.

As part of his program, Griffin strictly adhered to General Orders No. 26, issued by the Adjutant General's Office the preceding spring. This order called upon officers and men to honor President Johnson's proclamation ending the rebellion in the Southern states and restoring the civil government's authority over army jurisdiction, especially in legal cases. The army was to give way to civil courts in all cases, unless these tribunals refused to act.[31]

Griffin went so far as to order the army to yield in all cases, to the amazement of bureau officers, who predicted rebel defiance and intimidation of black defendants. Throckmorton, however, appreciated Griffin's policies. "Such evidences on the part of the military to uphold and sustain the laws and respect the civil authority of the state will have the most beneficial influence," he told the general.[32]

Another segment of Griffin's program was to consolidate the semi-independent bureau chain of command with that of the army in Texas. This realignment meant that Griffin would replace General Kiddoo and assume responsibility for the bureau himself. Kiddoo had an uneven image in Texas. Many of the things he did in regard to labor contracts and working conditions were well liked by the planters. He insisted that contracts be made to the mutual advantage of the freedmen and the planters, and he recommended that blacks work for a share of the crop rather than wages.[33] But his interest in bureau courts and black education greatly negated his initial popularity among whites.

In January, 1867, Kiddoo completely compromised his position with white Texans in two decisions. The first was to allow bureau agents to charge each employer one dollar and each laborer twenty-five cents for approving labor contracts. The other was to cancel the November 1, 1866, section of the Black Codes entitled "an Act Regulating Contracts for Labor." Kiddoo held that this law was already enacted through army orders and those sections that were not would reduce blacks to involuntary servitude.[34]

On January 29, 1867, Griffin relieved Kiddoo from duty, allegedly to allow him to rejoin his regiment on the Great Lakes. In reality his health was worsening, he made a good scapegoat for the bureau's unpopular actions in the past months, and the vacancy created allowed Griffin to combine command of both bureau and army, an action which Kiddoo had opposed, not wishing to be subordinated to the regular chain of command.[35]

Many Texans expressed mixed feelings at his departure. "That he is a Radical we will not attempt to deny," said the *Galveston Daily News,* "but the peculiarity about him is that he is an unprejudiced one." The editorial concluded that "Gen. Kiddoo had managed the Bureau rather satisfactorily, which is more than can be said of any other of the heads of the Bureau."[36]

Rumor had the popular General Getty returning to run the bureau operations, but Griffin had no intentions of sharing command responsibilities in Texas. He let Kiddoo take the blame for negating the Black Codes and harassing the civil administration, and he canceled the contract tax. As part of his consolidation program, Griffin issued an order instructing all post commanders that, in addition to their normal assignments, they would henceforth be the local sub-assistant commissioner should no bureau agent exist in their command area.[37]

A final concession Griffin made to Throckmorton that spring of 1867 concerned Indian problems. The governor wrote Griffin early in December, 1866, asking his cooperation in frontier defense. He barraged headquarters and Washington with information about Indian raids that had occurred in recent weeks.[38] At the same time that he kept up the pressure on Griffin, Throckmorton expressed appreciation to Sheridan for moving the two cavalry regiments into the west, in response to earlier complaints. The governor also suggested several possible fort locations, drawing on his own vast knowledge of frontier defense.[39]

Sheridan responded to Throckmorton's letter the following month. He listed a dozen proposed fort sites and told the governor that he would garrison each one with large infantry and cavalry detachments. He hoped to supplement each fort with smaller picket posts approximately twenty miles apart and to connect the whole line with a series of roving patrols, particularly at the time of the full moon—the "Comanche moon"—whose light guided the raiders to their targets.[40] General Grant had already approved of the new posts and authorized expenditures of $250,000 for Texas defense against the Indians, to all of which Sheridan vehemently objected. He still believed that the frontier problem was largely mythical, designed to remove proper military protection from the freedmen and Loyalists of the interior.[41]

Aware of Throckmorton's feelings on the frontier problem, Griffin sought successfully to allay the governor's suspicions by reporting every battle between troopers and Indians or outlaws in the western areas. This action so pleased Throckmorton that he asked Griffin to help restore all recovered property to its rightful owners. Proper identification of such recovered items could be a most difficult task, which caused Griffin to try to avoid responsibility. A prompt letter to Secretary of War Stanton led to Throckmorton's success in restoring stolen goods, too. The governor also made independent efforts through his own investigators to obtain stolen property from various tribes.[42]

Sheridan's promise to set up frontier forts was nearly wrecked by the national political situation during the spring of 1867. Because of the initial confusion caused by the enactment of the congressional Reconstruction Acts, Grant ordered Sheridan to postpone his impending trip to Texas and stay in New Orleans until the new Reconstruction process was running smoothly in Louisiana. This change of plans delayed Sheridan's arrival by a month, and when he came to Texas he canceled plans for a lengthy personal inspection of the frontier in favor of a short stay in Galveston.[43]

At first Sheridan thought the congressional legislation would force Griffin to reduce the frontier garrisons. Washington directed otherwise, however, and Sheridan told Griffin to proceed with the original plans for the western posts without delay, especially the camp at Buffalo Springs. During the summer of 1867, the army established four new forts in Texas and reoccupied five abandoned prewar posts. This action was made possible largely through the arrival of the Ninth (Colored) Cavalry in Texas, although Griffin had offered to detach a full regiment from the interior if Reconstruction proceeded smoothly.[44]

Griffin's efforts did not go unappreciated by Governor Throckmorton, who had expressed hope for such concessions in his farewell letter to Heintzelman,[45] and he responded to Griffin's concessions by cooperating on Reconstruction issues affecting the interior. When Throckmorton learned, for example, that freedmen in Prairie Lea were being chased by horsemen, run out of town, whipped, and shot at, he asked the army to send a detachment to restore order. Throckmorton requested that Griffin keep the troopers there until the local citizens could learn to behave themselves.[46]

In Brownsville, local authorities agreed with the area commander's assessment of an incident in which black soldiers shot and killed a local policeman and barkeeper. The mayor confirmed that the military patrol had been fired upon by a drunk from the saloon in question, and he condoned their conduct. Throckmorton agreed.[47]

Other examples of civil cooperation with the army followed. When a black orderly from the Seventh Colored Infantry died at the hands of horse thieves, the governor told Griffin that he had sent the information to the local judge,"and I trust I may be able to report hereafter that the parties have been arrested and punished." Throckmorton further assured the general that he expected all civil officers to punish all lawbreakers, whether the parties were white or black, civilian or military, and he asked for army help when local officials were lax in doing their duty.[48]

After the Harrison County Board of Commissioners refused to care for four orphaned black children, Throckmorton again intervened on behalf of the Freedmen's Bureau. The governor quelled the hostile attitude of the commissioners, one of whom said that "he ignores all the G——d——d Radical laws and the D——d Niggers should not be allowed the benefits of the poor fund." Throckmorton discovered that the problem was a feeling on the part of the board that blacks did not pay sufficient taxes. He hoped Congress or the bureau might supplement the poor fund in behalf of the children. In the meantime he ordered the county court to supervise proper care.[49]

When the bureau agent at Marshall, the same man who reported the pauper case, disclosed continued mistreatment of freedmen in the area, Throckmorton admitted his suspicions as to the man's reliability ("as a matter of course, I do not believe one word of this"), but he ordered the county judge to make a full investigation and a written report on the matter immediately.[50]

As he made clear to the chief judge in Panola County, Throckmorton would allow no mistreatment of blacks or anyone else in the courts. He warned the judge to maintain impartial law and order for "every class of the people." To a Parker County attorney, Throckmorton sent a note urging the law to be "rigidly enforced. It can only be done by the officers energetically discharging their duty," a plea he continually reiterated in his correspondence with all local authorities.[51]

Waco was the scene of controversy that winter. The bureau agent, First Lieutenant A. F. Manning, was angered when one Logswell, accused of murdering a Negro, escaped civil authorities before the bureau could take custody of him. Manning disgustedly wrote that a McLennan County grand jury had refused to indict Logswell, even though two blacks served on the panel. Manning thought him guilty anyway, and Griffin asked Throckmorton to assist in Logswell's recapture.[52]

A second incident in Waco shocked Lieutenant Manning. He discovered that two local physicians and a white man had castrated Manning's young Negro ward. Although one suspect, a Dr. Irving, was still at large, Manning had arrested a J. C. McCrary and a Dr. Bell. Manning was admittedly in violation of Griffin's orders to allow civil authorities to act first, but after the Logswell matter he did not trust them. Although he knew an outrage had been committed, he did not know exactly what charge to bring against the defendants.[53]

The men's attorneys produced a writ of habeas corpus which Manning refused to honor, a decision which led to immediate protest. The town's population became so agitated at Manning's "tyranny" that he felt compelled to use a whole company of cavalrymen to guard the jail. "The course taken by the Bureau agent here has given great dissatisfacton," asserted the lawyers to Throckmorton, "and is creating the impression that no man is safe in his rights if such things can be done."[54]

Not realizing the nature of the case, Throckmorton wrote Griffin asking about the two Waco men held in violation of a writ of habeas corpus. The governor believed that such action violated the Freedmen's Bureau Act and the Civil Rights Act. Griffin replied with full particulars on the event, which he called "a gross outrage on the person of a colored boy." He said that the bureau would hold the suspects for trial unless Throckmorton thought the civil courts would act.[55]

Throckmorton thanked the general for the information but asked the Texas commander to give the civil process a chance to work first in the future. He believed that aggrieved parties were going to the army first and not to state authorities, which gave the incorrect impression that state officials would not try to preserve justice. This also placed the army in a primary support role in civil affairs, not a secondary role as intended under law. Agreeing with the governor's criticism, Griffin agreed to let Waco courts proceed, under the observation of Lieutenant Manning.[56]

Unfortunately, in spite of his good intentions, Throckmorton could not convince local officials of the necessity for fair treatment of Unionists, Freedmen, and soldiers. Not even the army could alleviate this problem through five years of Reconstruction. But in 1867, such lack of cooperation on the part of local civil officers gave Throckmorton's assertions of loyal government a hollow ring.

Bureau schools, for example, still had trouble all over the state. In Houston, the subassistant commissioner had difficulty in finding a house in which to board his teachers, and when he did, the school-house was burned. The Goliad office of the bureau reported its schools doing well and the buildings undisturbed, but the teachers were shot at from ambush. They threatened to leave town unless troop protection were provided them. Indianola reported a different problem. The blacks there had shown an uncommon indifference to education, which caused the local agent to close the school from lack of interest.[57]

Planters still ignored bureau edicts on labor. At Liberty, the Freedmen's Bureau agent discovered that a plantation owner was making contracts on behalf of himself and a half dozen others, bypassing the agent's approval by taking the documents directly to the Galveston headquarters. He asked that Galveston refer the contracts back to him that he might regain his rightful authority. He also requested that the planter's cotton aboard the *Abie M* be seized in lieu of wages he owed his black laborers.[58]

A Corpus Christi planter allegedly held his slaves in bondage until February, 1866, through threats and intimidation. When three of the blacks escaped on horseback, the white man had them charged with horse stealing in a local court. The county judge feared that a civil court jury would find them guilty, contrary to his instructions, and would hang the freedmen unless the bureau interfered.[59]

Loyalists and soldiers complained of mistreatment in state courts. One Loyalist who fled Texas during the war returned, only to be indicted for an assault he allegedly committed before the war. When he left town for safety, he was tried in absentia. He asked the army to intervene in his case.[60]

A Fourth Cavalry sergeant, on leave and headed for Carlisle Barracks in Pennsylvania to recruit for the regiment, stopped in Gonzales to visit a friend. He hired a horse to ride out to his friend's house, stayed longer than expected, and returned to Gonzales four hours late. The liveryman meanwhile accused him of stealing the rented horse. Tried and convicted for horse stealing, the trooper was sentenced to seven years at Huntsville. Repeated attempts to contact his commanding officer were intercepted by local authorities. He finally got in touch with Lieut. Col. William Sinclair, the inspector general of the bureau, on his prison investigation. Sinclair believed the sergeant "looked like a good man," and he was not surprised that Texas courts could act in such an unjust manner.[61]

The frequent requests for soldiers to assist the state courts and to protect Loyalists and freedmen led to encounters with irate citizens.[62] On an expedition to Navasota to arrest two men charged with the murder of soldiers, First Lieutenant William A. Sutherland and his company of infantrymen were blocked by a crowd of thirty or forty men. Sutherland gave a quick order to surround the citizen group and then demanded that the civilians surrender their weapons. He was careful not to search anybody or allow his men to roam the streets while in town, even though it compromised his mission.

Later a citizen wrote an apology to Governor Throckmorton for the town's action, blaming it on drunks and rowdies, but the town newspaper editor had informed Sutherland that, had he made the arrests, a citizens' group would have assaulted the army camp in retaliation. Such harrowing possibilities led troop commanders to instruct subordinates to use only "picked men" and "competent" officers and sergeants for such squads. Reports of private arsenals abounded, necessitating well-armed detachments in all areas, lest the army's ability to act be compromised by a lack of firepower.[63]

Although Griffin's policy alleviated much of the army's previous difficulties with the state administration, it meant that military protection of Loyalists, black and white, became minimal. Unionists were understandably mystified and annoyed by this inability of the army to act. District Attorney Baldwin wrote Washington that Texas was on the "very vortex of war" and that murder was so rampant that "a bad man will shoot down his fellow with as little apparent compunction as he would a wolf or a bear." This complaint echoed A. J. Hamilton's observation a year earlier that human life was worth less than that of domestic cattle. Baldwin was angry that the military authorities could not or would not act to stabilize the situation in the Loyalists' behalf.[64]

Baldwin was correct in assuming that Griffin could not act to reassert his authority, but things were about to change decidedly for the better, at least as far as the Loyalists were concerned. In March of 1867, Congress passed the first two Reconstruction acts over the president's veto. This legislation divided the South into five military districts, each to be commanded by a general officer appointed by the president.

These generals were ordered to protect the civil and property rights of all persons; to suppress insurrection, disorder, and violence; and to punish, or cause to be punished, all criminal actions. The commanders were to use the civil courts or, if they believed it necessary, military tribunals. Existing state governments in the South were declared to be provisional in nature and were warned not to interfere "with the exercise of military authority." The generals were to review all prison

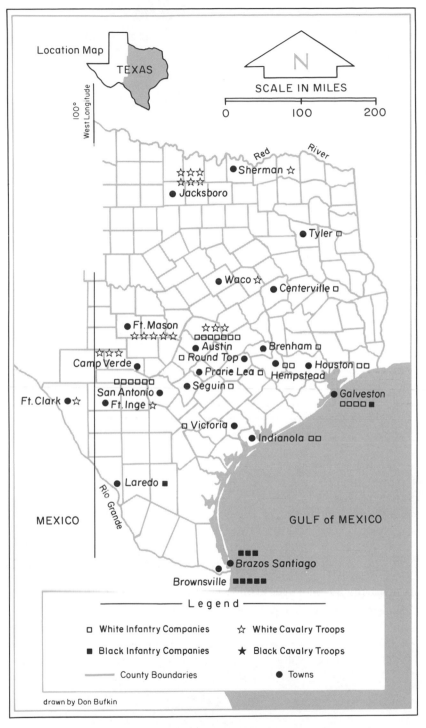

Location Map

TEXAS

100° West Longitude

N

SCALE IN MILES

0   100   200

Red   River

☆☆☆
☆☆☆
● Jacksboro   ● Sherman   ☆

● Tyler □

● Waco ☆
● Centerville □

● Ft. Mason   ☆☆☆
☆☆☆☆☆   □□□□□□□
● Austin
□ Round Top   ● Brenham □
☆☆☆   ● Prarie Lea   ● □□   ● Houston □□
Camp Verde ●   □ Hempstead
□□□□□□   ● Seguin □
San Antonio ●   ● Galveston
Ft. Clark ●☆   ● Ft. Inge ☆   □□□□ ■

□ Victoria
● Indianola □□

● Laredo ■

MEXICO   Rio Grande

GULF of MEXICO

■■■
● Brazos Santiago
Brownsville ■■■■■

Legend

□ White Infantry Companies   ☆ White Cavalry Troops

■ Black Infantry Companies   ★ Black Cavalry Troops

— County Boundaries   ● Towns

drawn by Don Bufkin

Map 5. Griffin's Troop Assignments, March, 1867: Creation of
the Fifth Military District

sentences pronounced by military courts and to submit death sentences to the president for approval.

Each state was to call an election for delegates to a constitutional convention. Should the state officials fail to do so, the district commanders could issue the convention call. The state convention delegates were to be elected by all males over the age of twenty-one who had lived in the state for one year and had been registered by boards composed of three loyal persons appointed by the district commander. No one who was barred from holding office under the proposed Fourteenth Amendment could register to vote or serve in the convention.

The convention was to provide for universal male suffrage and bring the state's organic laws into agreement with the United States Constitution in all respects. Once the new state constitution had been ratified by a majority of the registered voters (later amended to a majority of those voting), the new government elected thereunder was to ratify the fourteenth Amendment, whereupon Congress could readmit it into the Union.[65]

After he was notified of the substance of the congressional plan, Grant recommended Sheridan as officer in charge for the Fifth Military District of Louisiana and Texas. The president agreed.[66] Grant then ordered Sheridan to send all orders issued under the Reconstruction Acts to Washington, by telegraph if time was critical, and to take no action until official copies of the acts and corresponding orders were received in New Orleans.[67]

On March 19, Sheridan issued General Orders No. 1, which announced his assumption of command of the Fifth Military District. Each state was to keep its present military commander; Griffin thus retained control of the District of Texas. Sheridan declared the elected governments of both states to be provisional in nature, but he promised there would be no wholesale removal of civil authorities from office unless officeholders failed "to carry out the provisions of the law or impeded reorganization."[68]

All matters relating to state government would be supervised by Sheridan, assisted by Major George A. Forsyth as his secretary of civil affairs. Sheridan soon wrote Griffin and told him to take the necessary steps to reorganize Texas as soon as he received official copies of the Reconstruction Acts, which were already on the way.[69]

Throckmorton was slow to realize how the Military Reconstruction Acts altered his relationship to Griffin. He believed that the tenuous cooperation that Griffin had inaugurated in December was still in effect, and he wrote the general to say that he would cooperate fully in the new order and asked for a personal conference with Sheridan when he arrived.[70] Griffin, however, went on an immediate offensive. In a Prairie Lea case, where soldiers had shot two citizens and ordered another to leave the country, Throckmorton appealed to Griffin to investigate the "most unfortunate incident." The governor said he did not wish to shield any citizens if they were to blame.[71] Griffin replied angrily that the army was innocent in the matter. The townspeople, he said, had fired on the soldiers first, and the threatened man had been merely warned about his "disloyal actions." Griffin told Throckmorton bluntly to enforce the law there or stand aside and let the army do it.[72]

Griffin had deeply resented Throckmorton's skillful use of civil power to subordinate the army to many of his demands. In a biting letter to Forsyth, Griffin called to Sheridan's attention the necessity of removing "the chief civil officers of this state." Griffin complained that he could not "find an officer holding position under the state laws whose antecedents will justify me in reposing trust in him in assisting the registration" of voters.

The Texas commander particularly wanted to get rid of Governor Throckmorton and Lieutenant Governor G. W. Jones. The general admitted that the two men submitted fully to the letter of the laws but not to the proper "*spirit*" (his emphasis). Griffin said that he had repeatedly "called the notice of the Governor to outrages and murder on loyal men" and that he had yet "to ascertain a single instance in which the offender had been punished."

Other officials should be removed, too, maintained Griffin, but they could await the completion of registration. He recommended that Judge Colbert Caldwell or District Attorney David J. Baldwin be appointed in Throckmorton's stead. Under Griffin's influence, and still smarting from his own defeat by Throckmorton the fall before, Sheridan curtly informed the governor that state authorities could help Reconstruction only by supporting the army with good feeling.[73]

The Unionists lost no time in announcng their pleasure at the army's new role in Texas. Loyalists reported continued slavery, intimidation of Union men, "rebel rule" in local courts, and the need of more federal troops to prevent law from becoming, in the words of one man, "a farce." Another Unionist closed his letter to Pease with the wish that "you will do all you can to save the country & Republican Govt from destruction." Union men anxiously awaited word of what action to take to assist in Reconstruction efforts. They volunteered to serve in office, recommended others who were loyal and would serve, and sent suggestions on how to install a loyal government most effectively. [74]

Loyalists all over the state rejoiced at Griffin's avowed intention to cleanse the state of disloyal acts committed by "those whose hands are red with the blood of loyal men" and who "range at large untouched by justice." On its way to New Orleans to see Sheridan, a delegation of Unionists stopped in Galveston and had a "most cheering and satisfactory interview" with Griffin. The general agreed to consult white men and black men in each registration district when he appointed registration boards. He also asserted that the removal of Throckmorton was imperative to deny patronage to the disloyal. [75]

Griffin made similar assurances to Ferdinand Flake, a Galveston Loyalist and editor. The commander promised Flake that, unless Throckmorton did not clearly show that he "intends to do right" (his emphasis), Griffin would remove the governor and replace him with a true Unionist. This time Griffin favored Elisha M. Pease, if the latter wished to serve. [76] The Loyalists had reason to be happy. Military leadership had at last been restored to Texas and General Griffin was completely their man. Now, as loyal men had desired for months, there would be "real military occupation." [77]

6

The Pyrrhic Victory

TEXAS REPUBLICANS IN 1867 wanted to establish a completely new power structure in the state, a goal they hoped to accomplish by reconstructing the state's politics and government with loyal men. "He, who occupying an official position does not aid us in Spirit, is an *obstruction,* and ought give way (*voluntarily*) to those who will," thundered Judge Colbert Caldwell.[1] The Republicans, as the Loyalists were now becoming known, expected their agency for reform to be the officers and men of the United States Army.

General Charles Griffin did not disappoint the party. He had already promised to send a loyal man and ten soldiers into each voter registration district. If any area was without suitable Loyalists, Griffin would have outsiders brought in to supervise the registration boards.[2] Republicans knew that Griffin meant well, but they feared that half measures might cost them the new convention election just as had happened the year before. They believed that the Black Codes had given the black vote to the rebels through economic intimidation. Besides, most of the state offices were held by Throckmorton's disloyal cronies, and party newspapers still needed to be organized.

The Republicans thought none of these steps could occur unless all laws passed since 1861 were nullified, the old guard was removed from office, and, most important, Governor Throckmorton was deprived of all patronage. Such a comprehensive program was agreeable to Griffin, but because of the army's deference to the chain of command, he needed approval from higher up. "All depends upon Sheridan," said a knowing Loyalist.[3]

Initially Sheridan, Griffin, and the Texas Republicans supported each other, at least superficially, on all issues, and agreed particularly in their dislike of Governor Throckmorton's administration. Continual complaints rolled into headquarters concerning unfair court procedures. One Unionist said loyal men could not obtain justice in the Nineteenth Judicial District, centered around Waco. He suggested that court proceedings be stopped until a Republican could be appointed district judge. Otherwise, he asked that trials be postponed if either party objected to the conduct of the proceedings.[4]

In San Antonio a local rebel judge was accused of making more "property confiscations than Cromwell." The *San Antonio Express* theorized that "a good punching with a Federal Bayonet" was needed. "Arguments, reason, common sense, decency has no effect on this sort." When the public prosecutor in Harrison County shot a Loyalist, Governor Throckmorton retained the accused in office over the protests of Union men.[5] The ultimate in rebel defiance had occurred the previous fall when the Eleventh Legislature gerrymandered the state district court system, depriving five Unionists of their places on the bench. Eight of twenty district judgeships had been won by Loyalists in the state election held in the spring of 1866, not a bad showing in disloyal Texas.

On October 11, 1866, the legislature decided to "purify" the state court system by consolidating and abolishing five district courts, all of which had avowed Unionist judges. Geographic factors eventually forced them to reconsider, however, since all the districts but one were located in western counties of the state.[6]

Immediate protests flooded headquarters. Most of these complaints centered around the Fourth and Eleventh districts, headed by judges Thomas H. Stribling and W. P. Bacon. Stribling's district included the area around San Antonio, and its abolition forced citizens to use courts in Corpus Christi, which involved a one-week trip to a rebel judge. Bacon's jurisdiction centered in El Paso, an area so isolated by the loss of his services that cases had to be sent to Corpus Christi, an impossible journey through seven hundred miles of Indian country, which necessitated a cavalry escort.[7]

In response, Sheridan decreed that the districts of Stribling and Bacon be reestablished as they originally were. He remarked that the only reason the districts had been abolished was the Unionist opinion of the jurists and that the new districts were "of such extent as to make it impossible to administer justice within them through the courts."[8] Sheridan informed Grant that reports of Bacon's unfitness were "humbug" and that his El Paso court was necessary to prevent citizens from having to use courts in New Mexico Territory. Griffin later tried to have all five districts restored as they were in June, 1866, but he apparently did not succeed.[9]

Sheridan's reinstatement of Stribling and Bacon turned out to be a rather mild interference with states' rights when compared with another development, which became the most celebrated example of military interference with the civil courts in Texas. This event occurred on April 27, 1867, when Griffin issued Circular No. 13. The general was concerned over the discriminatory treatment Negroes and Loyalists had been receiving in Texas courts, and he was determined to act. Part of his motivation came from Governor Throckmorton's refusal to free black prisoners incarcerated at the Huntsville penitentiary.

Circular No. 13 was to prevent "persons disqualified by law" from serving as jurors. The circular required that all potential jurymen take the "ironclad oath," namely, that they had not voluntarily given "aid, countenance, counsel or encouragement" to the Confederacy. In the same order, Griffin printed section 2 of the Civil Rights Act of 1866, which provided that anyone who, "under color of any law, statute, ordinance, regulation or custom," deprived any citizen of his civil rights was guilty of a misdemeanor and subject to a fine of one thousand dollars or one year in jail or both.[10]

The effect of the jury order was to exclude the Secessionists from courtroom juries, which produced a howl of rage from whites throughout the state. A Houston man wrote President Johnson pleading with him to alleviate "the helpless, wretched condition of a people denied the protection of the courts of law," for he believed the circular would destroy the state civil court system.[11]

A lawyer from Rusk wrote the president that there were not twelve whites in the entire county that could take the ironclad oath, and he protested the use of uneducated blacks as jurors. He feared they knew nothing of the duties and responsibilities of courts. The attorney also believed the jury order exceeded the authority granted in the Reconstruction Acts and would only serve to prolong the process of readmission and expose the state to increased robbery and murder. He also stated that he had recently represented a Negro client who had sued a white man and received justice from a white court.[12]

Fifteen attorneys from Jefferson sent a petition to the White House in which they expressed fears that the oath was too strict and that blacks were too ignorant to be jurors. They thought that no county could provide an adequate number of jurors under the new rules and recommended a return to the state code, which required only that a juror be a voter and over twenty-one years old. Another lawyer told Governor Throckmorton that the inability of whites to serve on juries would prevent the trying of all cases in his area unless the defendants would waive their right to a jury trial. He expressed hope that circular would be revoked before court convened that year. Even some

Unionists believed the jury order was excessive. One unidentified correspondent called for the use of the amnesty oath of future loyalty and maintained that the ironclad oath was required only of Federal officials.[13]

The *Brownsville Daily Ranchero* printed a plea for white jurors to come forward and counteract the effect of the circular. The article noted that for some reason there was a great aversion to taking the oath. In spite of Griffin's insistence that Circular No. 13 was to be applied to all jurors from its date of issuance and his order that no discrimination was allowed between black and white testimony, confusion prevailed all over Texas. A Union man who had stayed in the state during the war wanted to know if he could hold court without jurors. He was particularly annoyed by freedwomen suing their husbands for nonsupport and freedmen suing each other over what he considered to be trivial, nonjury matters. Throckmorton suggested that Griffin clear up these perplexing questions and others now plaguing state judges through a new order.[14]

Many whites simply boycotted the courts. Alexander W. Terrell, a prominent Houston attorney, argued a case before a black jury, the members of which had been conscripted from a construction site across the street from the Harris County courthouse. The clerk of court had to write out the verdict and note each juror's name after his X mark. Terrell was too outraged at the whole idea to mention whether the decision was a reasonable one. He disgustedly abandoned his profession and took up managing a Brazos plantation. Terrell explained, "I found it more congenial with my nature to direct negroes in the field than to bow before them and call them 'gentlemen of the jury.'" Another white complained about an excessive fine and incompetent jury and asked the army to reverse his conviction under Circular No. 13.[15]

Governor Throckmorton placed the plight of his constituents before the president, but at the same time he advised all judges to follow the circular until further notice.[16] Throckmorton told Griffin he thought it unfair that federal juries in the state did not have to take the ironclad oath, while those in state courts did. When Griffin read this charge, he investigated and found that the oath was required at the discretion of the judge in federal proceedings. Throckmorton had sent Griffin a copy of his letter to Johnson because he feared the document had been misrepresented to the general. He also sent copies of his communications with Griffin to the president for the same reason.

Privately, Throckmorton was convinced the general had issued the jury circular in order to force him to oppose it, thus giving Griffin cause to remove him from office.[17]

The widespread attack on Circular No. 13 put Griffin on the defensive. He justified his order to Grant by stating that its purpose was not to force Texas to accept black jurors but rather to ensure that loyal whites and blacks were able to serve and to protect themselves from injustice. The oath was the same that Congress required of federal officials, said Griffin. He further maintained that he had not interfered with the state requirements that a juror must be a qualified voter, a householder of the county, or a freeholder of the state. These existing regulations excluded nearly every black person in the state from serving on a jury.[18]

Griffin dismissed complaints that there was a lack of jurors in many counties because of the jury order. The problem could be solved, asserted the general, by going to neighboring counties for jurors. In one specific instance, Judge J. J. Holt of the Tenth Judicial District erroneously reported he had no jurors to draw on; Griffin personally knew of sixteen qualified whites, and Governor Throckmorton had a list of thirty-eight more.

The general reiterated that the purpose of the jury circular was to protect "loyal residents in their lives, liberties, and property." He believed Unionists were all of it and would rather be tried by blacks, regardless of their education, than disloyal whites, whose motto seemed to be "rule or ruin."[19] Sheridan agreed with his subordinate that "the disaffected element" must be removed from juries because of their opposition to Reconstruction. He told Griffin that, if Texas officials tried to embarrass him by including unqualified blacks, Griffin should report them and Sheridan would remove them from office. One officer was so pleased with the effect of the jury order in his command area that he recommended its adoption throughout the whole Fifth Military District.[20]

This step was opposed by Grant, however, who said that the rules for selecting juries should assure "equal justice for all classes." Grant insisted that, if a man could be considered loyal enough to vote, he was loyal enough to serve as a juror. This policy became standard by the end of September, 1867, and the jury lists were revised accordingly.[21]

The most effective method of regulating justice in Texas was the use of military commissions to try civilians. But military tribunals were very unpopular with the disloyal element, both because they would convict those who persecuted blacks and Unionists and, more important, because they followed different rules of procedure than civil tribunals and could be more arbitrary. They required no juries, a two-thirds vote of the bench could condemn a prisoner to death, a majority of the board could convict noncapital offenders, and military officers could refuse to honor the writ of habeas corpus and hold prisoners indefinitely.[22]

Sheridan and Griffin used military commissions to try civilians, as authorized by the March 2, 1867, Reconstruction Act. Sheridan said that he used them only occasionally because civil courts "neglected their duty" and it was the only way to punish offenders. He "did not favor their use in governing the district, and probably would never have convened one had these [Reconstruction] acts been observed in good faith."[23]

Reflecting the attitude of a majority of Texans, the *Brownsville Daily Ranchero* spoke out bitterly against military trials of civilians in time of peace. The editor asserted that he expressed his ideas with "no unkind feeling, nor from a disposition to prejudice the case" being considered, but he held that these trials were "an unpardonable farce." Texans were helpless before them, continued the editor, and could only invoke "the coward's power—appeal to God for protection. The Goddess of Liberty has been in labor; the issue is before us. Liberty!—A base mockery."[24]

Even more controversial were military orders setting aside judgments or demanding that select cases be dismissed before they were concluded. On April 5, 1867, Griffin issued Circular No. 10 under his responsibility to protect the civil rights and property of all persons in the District of Texas. The circular ordered any post commander to take charge of any case in a local court when he believed the proceedings to be unfair and to present them to headquarters at Galveston for review.[25]

Acting under the authority of this order, a Freedmen's Bureau agent called Griffin's attention to a Prairie Lea case and ordered a stay in the proceedings of the Second Judicial court. The judge, John Ireland, had once served as a "rebel receiver" and was hated by Unionists. Later Griffin threw the case out of court and dismissed further action against the defendants.[26]

In another instance, the property of a Mrs. Helen B. Chapman of Corpus Christi had been seized by the Confederacy during the war.

She located it and filed a complaint with the army. Acting under Circular No. 10, Griffin ordered it returned forthwith and charged the local bureau agent with the responsibility of seeing the command carried out.[27]

The proceedings of a grand jury in the Third Judicial District were canceled and reversed when Griffin alleged that they acted "in a spirit of malicious prosecution fostered by vindictive and disloyal sentiments" in finding a true bill against an officer of the Seventeenth Infantry. Griffin also freed Santos Benavides, a former Confederate officer now an agent of the Federal government, when he was falsely convicted of murder. Benavides, who had defeated E. J. Davis's Union unit at Laredo during the war, had been acting in an official capacity at the time of the shooting assisting the army capture a band of killers and thieves on the San Antonio–Laredo mail route.[28]

Another area of some controversy in whch the army participated during Reconstruction was taxation. Reconstruction was financed on both the state and Federal levels. The initial congressional appropriation set aside $500,000 for the five military districts of the South, which was apportioned among the districts by the paymaster general in Washington. District commanders were to make requisitions on the sum deposited in their district's account held by the paymaster, who paid all legitimate bills. At times the various district commanders did not have to spend their whole account, and by mutual agreement, supervised by the paymaster general, such funds were reapportioned to districts having greater expenses.[29]

Most of the cost of Reconstruction was borne by the states themselves. Griffin quickly dispelled any doubt on this point when he announced that all taxes except those levied by the Confederacy were due and payable at once. During Griffin's term as district commander and throughout the rest of Military Reconstruction, the army closely supervised the collection and disbursing of state funds. Griffin collected all back taxes due the federal government to 1861, but his successors merely collected taxes due from the beginning of Military Reconstruction in 1867.[30]

The army appointed state tax assessors and collectors, collected bonds for them and other officeholders, authorized or levied taxes for the support of government at town, county, and state levels, provided military escorts to safeguard the collectors' lives and the monies obtained, and audited the accounts of state officials for accuracy. The army jealously guarded the state purse. When the state convention attempted to levy taxes in 1868, military headquarters annulled the ordinances. On its own authority, the army raised a tax to support the convention and seized and sold property of those who refused to pay.[31]

Although Sheridan, Griffin, and the Texas Loyalists agreed on the more mundane problems of Reconstruction, they did not always concur in one of the most important political problems facing the state: the establishment of a Republican coalition with military assistance under the Reconstruction laws. When he was informed of the passage of Military Reconstruction, General Griffin had acted rapidly to locate loyal men. He requested and received from Throckmorton the state records giving the names and residences of all who had been appointed to office during Hamilton's provisional administration two years before.[32]

As early as March 25, Griffin had informed the Loyalists that, if Throckmorton failed to indicate clearly that he intended to "do right," the general would remove him from office. Other "most cheering and satisfactory" interviews with Griffin established the district commander's interest in making more substantial changes in the composition of Texas civil government after Throckmorton's demise. An informant notified Pease that "the General believes, as we do, that the car of progress has received a start in the State of Texas that is to end in the triumph of liberty and confusion to treason." The same man told Pease that he was to be "the bulwark against which unrepentant treason is to dash itself to pieces."[33]

In a similar vein, Pease received other letters urging him to return to Texas to lead the new Republican party. Equipped with a certificate authorizing him to organize Union Loyal League branches throughout Texas, Pease hastened home. There he followed the proposal outlined by the astute Edmund J. Davis the year before. In Houston, Pease presided over the first Republican convention in July, 1867, which was attended by black and white delegates from twenty-seven counties.[34]

The Negro had at last entered Texas politics to fill loyal ranks. The blacks expressed an immediate interest in politics and requested league branches to help them organize. The Conservative press called the meeting a "Radico-Congo" convention, but Pease correctly believed that such derogatory statements merely showed that the opposition feared the increasing strength of the new party.[35]

One of the first important steps in organizing the party's strength was the registration of voters who would elect a new constitutional convention. In Texas the search for qualified registrars began in March,

1867, but the actual registration did not start until May, because Sheridan wanted to consult with Griffin first. The latter feared that the disloyal Throckmorton would hinder the enrollment of voters; to Griffin's surprise, however, the governor cooperated fully in obtaining the names of qualified registrars.[36]

Registration was carried out under a series of circular orders that Griffin issued in April, May, and June. In the circulars Griffin established fifteen registration districts, corresponding to the state's judicial districts. Each registration district was entitled to two registration supervisors and a clerk, who would be designated by army headquarters in Galveston. The three men had to take the ironclad oath.

The supervisors were to provide books and stationery, organize the actual registration boards (consisting of three men appointed by the supervisors who could subscribe to the ironclad oath), adjust causes of complaint, detect fraud, and forward the returns to headquarters together with a report from each supervisor. Initially they were allowed to set up precincts within the registration district, but Griffin later declared each county to be its own precinct.[37]

In the precincts, the appointed registrars were to enroll all legal voters, beginning at the county courthouse and moving to those points necessary to effect a full registration. All county officials were to assist in the enrollment.[38] Registration was to be completed in the shortest time possible and at the latest by September 1. Each voter had to take an oath that he was not excluded by law from voting because of actions committed during the war. This oath pledged future loyalty to the United States and affirmed that the individual had not sworn allegiance to the United States government and then later supported the Confederacy. Those who were in the army or who held state or federal government positions in 1861 and then served the Confederacy were thus excluded.[39]

The precinct registrars gave each voter a certificate of registration upon enrollment. They also took special care in registering black voters. Their registration certificates were marked "colored voter" in red ink on the back. Planters were cautioned not to use terms of labor contracts as a basis for denying freedmen the time necessary to register.[40]

Because Griffin suspected that many blacks had been unfairly discriminated against, he ordered the boards to be reopened for six days in late September, a decision which caused much animosity among landowners. "The prospect of military registration to enforce negro suffrage, together with mismanagement here, rendered all my efforts well-nigh in vain," said Thomas Affleck. It also cost the Texas Land, Labor, and Immigration Company its European support.[41]

The boards kept separate lists of registered voters and those rejected for enrollment, with the cause of rejection. The ambiguous language of the Reconstruction Acts made it almost impossible for the army to know exactly what could disqualify a man from registering. Sheridan requested advice from Grant, who told him to use his own judgment until an advisory opinion could be obtained from U.S. Attorney General Henry Stanbery. Sheridan decided to give the most rigid interpretation to the law and "exclude from registration every person about whose right to vote there may be doubt."[42]

Although Attorney General Stanbery's opinion recommended a more liberal approach, Sheridan received Grant's permission to continue his more restrictive policy until further notice. The two generals rationalized their refusal to adopt Stanbery's viewpoint (which paralleled that of President Johnson) by noting that the intent of Congress was superior to that of the president.

Since Congress had passed the Reconstruction Acts over Johnson's veto "so overwhelmingly," in Sheridan's words, the congressional opinion was obviously "the policy endorsed by the people of the country. It was, therefore, my determination to see to the law's zealous execution in my district." To do otherwise would defeat the intent of Congress, "as well as add to my perplexities," declared Sheridan.[43]

The result of Grant's action was Sheridan's famous secret memorandum on voter registration. This notice, kept from the press to avoid "intricate questions as to the restrictions imposed," allowed registrars to disfranchise anyone who had served as a civil officer before 1861 on federal or state level, from senators to sextons. Sheridan instructed registrars to use their own judgment and disfranchise anyone they suspected of false answers to a half dozen key questions used to determine loyalty. Congress vindicated Sheridan's position in the July 19 Reconstruction Act, giving the registrars wide discretionary power in voter registration. Griffin, for party reasons, had adhered to the hard line all along.[44]

Unexpectedly, a large number of blacks listed Africa as their birthplace, over five hundred in one registration district alone. The supervisor of this district did not know if they qualified to register, because the terms of the as-yet unratified fourteenth Amendment limited citizenship to those persons "born or naturalized in the United States, and subject to the jurisdiction thereof." The Africans appeared to be neither. He suspected they were to be disqualified but recommended that they apply anyway, with all facts to be sent to General Griffin in Galveston. Griffin readily approved of their registration.[45]

When registration was completed, the registrars had to fill out full reports showing the total number of voters registered, the number of colored voters registered, the number of applicants rejected, the reasons for the rejections, and an explanation as to whether or not the board felt the returns were complete. Neither the supervisors, the clerk, nor the precinct registrars were allowed to be candidates for public office while engaged in registration duties. The performance of their duties was subject to review, and irregularities were liable to adjudication by a military tribunal.[46]

In spite of promised military supervision, the registration boards often exercised power subjectively, which greatly dissatisfied Texans. Numerous letters arrived at headquarters accusing boards of arbitrary action in refusing to register qualified whites. Some of these rejected applicants were enrolled later after an investigation proved their suitability. Texans also believed that the registrars had enrolled blacks ahead of the registration period, had allowed blacks to register without having to stand in line to wait, and had registered freedmen who were under voting age or could not meet residency requirements.[47]

Such beliefs resulted in continued trouble at the registration sites. In Dallas, a rejected white applicant "grossly insulted" Dr. B. F. Barkley of the registration board, but the latter "replied effectively in kind."[48] One disgruntled white related how he had gone into Clarksville to register, but "a big black nigger, with a nose like a dormant window, and a pair of lips that looked like he had been sucking a bee gum and got stung in the operation" objected to his enrollment.

The rebuffed applicant turned on the black registrar and "took him a club over the head that would have stunned a beef, but he never winked." Undaunted by that failure, the angry white then "gave him twelve inches of shoe leather on the shins that brought him to his milk in short order." But the assailant had to flee into Indian country to avoid a military trial for assaulting a registrar.[49]

Many whites simply refused to register when they discovered black registrars on the boards, which led one supervisor to comment: "The more I think of the folly of men refusing to act because of a freedman being on the local board—the more I am convinced of their unfitness to give a helping hand in the reconstruction."[50] Many board members would have considered a cussing, a kick in the shins, or a refusal to register as mild responses when compared to the violence that registrars frequently suffered. In the spring of 1867, many people had volunteered to serve on the registration boards. By the following fall, however, intimidation had caused many registrars to resign or to demand more pay to offset the hazards of the job.[51]

Griffin had promised Loyalists in April that he would send escorts of ten soldiers into each district to guard the boards, and on June 1, with the approval of higher authorities, he ordered all post commanders to afford full protection to the registration boards in the performance of their duties. Registrars frequently traveled in army ambulances, followed by their escorts on horseback or in wagons.[52]

Although sporadic violence continued, Griffin was pleased with the progress made by Republicans in the spring and summer of 1867. Unfortunately for the Republicans, affairs were moving too rapidly toward a quick registration and election of the new convention. This problem had destroyed their chances of success in 1866, for there had not been enough time to organize a viable party structure at the grass-roots level.[53]

One big weakness remained in Republican plans to take over the state government. As a Republican organizer in Hidalgo County explained, Throckmorton's rebels still held all of the county offices, and "a Union man has no more a chance of getting elected to office than Satan has of getting to heaven."[54] Throckmorton was politically astute and was well aware that the vagaries and gaps in the Reconstruction Acts could allow the elected government to retain much power. He wrote to Griffin, asking him to clarify who was to fill vacant state offices. According to the state constitution Throckmorton was, but the congressional acts asserted that a new constitution was necessary and implied that the old one was null and void. Throckmorton emphasized his willingness to cooperate in every way with the new laws.

In response to the governor's query and instructions from Sheridan, Griffin issued an order declaring that no further elections were to be held in Texas. He told Throckmorton to appoint replacements for vacancies in the state executive department and report all other vacancies to headquarters. But in a personal letter to the state executive two weeks later, Griffin said he would assume the right of making all appointments to office in Texas. Again Throckmorton smilingly acceded.[55]

Throckmorton's plan was the same one used so effectively against Sheridan the previous fall. He would uphold the law, ride close herd on state officials to do the same, assist in registration, and pardon a few freedmen and Loyalists at Huntsville, while at the same time he would obstinately criticize army policy, quietly recommend Conservatives to Griffin for appointment, and occasionally authorize illegal elections to fill vacant offices.[56]

But this time the army was not to be fooled by Throckmorton's tactics. The governor's independence angered Griffin, and in late March he asked Sheridan to remove Throckmorton from office. Sheridan passed the request on to Grant, at the same time recommending the removal of the governor of Louisiana, James Madison Wells. Grant, however, demurred because he was not sure that the removal power existed under the current laws.[57]

A few days later, Grant changed his mind. He wrote Sheridan that he believed Congress had intended that a commander should have the right of removal, but that it should be used sparingly.[58] Sheridan tested Grant's theory by removing governor Wells and the Louisiana Levee Commission from office. These acts created such a furor that he deemed it wise to refrain from removing Throckmorton. Grant sought to sooth Sheridan by informing him that he, Secretary of War Stanton, and the "loyal people generally" had the fullest confidence in him. But Sheridan was more worried about the reaction of a hostile president and commander in chief, not Grant and his friends.[59]

Griffin and the Texas Republicans were dismayed at Sheridan's reluctance to move ahead. Only the Fifth Military District commander could authorize Throckmorton's ouster. One anxious Loyalist warned that, so long as the "Seditious element" held office in the Southern states, life, liberty, and property would be insecure. He demanded the completion of Reconstruction through removal and appointments. In a like manner, Griffin begged his senior commander to act. "Give me assistance by removals, soon as possible," he urged.[60]

Griffin and later historians failed to realize that, as much as Sheridan was in agreement with the goals of Congressional Reconstruction, he was not a party man. Sheridan would allow no wholesale removals from office in Texas without due cause. His policy was consistent during the whole period, both in Texas and in Louisiana.[61]

Sheridan stated his attitude some months before in a letter to an acquaintance in New York. The pressure of the job had not given him "any more grey hairs," said Sheridan, because he never permitted anyone to approach him on politics. Instead he went along each day, "minding my own business and my legitimate military duties as though I did not care whether the Southern States were admitted tomorrow or kept out for twenty years."[62] Sheridan was not a Radical Republican sycophant during Reconstruction. Indeed he was as much of an impediment to Reconstruction at this stage of his career as Governor Throckmorton. Only Sheridan's acid personality, his dislike of rebel sentiment, and his spectacular, unprecedented removal of the governor of Louisiana prevented contemporaries and recent historians from correctly comprehending his stand.

Sheridan soon made his position abundantly clear to Griffin and his political allies. When Griffin, for example, recommended the removal from office of Judge J. J. Holt, whom reputable Unionist John L. Haynes had described as a "secessionist politician," Sheridan refused, saying that there was no proper reason. "Of course it comes back to what I remarked to you, whilst in Galveston," wrote Griffin to Elisha M. Pease, "that no reason should be assigned for removals." By insisting upon valid motives, other than purely political labels for removals, "Sheridan, in my opinion, makes a great mistake," declared Griffin.[63]

The only hope left was for Congress to authorize the removal of public officials, a matter that Pease recognized when he informed his daughter that such an act "would greatly aid the Union cause in this state by placing its government in the hands of loyal men." Griffin reluctantly admitted that Pease was correct; Congress would have to move before Sheridan would. "I trust so soon as the law will permit," he wearily wrote Sheridan, "there will be changes in the civil affairs of this state."[64]

In the meantime, Griffin did his best to act for the Republicans without being too antagonistic or disobedient to his superior officer. Everyone agreed that vacant offices needed filling, so the Texas commander began to fill those positions as they were brought to his notice. He named a county assessor and collector of taxes for Bastrop and Harris counties and a constable for the town of Bastrop.[65] But this process was much too slow and haphazard for the energetic and efficient Griffin. He impatiently awaited what he believed was patriotically and politically necessary and searched for a way to commit Sheridan to removing Texas officials.

The issue crystallized in early June. Sheridan had authorized Griffin to make any change he thought proper in the composition of the Galveston police force to prevent the occurrence of "riots and breaches of the public peace." Grant feared that the frequency of such disturbances indicated conspiracy.[66] Under the cover of this limited sanction, Griffin recommended several Republican police appointees to Mayor J. E. Haviland. The mayor agreed to nine of the suggested loyal men but rejected the others. He said the whites did not have the proper residence requirements according to city law. None of the blacks could read or write, which were legal requirements for policemen under the same law. Haviland advised Griffin that other recommendations might be more favorably received. The general instead removed Haviland from office for his own man, subject to Sheridan's approval.[67]

Griffin sent a complete account of the matter to Sheridan, accusing Haviland of what Sheridan later described as "contumacious conduct." When Sheridan indicated approval of Haviland's ousting, Griffin further suggested that at least three judges of the state district court be fired for refusing to follow the conditions set forth in Circular No. 13. Sheridan dissented, even though Griffin assured Sheridan that he was trying to keep from instituting wholesale removals, and even though Griffin warned that other treasonous officials were still in their offices undisturbed.[68]

Disappointed by Sheridan's reluctance to replace more disloyal men, Griffin again inquired among Unionists for open positions to which he might appoint someone. He encouraged local Republicans to send in ironclad oaths and recommendations for appointments, which he readily acted upon.[69] In this manner, he made eleven more appointments, including the mayor and city council of new Braunfels, the mayor of La Grange, the district court clerks of Matagorda and Liberty counties, the sheriff of Victoria County, the justice of the peace in Lavaca County, and the mayor of Harrisburg.[70]

Griffin's earlier hope for congressional action was not in vain. In the middle of July, 1867, Congress passed a third Reconstruction Act, which authorized military commanders to remove any civil officer who obstructed the Reconstruction process.[71] About this same time, Griffin wrote to Sheridan describing the "lawless" condition of Texas and the uncooperative actions of "rebel" officials, including the governor, who obstructed the laws. Griffin feared that he would have to move some garrisons from the frontier back to the interior.

Griffin believed much of the problem could be solved by replacing Governor Throckmorton with a loyal man, preferably Elisha M. Pease. Sheridan forwarded all of Griffin's warnings to Grant in Washington, noting that Griffin "attributes this condition of affairs to a disloyal governor and his subordinate civil officeholders."[72]

In late July, Grant wrote Sheridan and informed him that he now had the power to remove civil officials and to fill the vacancies with appointments of his choice. Sheridan did not delay in exercising this authority. "A careful consideration of the reports of Brevet Major

General Charles Griffin," Sheridan decreed, "shows that J. W. Throckmorton, Governor of Texas, is an impediment to the reconstruction of
the State, under the law; he is therefore removed from office." Sheridan appointed Elisha M. Pease as the new provisional governor—
the man who had overwhelmingly lost the election that had placed
"Throcky," as the Republicans now derisively called him, in office one
year before.[73]

Griffin sent copies of Sheridan's removal order to both Throckmorton and Pease. At ten o'clock in the morning, August 8, 1867,
Elisha M. Pease took over the governor's chair, making true in fact
what had been true in principal since Sheridan issued his July 30
order. The Republicans were in power at last. "Gen. Sheridan has done
so much for the Union men with his sword," commented one jubilant
Pease supporter; "he now completes the job with his pen."[74] Republicans saw Pease's appointment to the provisional governorship as
merely the first step in the process of necessary change. "I hope Gov.
Pease may be invested with full authority to make further changes
among state officials as he may deem necessary," said Judge T. H. Duval. Another party member wrote to Griffin that he understood there
was to be a general removal of state officials and hoped his own name
would be remembered when new appointments were made.[75]

In consultation with Pease, General Griffin slowly began to fulfill
the Republicans' hopes. He placed loyal men in the posts of city
recorder and chief of police in Galveston.[76] Griffin suggested again
that the state district court be purged and recommended the replacement of judges John Ireland, James E. Sheppard, H. P. Mabery, and
J. J. Holt.

All of these men were described as "confederate colonels" or "secessionist politicians" and were known for "disloyalty and hostility to the
General Government," said Griffin. Sheridan approved the replacement of Ireland, Sheppard, and Mabery but told his Texas subordinate
to keep Judge Holt in office until more specific charges of malfeasance
could be established.[77]

Griffin was furious at Sheridan's refusal to sweep Texas clean of tyranny and disloyalty. He told Pease that he was amazed at Sheridan's
obtuseness in this matter. Pease concurred and wrote Sheridan, asking
him to allow removal of all officials who were known not to be friendly
to the federal government, its policies, and its principles.[78] But Sheridan stood firmly behind his promise of the past March and refused to
allow wholesale removals.

Only two other Texas officials were replaced in the ensuing weeks, the sheriff of Harris County, who "abscounded," and Judge Edward Daugherty, who had the temerity to tell a general officer personally that he would not obey those laws of the United States which conflicted with those of the state. Meanwhile Griffin issued the only order forbidding discrimination in public accommodations endorsed by any of the Reconstruction authorities during the period.[79]

Although it is doubtful that Sheridan would have violated his announced position on removals, he had good reason to be circumspect in his actions as head of the Fifth Military District. President Johnson wanted to replace the controversial, outspoken commader at New Orleans. In early August, shortly after Congress adjourned, the president removed Edwin M. Stanton as secretary of war. Stanton had been leaning toward Congressional Reconstruction, had leaked details on confidential cabinet meetings to the press, and had revealed some ignorance in his own frontier defense policy.

Gaining Grant's reluctant promise to obey orders and cooperate, Johnson suspended Secretary Stanton from his position and appointed Grant secretary ad interim. Having dealt with the objectionable Stanton, the president now moved to purge selected district commanders whose policies he disliked. Sheridan was at the top of the president's list.[80]

On August 17, the president asked General Grant if he thought Major General George Thomas might be a good replacement for Sheridan. Grant implored Johnson not to change the commander to the Fifth Military district, for, he asserted, Sheridan had done his job "faithfully and intelligently." Grant found "military reasons, pecuniary reasons, and above all patriotic reasons why this should not be insisted upon." Sheridan's removal could be taken as a sign by unreconstructed Southerners to increase their resistance toward the federal government. Grant believed it was the "expressed wish of the country that General Sheridan should not be removed from his present command." He reminded the president that the United States was "a Republic, where the will of the people is the law of the land." Grant also informed the president that General Thomas did not wish a Southern assignment.[81]

Johnson replied that he was not aware that the question of Sheridan's removal had ever been submitted to the people. He reminded Grant that the little Irishman was not the only officer capable of running the Fifth Military District. The president found Sheridan's reign "exceedingly obnoxious" and believed his arrogant attitude discredited the army and Reconstruction. "His rule has, in fact, been one of absolute tyranny, without reference to the principles of our government or the nature of our free institutions," said Johnson. Sheridan's course of action "has seriously interfered with a harmonious, satisfactory, and speedy execution of the acts of Congress, and [this] is alone sufficient to justify a change." The president concluded that he failed "to perceive any military, pecuniary, or political reasons why this order should not be carried into effect." He had not liked Sheridan's original appointment anyway. Johnson therefore designated Thomas head of the Fifth Military district on August 19.[82]

Grant assented to Sheridan's replacement by Thomas only on condition that the latter continue in force all orders in effect in the Fifth Military District when he arrived to assume command. But Thomas would not accept the responsibility, pleading poor health. Thomas suggested that the president appoint Major General Winfield S. Hancock instead.[83]

Grant protested Hancock's assignment to New Orleans even more vehemently than he had Thomas's. Hancock was a known Democrat in sympathy with the president's policies and opposed to those of Congress. Johnson called Grant in for a personal conversation, during which Grant agreed to withdraw his protest and the president agreed to order Hancock to observe all orders existing at the time of his arrival in the Fifth Military District.[84] Because of the intricacies of the command system, Sheridan received orders to proceed to Saint Louis and relieve Hancock, who commanded there. Hancock then went to Washington to consult with President Johnson before going to New Orleans.[85]

If Griffin and Pease had considered Sheridan an obstacle, Hancock would be impossible to work under. The Texas Republicans had but one chance to organize their own state government: they would have to act in the interval between Sheridan's departure and Hancock's arrival from the North. Fortunately for the Republicans, Griffin, as the senior officer in the Fifth Military District, would handle both his and Sheridan's functions until Hancock arrived. He also had permission to run the Fifth Military District from Galveston, rather than New Orleans, where he could more easily cooperate with Pease and his allies.[86]

Sheridan fully realized that Griffin's takeover would allow the latter to institute his own policies. Ironically Johnson's intercession in the Fifth Military District served to augment the very replacement policy that the president had hoped to curtail. Perhaps Sheridan realized this irony and sought to get even with Johnson for his own removal. Possibly he merely wished to make the transition to a new commander more smooth. In any case, before Sheridan formally turned the Fifth Military District over to Griffin, he gave Griffin a blank check to remove all such Texas officials "as are disloyal to the government." He also allowed Griffin to announce immediately his own secretary of civil affairs.[87]

Griffin took over actual control of the Fifth Military District on September 6. He had not waited, however, to exercise the rights granted in Sheridan's letter ten days earlier. Griffin removed the remnants of Throckmorton's executive arm by making changes in the offices of attorney general, treasurer, comptroller, and state land commissioner.[88]

He then dealt with the state court system. On September 11, he replaced three more disloyal judges, including the durable Judge Holt, with Republicans. He also removed the entire state supreme court because of its "know hostility" to Reconstruction.[89] Other minor appointments followed. As Colbert Caldwell, one of the new Republican justices on the state supreme court aptly noted, Sheridan's loss was the party's gain because Griffin now had a free hand to save Texas before the coming of Hancock.[90]

Then, in the midst of Republican success, came an unexpected interruption: the entire Gulf coast was inundated by yellow fever. Griffin turned his attention from politics and attempted to organize Galveston to combat the feared disease. Higher authorities recommended that the general move his headquarters as a safety precaution. Griffin refused. The city was without doctors, as nearly all civilian and military surgeons succumbed to the disease. Griffin maintained that "to desert Galveston at such a time was like deserting one's post in time of battle." Griffin's own family contracted yellow fever, and still he refused to retreat. Then the general himself fell ill. He struggled on with his duties until September 15, when he died from advanced complications.

General Griffin's death was a grievous blow to Reconstruction in Texas. With his passing, the Republicans lost their chance to work with an understanding, cooperative officer to install their men into office before Hancock's conservative influence could be felt.[91] The Texas Republicans desperately needed a miracle to institute their patronage program. It came in the person of Brevet Major General Joseph Jones Reynolds.

PART THREE
Military Reconstruction:
The Reynolds Era,
1867–70

The pious, doubled-faced, double-dealing, smiling, fawning, sycophantic Maj. Gen. Reynolds, by brevet, . . . is now the law-maker, law-giver, judge, jury, pettifogger, and teazer over the whole State of Texas.

—Brownsville Daily Ranchero,
December 11, 1867

7

Another Setback

BECAUSE OF THE LATITUDE ALLOWED by the Reconstruction Acts, the personality of each district commander largely determined the character of Military Reconstruction in his area. Although the new commander of the District of Texas, Brevet Major General Joseph Jones Reynolds, allegedly possessed little administrative ability, he developed a definite flair for political intrigue. Reynolds demonstrated an ability to extract information from those bent on keeping secrets; he was, in the words of one Conservative editor, "a most powerful force pump. When applied to [a] man it leaves him with nothing to say in less than five minutes, or, in other words, it leaves him without a secret in that time." This same critic concluded that Reynolds was the most "affable or oily man" alive in Texas during the whole Reconstruction era, an assessment that future events tended to confirm.[1]

As Griffin's replacement in the District of Texas, Reynolds was the key to Republican success or failure in their patronage program. The outlook in September, 1867, however, was not promising. Reynolds had been an extremely popular officer in Brownsville, where he had supervised the Subdistrict of the Rio Grande before assuming the Texas command. He was close to the people and highly praised by the uncompromising archenemy of Reconstruction, the *Brownsville Daily Ranchero*, which did not recommend him to Texas Loyalists. "I do not know what to advise our friends in Texas to do except to prepare (secretly) for defense," a worried A. J. Hamilton informed his brother.[2]

Born in Kentucky, Reynolds was graduated from West Point in 1843. He served in the army until 1857 in various frontier and eastern garrison positions, including a term as an instructor at the Military Academy. He resigned his commission to accept a teaching position in mathematics at Washington University in Saint Louis. The beginning of the war found him in Indiana assisting in the family grocery business. Reynolds became colonel of the Tenth Indiana Infantry, was soon promoted to brigadier general, and fought in the early campaigns in western Virginia.

In 1862, upon the death of his brother, he resigned his commission a second time to settle family affairs back home. While in Indiana he was active in recruiting new soldiers, which led to his reappointment and promotion to major general in late 1862. He returned to active duty with the Army of the Cumberland and was breveted for heroic action as a division commander at Chickamauga and as chief of staff to the Army of the Cumberland at Missionary Ridge. Reynolds finished the conflict as a corps commander in Louisiana and Arkansas. Because of his war record, Reynolds realized a permanent commission as colonel of the Twenty-sixth Infantry in 1866, and in January, 1867, he became commander of the Subdistrict of the Rio Grande.[3]

Reynolds received his assignment as chief of the District of Texas on September 16 and assumed command a few days later. He temporarily established his headquarters at Austin because the yellow fever epidemic along the coast made travel to Galveston perilous. Seeking to make a good impression on Reynolds, Republican leaders consulted with friendly local commanders and asked them to present the party's program to him.[4]

To their pleasant surprise, a first sign of hope came soon after Reynolds's arrival in Austin, when his secretary of civil affairs wrote Governor Pease to ask his advice on a list of names submitted for appointments.[5] One month later the alliance between Reynolds and the state executive was completed.

The basis for cooperation between Reynolds and Pease was the latter's denial of the principle of ab initio. First made public in the 1866 Convention, the doctrine viewed secession and all ensuing acts of the state and Confederate governments as null and void from their inception. The 1866 Convention had rejected the principle, but led by Morgan C. Hamilton, its adherents bided their time, waiting for an opportune moment to reintroduce the question. With Pease's assumption of the governorship and Griffin's elevation of party leaders, including Morgan Hamilton, to high state offices, ab initio raised its controversial head once again.[6]

Up to this moment, neither the Republican party, Congress, nor the army had taken a formal position on the question. But there were hints that the army might adopt the position if state Republicans merely pressed the matter. Sheridan had indicated to Granger that, upon his arrival in Galveston in 1865, he should declare all actions since secession illegal, which Granger had promptly done. A. J. Hamilton had also taken this position in his July 24, 1865, proclamation announcing his assumption of the state government. But the army and the provisional government had not acted to enforce these statements.[7]

In October, 1867, Morgan Hamilton, the foremost advocate of ab initio and the comptroller of the state, revived the controversy by refusing to issue salary warrants to certain state officials. Hamilton said that the Eleventh Legislature, which had created the offices and appropriated the money for them, had no validity as a legal assembly of the people because it had not been recognized by Congress and the state had not been readmitted to the Union. This ab initio declaration was upheld by the state attorney general, William Alexander. Like Hamilton, the state's legal advisor contended that Congress had never readmitted Texas to the Union. Quite the contrary, said Alexander; in the Reconstruction Acts, Congress had declared all Southern state governments illegal, including Throckmorton's Eleventh Legislature. Hence Hamilton was correct not to pay salary warrants authorized by an illegitimate legislative body.[8]

Although in the aftermath of the tensions of war it was natural to expect the victorious Yankees to demand that the South repudiate all disloyal acts, Hamilton's concept of ab initio, as upheld by Alexander, was totally impractical by 1867. If all laws were truly illegal upon their inception after February 1, 1861, then taxes, salaries, marriages, deeds, all criminal convictions, and the simple, everyday business of the state could be challenged in courts of law.

Judge Chauncy B. Sabin brought these implications to the attention of the temporary head of the Fifth Military District after Griffin's death, Brevet Major General Joseph A. Mower, who also commanded the Department of Louisiana at New Orleans. Sabin claimed that ab initio and such "nonsense" would create a "confused and chaotic mess" of Reconstruction if allowed to develop unchecked. A. J. Hamilton opposed his brother's stand vigorously in a letter to Governor Pease in which he reversed his earlier position, now calling ab initio "senseless" and "pernicious."[9]

The ab initio controversy gave the new Texas commander, General Reynolds, an excellent opportunity to consolidate the army's position in the state. Griffin had barely begun the Republican party's removal program. His death had greatly impaired the Republicans' ability to install their own men in office—unless Reynolds would cooperate in the same spirit. Yet Reynolds could not see the necessity of an ab initio declaration, which would throw the state into more confusion than already existed. A simple statement that all laws in conflict with the results of the war were cancelled would be sufficient. Agreement with this position as well as a statement from Governor Pease recognizing the army's supreme control of the state became Reynolds's price for appointing a Republican administration. Reynolds illustrated his desire to forget the past and begin anew in an order that changed Griffin's policy of collecting back taxes due before the commencement of Military Reconstruction in 1867. Reynolds now decreed no forced collection of back taxes and later canceled the penalties for late payment.[10]

Pease indicated his willingness to cooperate with the general in a proclamation issued on October 25. He declared that the powers of his government rested on the March Reconstruction Acts, Sheridan's orders placing them in effect, the July Reconstruction Act, and any orders promulgated by the head of the Fifth Military District. There was no legal state government in Texas, continued Pease, but he would allow the laws of Texas existing in March, 1867, except those that had been nullified by Congress, to continue in effect. Those persons in office when the March Reconstruction Acts were passed and who had not been removed were the representatives of the provisional government.[11]

The Proclamation of October 25 was Pease's way of recognizing the army's supreme control in the state, something both A. J. Hamilton and Throckmorton had resisted. In addition, Pease adopted Reynolds's interpretation of the validity of all laws passed since secession except those held null and void by federal laws. Pease thus challenged the ab initio faction of his party and initiated a split that would cause trouble in the constitutional convention of 1868 and the election of 1869. The governor also ordered all state officials to obey the principles set forth in the proclamation.[12]

The ab initio faction pilloried Pease for his adoption of the milder position advocated by General Reynolds. Alexander resigned his position as attorney general, defending the wisdom and justice of ab initio and decrying the recognition of any action committed by the treasonous, illegal administrations in power since secession.[13]

Morgan Hamilton retained his office, but he wrote an acrid letter to General Mower in New Orleans criticizing Pease's proclamation. Hamilton argued that the Pease-Reynolds doctrine would sanction property confiscation by rebels during the war, the imprisonment of loyal men during the conflict and untold other evils. He attacked those Loyalists who were willing to endorse the injustices perpetrated under "these bastard statutes." Mower, however, had already endorsed Reynolds's acceptance of Pease's proclamation as the wisest course.[14]

Forsaken by military authorities, the ab initio advocates transferred their operations to the Union Loyal League, which became their principal area of concern because of its influence among black Republicans. On December 11, the corresponding committee of the Travis County chapter issued a report at Austin which proposed to amend the Republican platform adopted at Houston in July. Included in this paper was a statement defending ab initio, a proposal to invalidate the statute of limitations against suits to recover property or damages for Confederate actions initiated against Loyalists during the war, a clause declaring that the Emancipation Proclamation had legally freed Texas slaves (opening up the possibility that blacks could sue their masters for compensation for their last two years of "illegal" bondage), an endorsement of the proposed Fourteenth Amendment, a demand to disfranchise former rebels, and various economic improvements clauses and land tax proposals. The Austin league called upon Republicans to vote only for those convention delegates who would support these revisions of the party platform.[15]

Meanwhile, in exchange for the governor's proclamation and without General Mower's knowledge, Reynolds agreed to appoint a Republican administration before Hancock arrived. Reynolds was able to keep his agreement because the yellow fever epidemic had delayed Hancock's coming. The army had already lost one general to the disease and was not willing to risk Hancock's life unnecessarily.

Mower, as interim head of the Fifth Military District, unwittingly assisted Reynolds when he wrote to Grant and recommended that Hancock stay in Amite, Louisiana, until it was safe to come into New Orleans. Acting on Mower's suggestion, Grant decided instead to keep Hancock in Saint Louis until mid-October. He later extended his stay there to the end of November.[16]

Mower, like Sheridan, became so involved in Louisiana politics that he had little time for Texas matters. Furthermore, he received no reports from Reynolds beyond some letters on the ab initio quarrel. Mower, and thus Grant, knew only that the Texas Republican party disagreed on a philosophical issue and that Reynolds was rumored to have replaced some Texas officials. When Reynolds finally communicated with New Orleans, he received Mower's permission to remove several state judges, district attorneys, and the state attorney general. Mower himself had replaced some Louisiana civil authorities. When Grant heard of Mower's action, he telegraphed a new order to suspend all removals until Hancock arrived; Mower complied, but it was too late to deter Reynolds in Texas.[17]

Because of Mower's preoccupation with Louisiana, Reynolds was free to carry out his agreement with Texas Republicans. On October 28, Reynolds appointed 33 men to vacant offices. A week after Pease issued his proclamation, Reynolds announced Special Orders No. 195, a thirteen-page document that removed 400 Democrats from office and appointed 436 Republicans.[18]

During the next six days, the general appointed Republican officials to the city governments of San Antonio and Austin and filled eighty-eight miscellaneous state offices, removing incumbents from all but fourteen of these positions. Then, between November 18 and the end of the month, Reynolds appointed eighty-seven more men to local government jobs, twenty-five of which had been vacant. The miracle had happened—the Republicans were entrenched in state government as never before.[19]

Reynolds did not act a day too soon, because Hancock finally arrived in New Orleans on November 28. The new commander was a native of Pennsylvania and graduated from West Point in 1844. He served in the Mexican War as an infantry lieutenant and on the frontier primarily as a quartermaster. During the war, he had a meritorious career with the Army of the Potomac, rising from brigade to corps command. Hancock fought in nearly every battle in the eastern theater. He was instrumental in saving the Union army on the first day of Gettysburg, and his corps bore the brunt of the fighting during the next two days, when he received a serious hip wound. Hancock later returned to action and led his corps in the 1864 campaign against Richmond until his old wound reopened. Because of his fine record, Congress made Hancock the junior major general in the army in 1866. He had served as commander of the Department of the West until he was assigned to the Fifth Military district.[20]

Hancock finally took command at New Orleans on November 29. His first act was to replace Mower with Brevet Major General Robert C. Buchanan; Mower's effectiveness had supposedly been impaired when Grant told him to reinstate deposed Louisiana officeholders.[21] The officials set aside by Reynolds in Texas had been eagerly awaiting similar reprieve. Upon Hancock's assumption of command, they flooded the Fifth Military District headquarters with angry letters protesting Reynolds's action.[22]

Many of these complaints referred to Reynolds's removal of Judge James Love of the criminal court of Galveston and Harris counties. The bar associations of Galveston and Houston both attested to the judge's competency for the bench. Governor Pease, however, said that before the war the Texas bar had considered Love an incompetent judge and had forced him to resign. The governor marveled at how their tone had changed. He assured Reynolds that Love and the bar associations' members were former Confederates and that Love's successor, W. R. Fayle, was a "thoroughly loyal and educated gentleman."

Pease neglected to point out, however, that Fayle, a merchandiser and gospel minister, had no legal experience. Reynolds sent Pease's remarks to New Orleans, adding that Love's legal background was irrelevant, since he was disqualified from holding office because he could not take the oath.[23]

Prompted by the various complaints about the removal of Love and others, Hancock demanded that Reynolds detail his power and justification for the removal of so many state officials. He moreover ordered Reynolds to make no further changes in civil officials and to permit those who had been removed (but who still physically held their offices) to remain in their positions. After a long delay, Reynolds explained his course of action. The replacements had been made "after consultation with Governor Pease and were based on written evidence in this office," said Reynolds. He admitted that he did not know any of the men involved nor had he seen all of the evidence.[24]

His basis for acting without Hancock's authorization was Sheridan's letter of August 27 to Griffin, in which Sheridan had told Griffin to remove all disloyal persons from office. Reynolds also believed he had proper authority under the Reconstruction Acts to eliminate any officeholder who tried to "hinder, delay, prevent, and obstruct" the laws of Congress.[25]

The Conservatives in Texas were not satisfied with this explanation, and they pressured Hancock to reverse the November office changes. They also suggested that Reynolds should follow Mower to another, less sensitive assignment. The *Brownsville Daily Ranchero*, happy with Reynolds in September, now vilified him. "We sincerely hope that Major General Hancock may find a retired spot in the corner of New England for the pious, double-faced, double-dealing, smiling, fawning, sycophantic Maj. Gen. Reynolds, by brevet," said the *Ranchero*. The paper bemoaned the fact that Reynolds was "now the law-maker, law-giver, judge, jury, pettifogger, and teazer over the whole State of Texas."[26]

Unsure of how far he should go in disciplining Reynolds, Hancock explained the whole situation in a letter to Grant. Grant approved limiting Reynolds's right to make further removals, but he thought it would be wise to confirm the appointments already made.[27] Hancock followed Grant's advice but told the complaining Texas Conservatives that he could not act in their behalf because the Reconstruction Acts prevented reappointment of an official once removed. Although Hancock refused to replace local officials for political reasons, he did appoint some ninety men to offices already vacant.[28]

If Hancock did not overtly change the situation in Texas, he did effect a new spirit of administration. Hancock had had no desire to command the Fifth Military District because he knew that his feelings on Reconstruction differed from those expressed by Congress in the Reconstruction Acts. President Johnson, however, appointed him for just that reason. On his trip south, the new commander frequently voiced his apprehension to his wife. "I am expected to exercize extreme authority over these people," Hancock told her. "I shall disappoint them." The general said that he had not been educated to overthrow civil authorities in time of peace and that he intended to issue a proclamation to that effect.[29]

Hancock also expressed his fear that he might lose his commission, but he would rather do that than "retain it at the sacrifice of a life long principle." The night before he arrived in New Orleans, the general stayed up until 4:00 A.M. working on his proclamation. Gazing at the finished product, he sighed to his wife, "They will crucify me." Hancock knew President Johnson was on his side, but he realized that Johnson could do little to help him survive the impending political attack.[30]

On November 29, 1867, Hancock issued his proclamation as General Orders No. 40. The general announced his assumption of command and stated his principles. Hancock declared that he regarded "the maintenance of the civil authorities in the faithful execution of the laws as the most efficient [thing to do] under existing circumstances." The war was over, and it was time for the civil authorities to exercise full power. "The right of trial by jury, the habeas corpus, the liberty of the press, the freedom of speech, the natural rights of property must be preserved," continued the proclamation. If the civil authorities proved themselves unequal to the task before them, the general pledged military action to ensure "the liberties of the people."[31]

Conservatives in Texas rejoiced at Hancock's "patriotic" proclamation. The *Brownsville Daily Ranchero* summed up their opinion in a brief editorial: "That document sounds like a return to earth of the immortal spirit of '76." The newspaper was happy that Hancock was a responsible commander, but it objected to the idea that a military man had the right to issue any orders to the people at all. The Conservative sheet grieved that Texas and the South were still considered a "military kingdom."[32]

Texas Republicans found Hancock's principles reprehensible. Judge Colbert Caldwell wrote Pease about an incident that occurred in Marshall shortly after the issuance of General Orders No. 40. Charged with investigating a riot, a military commission had met in a law office with the mayor and a dozen rebel lawyers present, none of whom knew the facts of the case, according to Caldwell. Through the information supplied by two lieutenants, Caldwell concluded that the commission was twisting the available evidence to secure General Reynolds's court-martial. Caldwell had offered his services as the local district judge, but the officer in charge retorted that his help was unnecessary. Caldwell believed that the perpetrators of the riot were being ignored and that Reynolds and the "rest of us" were to be accused of interference with the town government for using troops to quell the riot. Something had to be done quickly, he concluded, to counter these rebel triumphs achieved under Hancock's order.[33]

In spite of various appeals, Hancock refused to compromise with Caldwell or the Republican administration in Texas on the principles enunciated in General Orders No. 40. When Governor Pease tried to obtain a military trial for three men accused of murder in Uvalde County, Hancock demurred, even though it was doubtful that the prisoners could be held long enough for the civil processes to take effect. The general noted that the right of organizing military commissions was "an extraordinary power" to be used only in the "extraordinary event that the local civil tribunals are unwilling or unable to enforce the laws against crimes."[34]

The general did not find Texas civil authorities unwilling to hold fair trials and refused the request for a military court. He suggested that, if an unfair trial was feared in Uvalde, the local judge could grant a change of venue under Texas law. If an escape from jail was feared, the courts should ask the army to hold the prisoners until their trial could be scheduled. If more judges were needed to fill existing vacancies and help end the legal backlog, Hancock would make the necessary appointments. Until the civil outlets had been exhausted, however, the army would not interfere directly with the courts, concluded Hancock.[35]

A few days after he wrote Pease, Hancock publicly condemned petitions sent to his headquarters which implied that he had the right to make arbitrary law in civil controversies. "One petitioner solicits this action, another that, and each refers to some special consideration of grace or favor which he supposes to exist, and which should influence this department," he said. "The rights of litigants do not depend on the views of the general," concluded the statement. "Arbitrary power, such as he has been urged to assume, has no existence here."[36]

Upon receiving Hancock's letter and new manifesto, Governor Pease quickly and irately responded to Hancock. The governor denied that Texas was in "full exercize of its proper powers." According to the acts of Congress, said Pease, there was no legal government in Texas, and any civil government which did exist was fully subordinate to the Fifth Military District command. The general in New Orleans was therefore the true executive head of Texas government.[37]

Then Pease challenged Hancock's assertion that Texas was in a time of "profound peace." A large majority of the white population was embittered against the United States, said the governor, which made it hard to enforce criminal laws in the state. Often civil officers refused to act or could not act because of continual intimidation. Pease blamed a "perceptible increase of crime and manifestations of hostile feelings" directly on Hancock's attitude as commanding general.[38]

Temporarily ignoring the governor's assertions, Hancock left New Orleans to make a personal inspection of conditions in Texas. Pease disgustedly told his daughter of the reception Hancock received in Austin, where more rebels had attended than Republicans. "The former expect great things from him," said Pease. There had been rumors to the effect that Hancock would remove both Pease and Reynolds, but the governor believed that Hancock would be superseded first by "some officer whose feelings are more in sympathy with the Union men of Texas."[39]

Back in New Orleans, Hancock continued his crusade against military intervention in local government. When a Freedmen's Bureau agent tried to secure military trials in his jurisdiction, Hancock refused because the agent made "only vague and indefinite complaints." He promised to consider any particular case on its merits, but the Reconstruction Acts gave the district commander "the duty of protecting *all* persons in their rights and property," said Hancock, including former rebels.[40]

Hancock firmly believed that the bureau was unfairly biased toward the blacks and Loyalists in its administration of justice. As with the issue of removals and appointments, Texans sent vociferous complaints detailing alleged bureau tyrannies. The subassistant commissioners were accused of false arrests, forced fines, unlawful seizure of property, and interference with civil courts. Hancock sent urgent requests to both Reynolds and the bureau staff that they identify the source of bureau authority in the state.[41]

Tired of what he saw as insubordination in the army and bureau staffs in Texas, Hancock ordered all freedmen's cases involving legal problems to be directed hereafter to the civil courts. The bureau was not to interfere with these civil judgments in any manner. The agents' only remaining powers included the right to seize a landowner's property for failure to pay his or her laborers, if civil authorities refused to act first, and the right to arrest anyone who committed an outrage upon a freedman, providing the civil authorities were unable to guarantee justice. Hancock also withdrew all separate detachments from bureau command to prevent unauthorized independent action.[42]

The bureau agents protested Hancock's orders, but to no avail. One said that the general had removed all authority from the bureau to negotiate contracts and that blacks were consequently being defrauded. Another contended that the civil authorities were unwilling to be fair and asked for soldiers and the suppression of disloyal newspapers. Others reported that mob scenes, murder, threats and intimidation all increased markedly when their troop contingents were withdrawn.[43]

The general continued to exasperate Texas Republicans by revamping the entire voter registration system. The total figures were announced to Texans about the time Hancock had assumed command in New Orleans. The military report showed 104,259 persons registered, of whom 56,678 were white and 47,581 were black. Rejected registrants totaled 8,005, but were not designated by color.[44]

Conservatives alleged the figures proved dishonesty in the registration process and estimated that white voters in the state ought to number close to 110,000. The *Galveston Daily News* claimed that nearly half of the potential white voters had been denied registration, not the few thousand listed by the army. Lack of participation, however, not direct rejection of voters, better explains the figures.[45]

Especially shocking to Conservatives was the large number of black registrants, about double the expected figure. Republicans were probably correct when they pointed out that Conservatives based their expectations on the black population listed in the 1860 census, while wartime migration had actually greatly increased the numbers of Texas blacks. Conservatives had hoped to outnumber black and white Loyalists by two to one and easily block any convention or the passage of any new constitution. Now if the white Republican vote in the upcoming election was anywhere near the 1861 vote cast against secession, the Conservatives would be dismayingly outnumbered by black and white Republicans. A new convention and constitution appeared to be assured.[46]

Conservative apprehensions were voiced by John Hancock (not related to the district commander), a former Unionist who had been disfranchised. He told General Hancock that Sheridan's instructions to registrars had been to disfranchise all state officials regardless of rank and anyone who had aided them in any manner. This order went far beyond the intent of the Reconstruction Acts. Negroes, said the Texan, have been registered without question as to their qualification, especially concerning their ages. John Hancock asked General Hancock to reopen the registration books for a fairer count.[47]

The commanding general of the Fifth Military District responded to Conservative complaints by mandating a new registration period opening January 27, 1868, and lasting for five days. He admitted that there was much doubt as to the intent of the Reconstruction Acts, but he negated Sheridan's guidelines because they were too strict and discriminated unfairly against white applicants. Hereafter, said Hancock, the only rules the boards were to follow were the disfranchising sections of the Reconstruction Acts and the officeholding disqualification clause of the proposed Fourteenth Amendment. If for any reason the registrars were unable to perform their duties, Reynolds should replace them with the county judge, clerk of the county court, or clerk of the district court, in that order, providing these individuals could take the ironclad oath. Otherwise, vacancies were to be filled by appointments made by the remaining board members.[48]

In addition to changing the rules of procedure, Hancock did his best to mitigate possible registration injustices by ordering doubtful cases to be registered. But the boards jealously guarded their own authority, and General Reynolds usually allowed them to pursue their own course with a minimum of interference.[49] Not until seven months later, after the constitutional convention was elected, did Reynolds institute new registration guidelines. Then he ordered Republicans in each county to do their best to find white registrars and told the boards to confine themselves to asking whether the applicant had ever held a Federal or state office, taken an oath to support the Federal government, or voluntarily engaged in rebellion.[50]

Ultimately Hancock's registration did little to change the overall registration figures, although a few thousand more voters of both races were enrolled.[51] By February, 1868, about 11 percent of the white population and 20 percent of the black population had been regis-

tered. Blacks controlled only 33 counties and represented over 40 percent of the voters in only 14 others, out of 119 counties reporting.

Nonetheless, Republicans would have to take the entire black vote
and 10 percent of the white vote to win any future election. An increase
in white registration, such as that of 1869, when twenty thousand more
whites enrolled to vote, or a decline in black voter participation would
cost the loyal element control of the state. It was essential for the Republicans to win additional white adherents if they desired to maintain
their initial electoral advantage.[52]

Because of the yellow fever epidemic, army command changes, and
new registration guidelines, the election originally scheduled for November, 1867, had been postponed until February, 1868; this delay
was partly responsible for the eventual Republican victory.[53] Initially
the Conservatives thought that no convention would meet unless a
majority of the potential electorate registered and voted. They soon
realized, however, that they were mistaken. The crucial factor according to the Reconstruction Acts was whether a majority of those registered voted in favor of the convention. The party leaders began to
urge their supporters to register and refuse to vote in February.[54]

Shortly before the election it became obvious that white Republicans and their black allies had sufficient strength to carry the state,
even if the Conservatives did not vote. The party's leaders once again
changed their tactics and told their backers to vote against the convention. At the same time, party members were instructed to cast
their ballots for Conservative candidates who would oppose black
suffrage.[55]

The continual changes in Conservative policy merely confused the
voters and resulted in an overwhelming Republican victory. With just
over half of the registered voters participating, Texans cast 44,689 ballots for the convention and 11,440 against. Since only 1,127 more
than half had voted, the 11,730 blacks who failed to show up at the
polls had nearly cost Republicans the right to hold the convention.[56]

After the election, Hancock again turned his attention to Governor Pease. "Your communication of 17th January last was received in
due course of mail," began Hancock, "but not until it had been widely
circulated by the newspaper press." The general asserted that he replied only now, "as soon as leisure from more important business
would permit." Hancock admitted that he had full power over civil
affairs in Texas and the right to order military trials. He believed, however, that "the power to do a thing . . . and the propriety of doing it,

are often very different matters." The main complaint that Pease had against the people of Texas, said Hancock, was that they did not agree with the governor's political views. "It would be difficult to show that the opponents of [the] government in days of the elder Adams or Jefferson, or Jackson, exhibited for it either [the] 'affection' or 'respect'" Pease demanded of his fellow Texans, continued Hancock.

Since the war had been over for two years, Hancock thought it was time "to tolerate again free, popular discussion, and extend some forbearance and consideration to opposing views." As for lawlessness in Texas and the failure of officials to arrest, indict, and convict, Hancock said, "There is no place in the United States where it might not be done with equal propriety." The general was not going to annul the state civil code to attain law and order.[57]

Hancock was incensed at Pease's accusation that General Orders No. 40 had caused an increase in crime. He tried to get more facts on the situation from Reynolds, but the latter evaded the question by sending incomplete information.[58] The governor claimed that over 100 cases of homicide had occurred in 1867, while the constitutional convention maintained that 331 cases occurred in the same year. Neither of these figures was really very large when compared with Benjamin C. Truman's assertion that Texas averaged 450 murders each year before the Civil War, and Hancock found it hard to see how his proclamation could be blamed for the 1867 crime level, since it took effect only in December of that year.[59] Hancock said Pease had not yet had enough time to ascertain its effect fully and accurately. Besides, all the order had done was declare "the great principles of American liberty." The general also asserted that many of the officials refusing to act to preserve the peace were recent Republican appointees.

Hancock professed to find little in Pease's letter "but indications of temper lashed into excitement by causes which I deem mostly imaginary, . . . an intolerance of others, [and] a desire to punish the thoughts and feelings of those who differ from you." Above all, the general was dismayed at Pease's "most unsound conclusion that while any persons are found wanting in *affection* or *respect* for the government, or yielding it *obedience*[,] from *motives which you do not approve*" they should be placed under martial rule.[60]

Hancock's biographers consider his general orders and the March 9 letter to Pease to be heroic documents that guaranteed fundamental civil liberties.[61] This analysis of Hancock, however, ignores his interference with the attempts of Texas and Louisiana Republicans to build up their party through military patronage. By restraining the army from intervening in the status quo and insisting that civil authorities assume full governmental responsibility, Hancock effectively maintained Conservatives in power. James Marin, a special agent for the Treasury Department in New Orleans, recognized this fact when he informed President Johnson that "Gen. Hancock's influence is most decidedly felt in our favor." Marin realized that the general, by avoiding military interference in politics, could act in the name of civil liberties—the rights of free speech, free press, trial by jury, and open dissent—to prevent further changes in the composition of local government.[62]

Believing in a restricted role for the army in Reconstruction, Hancock naturally turned the occupation forces to other fields of activity. In Texas, he concentrated on planning frontier defense against Indian attacks and directed the construction of forts Concho, Richardson, Griffin, and Burnham. He also ordered the army to establish a defensive line stretching from the new forts to the Rio Grande. Smaller picket details were placed at forts Chadbourne, Phantom Hill, and Belknap. Hancock recommended that a telegraph system be established to connect the forts which would allow a more efficient response to reported Indian raids.[63]

Hancock then commanded Reynolds to shift infantry "to the points most likely to be required for the performance of its legitimate duties." This involved moving the Twenty-sixth Infantry to the Rio Grande valley and forwarding the Seventeenth and Forty-first (Colored) regiments to the frontier. Hancock sent all of his cavalry to the west and ordered that no other work but frontier defense be required of it. Reynolds, however, delayed the troop movements as long as possible and thus negated some of their effect.[64]

Undoubtedly, white Texans were generally glad to see the bluecoats leave for "proper" frontier stations. Incidents between soldiers and civilians had continued unabated during the winter of 1867–68. A Fredericksburg man reported an attempted outrage on his wife by Fourth Cavalry troopers who visited his farm during his absence.[65]

In Weatherford, Sixth Cavalry soldiers broke into a local home and stole several items. The rancher involved had identified the men as members of a company led by a Lieutenant Winchester. The officer denied his men's culpability and dismissed the evidence presented as circumstantial and insufficient. The *Daily Ranchero* blasted the conduct of "nigger troops" in the Rio Grande valley. The journal asserted that assaults and robberies were at a new high and that the citizens anxiously awaited their transfer to the Indian country upriver.[66]

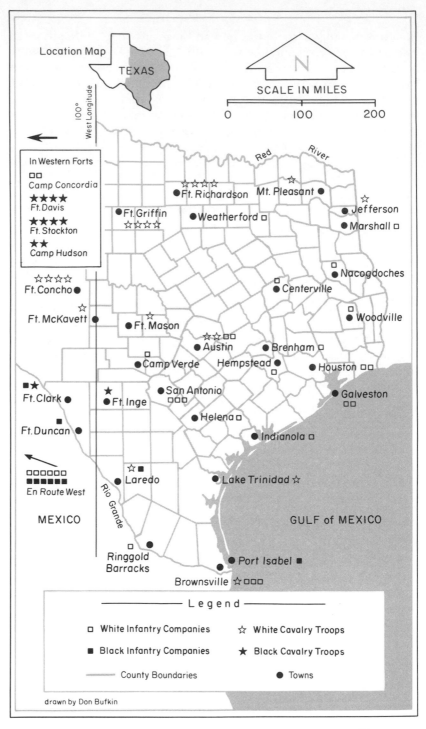

Map 6. Hancock's Troop Assignments, March, 1868: Troop Movement West

One of the most notorious examples of military-civilian misunderstanding occurred in Gonzales that spring. In February, 1868, a Gonzales County resident sent headquarters a complaint about the conduct of Sergeant Thomas Dwyer and his detachment from the Thirty-fifth Infantry. The protestor remonstrated that the whole area was being intimidated by armed soldiers and was completely at their mercy.[67]

The army failed to respond to this plea until a couple of months later when the county district attorney reported that Sergeant Dwyer and a private under his authority had been arrested for murdering a civilian. The district attorney recommended that the army intervene and save the soldiers by ordering a military court-martial or at least that it provide for a change of venue.[68]

Hancock's eventual successor, Brevet Major General Robert C. Buchanan, granted a change in venue but told Pease to have Dwyer tried in state courts. Shortly thereafter, Texas was transferred from Buchanan's control, and Reynolds intervened to have the suspect sergeant tried by a military court, which found him and his accomplice not guilty as charged.[69]

Much of the lack of discipline in the Texas command arose from a shortage of experienced officers to supervise the garrisons and from the boredom of occupation duty. The men often went unpaid for a year at a time, while their officers were harassed by civil courts and newspapers mercilessly, which led one Fourth Cavalry major to beg for reassignment to escape persecution.[70]

The officers and men tried to alleviate the situation by drinking, gambling, and, in the words of General Reynolds, "other vicious habits" to such an extent that he ordered suspect officers cashiered and enlisted men brought before courts-martial. At the same time, New Orleans warned commanders to be understanding and not to use Reynolds's orders to persecute the soldiers under their command.[71]

Yet, regardless of the inherent difficulties of military-civilian relations, throughout Reconstruction there were always areas where soldiers and citizens got along. The *Army and Navy Journal* reprinted a series of newspaper articles detailing such rapport in Indianola and Galveston. Similar reports arrived at various times from Centerville, Halletsville, Nacogdoches, Waco, and Hempstead. When the Seventeenth Infantry left Houston for its frontier assignments, the town threw a complimentary ball for the departing soldiers. Whether from sorrow or from relief, such an event was an improvement over the hatred of the previous year.[72]

Hancock's action in removing troops from the interior brought the number of soldiers on the frontier to just over 3,000 men, a new high. In fact, this total was the largest number of men stationed in the western part of Texas until 1873, and was above average for the entire period prior to the defeat of the Comanches at Palo Duro Canyon. The only year the troops dropped significantly below this level was 1869, when the army reduced the western garrisons to 1,976 men in order to combat increasingly disloyal acts in eastern Texas. Hancock also had removed the last black soldiers from the more populated areas of the state.[73]

Aware of Hancock's unenthusiastic approach to Reconstruction, congressional Republicans began to scheme for his removal, although they were unsure how to proceed. The Senate considered a bill that would reduce the number of generals in the army by retiring the ones last appointed. As the major general with the least seniority, Hancock would lose his commission. This attempt died in committee when party leaders detected signs that Hancock might become not only a martyr but also a serious Democratic contender for the presidency in 1868. As President Johnson was happy with the general's policies, the only other way to secure Hancock's removal was to force his resignation.[74]

Hancock conveniently provided the Republicans with the issue they needed by removing the New Orleans city council for holding an unauthorized election. At first Grant had approved the action, but ten days later he ordered the council's reinstatement. Grant reasoned that Hancock's General Orders No. 40 expressly stated that civil authority had been restored in the Fifth Military District, which gave the council the power to call an election. For Hancock to interfere, said Grant, was to deny the veracity of his own order. Hancock could do nothing but sullenly obey the command, the issuance of which marked another step in Grant's conversion to the Republican cause and his advance to the presidency.[75]

Shortly thereafter, Grant refused to allow Hancock to remove the New Orleans street commissioner. Hancock protested and wired the full particulars of the case to Washington. Grant told him to stop using the telegraph and resort to the mails when "there is not a greater necessity for prompt reply than seems to exist in this case." With his authority so severely compromised, Hancock asked for reassignment and left for Washington on March 14. Once again the Conservatives had been checked in their efforts to frustrate Texas Reconstruction.[76]

8

Confusion Reigns Supreme

THE DEPARTURE OF GENERAL HANCOCK left Brevet Major General
Robert C. Buchanan the senior officer in the Fifth Military District. Buchanan was an old regular officer whose career was very similar to that of General Heintzelman. Graduated from West Point in
1831, Buchanan had fought in the Black Hawk War, the Second
Seminole War, and the Mexican War. For his heroism he was breveted
twice in the Mexican conflict. Buchanan then served along the California coast, where at one point he forced U. S. Grant, then an unknown brevet captain, to resign his commission or face a court-martial
for drunkenness and neglect of duty.

Coming east from California for the Civil War, Buchanan led the
Regular Brigade of infantry in the Army of the Potomac. He covered
McClellan's withdrawal to Harrison's Landing and Pope's retreat from
Second Manassas, was present at Antietam, and led a charge against
the stone wall at Fredericksburg. In each of these actions, Old Buck,
as his men called him, was breveted for bravery. By March of 1863,
however, his temporary commission as brigadier general was not renewed by Congress, and he left the field. For the remainder of the war
Buchanan served on numerous investigation boards and with the
Freedmen's Bureau. Like Heintzelman, he had a regular rank of full
colonel and was ignored in favor of younger men during the war.
Buchanan had replaced Mower as the head of the Department of Louisiana in December, 1867, and when Hancock left for Washington, he
naturally expected to assume command.[1]

Unfortunately for Buchanan, the adjutant of the Fifth Military District mistakenly assumed Reynolds to be the senior officer and ordered
him to replace Hancock. President Johnson intervened upon Hancock's request and appointed Buchanan chief of the Fifth Military District. When Reynolds arrived in New Orleans he found a copy of the
order assigning Buchanan to command. He was enraged at the maneuvering that had gone on behind his back and stated that the whole
process was unfair and illegal. Rather than create trouble, Reynolds

returned to Texas and satisfied himself with a letter to the Adjutant General's Office in Washington requesting it to take such action "as the good of the service demanded."[2]

Buchanan's replacement of Reynolds had little effect in Texas, even though Buchanan announced that he would continue Hancock's policy of no interference with civil authorities. Like Mower, Buchanan was more interested in Louisiana. He was unfamiliar with the strange names, places, and events across the Sabine. Louisiana politics were especially demanding that spring of 1868 because the state was completing the final steps required by the Reconstruction Acts for readmission to the Union. Once again Texas was left in the hands of Reynolds and Pease, and they immediately began rebuilding the Republican party.[3]

Buchanan stayed out of Texas affairs until Governor Pease made the mistake of questioning the loyalty of Buchanan's appointee as mayor of Jefferson. Buchanan indignantly stated that he had approved of nearly all of the appointments suggested by Reynolds and Pease and that they had recommended any public officers who were now considered disloyal or incompetent. Buchanan also complained that Pease saw loyalty only as a party label, not as a characteristic of any efficient officeholder.

He further objected to the manner in which Pease was willing to overlook state residence requirements in selecting "loyal" appointees. Buchanan admitted that military appointees did not have to satisfy residence rules, but he believed it best to follow the state law as closely as possible. Accordingly, over Pease's violent protests, Buchanan removed several Republican officeholders and ordered the governor to submit a list of all state officials who lacked proper residence requirements along with comprehensive reasons why they should be retained in office. Buchanan also hinted that Pease himself might be removed next.[4]

Fortunately for Pease, Buchanan's reign was cut short by Louisiana's readmission to the Union on July 28. The general was retained in New Orleans as the commander of the new Department of Louisiana and Arkansas. The Fifth Military District now consisted solely of Texas, "a whole satrapy by herself, with Gen. Reynolds in command," wailed the *Denton Monitor*. "Oh the pity of it, the villainous pity of it!"[5] To control the state more fully, Reynolds moved his headquarters permanently from Galveston to Austin. There was much Conservative influence for the Republicans to neutralize in the Texas government, and the commanding general would not disappoint the Republican party.[6]

Part of Reynolds's assistance to the Republicans came in the form of political appointments. From August 10 to November 3, he appointed 190 men to local offices, 43 percent of which had been vacant.[7] Many Conservatives began to resign their posts, which included 40 of the 190 positions filled. Others indicated their willingness to do the same, such as the Wise County judge, L. L. Ward. But according to Ward, the army's appointees had not yet qualified (that is, taken the proper oath), and Wise County courts had a large backlog. Ward suggested that the former officials resume office until further arrangements were made, but the army never acted on his idea. In another instance, however, Reynolds followed Ward's proposal when he declared the actions of a Trinity County official to be valid, even though he had not taken the proper oath while in office, which did not endear the general to the ab initio wing of the Republican party.[8]

The major problem facing the army and the Republican party that summer of 1868 was the new state constitutional convention. The convention had been scheduled for June 15, but at Grant's suggestion Buchanan had advanced the date to June 1. If the convention acted quickly, the Texas electoral vote could perhaps be counted in the Republican column in the upcoming presidential election. Grant failed to realize, however, that, even though the Republicans held all but a dozen of the ninety convention seats, the party lacked a clear policy on what was necessary to purify the state for readmission to the Union. Hence the convention would drag on for months in partisan debate and delay the formulation of a new constitution.[9]

The delegates to the convention were primarily men who had been in Texas years before the Civil War. There were seven carpetbaggers and ten black delegates. The convention members were not leading members of the Texas business community, most of whom were prominent, disfranchised Democrats.[10] The delegates' income and educational levels were well above the Texas average. Many of them had served the state in political, administrative, and military positions dating back to the days of the Republic, although they were men who usually represented opposition factions within the traditional prewar Democratic party structure. The average delegate was a middle-aged person of moderate means and of some education who had lived in Texas long before the war and was a farmer, lawyer, or businessman by profession.[11]

The delegates quickly divided into factions over the major issues facing the convention: ab initio, formal division of the state into "loyal" and "rebel" areas, and disfranchisement of former Confederates. These items were highly important because they split Republican strength and gave Conservatives more influence than their small number of delegates would indicate.

The Republican party splintered into two groups. One called itself the Moderates. These Moderate Republicans opposed ab initio, division, and disfranchisement. They believed that the rebels had been sufficiently punished for the war, and they wished to proceed with the traditional state political contests. Eventually this group included about forty consistent supporters and constituted a convention majority on most issues. Andrew J. Hamilton led the Moderates, with assistance from Colbert Caldwell, Livingston Lindsay, and A. P. McCormick. Critical to Hamilton's parliamentary victories was the support of seven Conservatives, who agreed on many issues with him. The Conservative faction was headed by former U.S. Representative, Know-Nothing leader, and Unionist Lemuel D. Evans of Marshall.[12]

Opposed to the other factions, although gaining some Conservative support on state division, was a group of thirty Republicans, labeled Radicals. These men believed that further punishment and a close supervision of Texas politics by strictly loyal persons was necessary to cleanse the state of rebellion and its effects. Their program included support for ab initio, division, and disfranchisement of whites, while guaranteeing political rights for the freedmen. They also believed that the convention could act as a temporary legislature to correct past mistakes committed by heretofore disloyal administrations. Led by Edmund J. Davis, the Radicals included Edward Degener, Morgan C. Hamilton, and a shrewd black delegate from Galveston, George T. Ruby.[13]

The convention started off well for the Radicals when Edmund J. Davis was elected the convention president over Colbert Caldwell. Davis's election was not a fair test of strength for either faction. More than anything else it testified to an initial lack of organization by the Moderates. Shortly after Davis's election, Governor Pease entered the hall, accompanied by General Reynolds. Both men were escorted down the aisle, and Reynolds was even offered a permanent seat in the body, which he declined. He had come only to listen to and support Pease's message.[14]

Governor Pease forcefully presented the Moderate Republican program for Reconstruction. He asked for equal political and civil rights for all persons, regardless of former status, although he, unlike Hamilton, believed that the convention should disfranchise enough disloyal men to place political control of Texas in loyal hands. The governor urged the delegates to avoid discussion of so divisive an issue as making Texas into several states.

Pease called for decisive state action in education and internal improvements and for the creation of a state homestead law. Pease also mentioned that the state treasury had ample funds, which he hoped would eliminate any necessity to tax the people further for convention expenses. Finally, the governor issued a ringing repudiation of ab initio. He called for the resumption of payment on all state debts, except those incurred during the rebellion, and validation of all state laws passed since secession that were not in conflict with the results of the war.[15]

After Pease and Reynolds left, the Radicals ignored the governor's suggestions and asked the delegates to condemn the rebellion and Presidential Reconstruction. The Radicals maintained that the people and not the states had created the Union and its Constitution, that the Union was permanent, and hence that no state could secede. The Radicals believed that no state government was valid unless Congress recognized it. Under the Reconstruction Acts, the convention was not to recognize or sanction the state's secession ordinance or any provision that was not first recognized by Congress. The Radicals concluded that any person who honored the provisions of any government established since 1861 and not sanctioned by Congress was a traitor.[16]

The Radical contention was challenged by A. J. Hamilton and the Moderates, who managed to get a substitute motion passed by the convention. The Moderate proposal declared that only laws in support of secession and the Confederacy contrary to the Constitution of the United States were null and void. All other ordinances and court decisions relating to domestic affairs, so long as they did not aid the disloyal at the expense of the Union men and the public, were still valid.

Davis refused to admit defeat and introduced a modified ab initio proviso. This measure would allow the 1866 Convention and the Throckmorton regime provisional status, recognize private and domestic matters enacted since 1861 to be valid, and honor proceedings of military officers and courts since August, 1861. Morgan Hamilton amended the proposal into an extreme ab initio declaration in committee and castigated any who would disagree with him on the floor. Although Davis tried to compromise, the Moderates refused to give ground, and the measure was laid to rest. The bitterness within the Republican Party, however, lingered on.[17]

Republicans also disagreed on the issue of dividing Texas into two or more states. The size of Texas had been a continual problem in its history. The annexation agreement provided for division of the territory into as many as five states. During the debates over the Compromise of 1850, Congress had entertained a series of resolutions proposing to reduce Texas' size. At the same time, Senator William H. Seward of New York sponsored a petition from residents of Brownsville, who asked that the Rio Grande valley be made independent of the rest of Texas to help validate dubious land titles there. All of these attempts failed.[18]

During the secession crisis, the scattered population of Texas found their interests to be quite diverse. The eastern part of the state contained the bulk of the wealth, slaves, and population. It was also decidedly in favor of leaving the Union. Western areas of the state tended to back the Union, contained large numbers of immigrants, needed economic development, and disliked slavery, Negroes, and slaveholders. After the war, most white Republican support came from these outlying areas of the state. "In the interest of the *Union*," wrote Edward Degener of San Antonio, "the Republican element must be strengthened. *Strategically* it is important to shut off the old Secession element from the frontier." Both objectives could best be accomplished by dividing the state in half, he concluded.[19]

The constitutional convention heard several plans for dividing Texas into various states. Both Radicals and Conservatives supported these plans, each seeking to be rid of the unwanted influence of the other in a reconstructed Texas. Indeed, if any pattern could be discerned on division in Texas history, it would be one of politicians out of power manipulating the issue in order to dispose of their political competition. In general, delegates from frontier and coastal areas supported division, those representing northeastern and north central counties opposed it, while representatives from eastern Texas were evenly separated on the issue. Moderates finally managed to postpone a decision on division until the second session of the convention. Instead both sides sent delegations to Washington to gain Federal support for their viewpoint.[20]

In August, as the convention's first session was drawing to a close, the state Republican leadership assembled in a private meeting at Austin to work out a party platform and to present a united front in order to oppose the Conservatives more effectively in the convention and future elections. Unlike the meager participation in the meeting of the prior summer, this effort brought together 159 delegates, representing over one hundred counties. Sixty-five of the delegates were also members of the convention.

But two-thirds of the party's state convention were Moderates; hence the Republicans readily adopted the principles enumerated by Governor Pease, A. J. Hamilton, and General Reynolds. The state platform endorsed the national party's principles, the Fourteenth Amendment, the Reconstruction Acts, and U. S. Grant as their presidential nominee. Radicals objected to the absence of an ab initio statement but were voted down.

Understandably angry, the Radicals withdrew from the party's councils and held their own meeting, in which they endorsed the ab initio doctrine. Moderates invited them back but offered no concessions on principle. Since the Moderates held the patronage and the constitution still had to be written, an uneasy peace developed. As one reporter correctly observed, "The truth is that the two wings of the Republican party live sort of a cat and dog life. Like badly matched couples, divorce would be a blessing rather than an evil."[21]

Although Republicans disagreed among themselves on ab initio and dividing the state, all sides concurred in the approach to a third problem—law and order. Nearly all of the delegates had been threatened by night riders. In Jefferson, corpses of Republican dead reportedly could be found on street corners, attempts had been made to burn the Radical newspaper, and some feared renewed civil war as homicides increased. The Jefferson Union League doubted whether it could hold any further meetings.[22]

Governor Pease painted a bleak picture to the delegates in his message to the convention on June 3. The governor believed that crime was at a new high and asserted that 206 homicides had been confirmed in the preceding seven months and that even more had undoubtedly gone unreported. He praised General Reynolds for his vigor in law enforcement and blamed the trouble on Hancock's General Orders No. 40.[23]

Much criminal activity during this period was due to the clandestine operations of the Ku Klux Klan, Knights of the Red Hand, Knights of the White Camellia, Pale Faces, White Brotherhood, Constitutional Union Guards, and other secret terrorist organizations. According to rumor, Colonel Roger Q. Mills, a former Secessionist and later a Redeemer congressman, coordinated Klan activities, but the various groups seemed to operate more on a local level with no central direction.[24] The Klan often acted to fill the vacuum left by the disappearance of the old slave patrols and punished Negroes for many of the same "crimes," such as being out after curfew or acting "uppity." They also turned their ire on whites who allied with the freedmen in securing civil, political, and social equality.[25]

White Texans considered the Klan to be their "savior from evil and oppression" and thought that no other method "could have lifted us so easily and completely in so short a time." The movement was supposedly composed of citizens of high standing and local law-enforcement personnel who, "by vigorous but cautious action," re-established "the proper relationship between the white race and the negro element." Many asserted that little or no bloodshed or violence accompanied the Klan's activities and that its record read "more like a fairy tale than sober reality."[26] Major Guy M. Bryan, a member of Governor Murrah's staff during the war, in a letter to his personal friend, Ohio congressman Rutherford B. Hayes, insisted that the Klan stories were completely false and that no such organization existed in Texas. Bryan wanted reference to Texas eliminated from a congressional report, but he failed to persuade Hayes.[27]

Unlike Bryan, the United States Senate, the army, the state constitutional convention, and the state Republican party believed that the main problems in securing law and order in the Southern states came from Ku Klux Klan threats. Even some Klansmen expressed doubt as to the sterling character of their members. The Sulphur Springs branch of the Klan, for example, found it could not control its hot-bloods who insisted on violence to enforce the group's veiled threats against Negroes in Hopkins County. The cooler minds disliked violence because it attracted Federal military patrols into an area.[28]

Klan activities ranged from murdering the Goliad sheriff because he favored Negroes to whipping two men in Bell County who belonged to an odd religious sect and another man because he had no religion at all. In Matagorda County the local Klansmen deposited their arms at J. C. McNeill's house and were issued ammunition by McNeill's wife and children when he was absent on business. A similar tactic was used in San Augustine, where a Negro, Henry Garrett, organized a black militia company that drilled near a fortified house. The whites in the area also organized themselves and visited individual Negro militiamen at night to administer them a "good flogging." When the whites felt strong enough and army patrols were not nearby, they attacked and subdued the negro fort. Nightly raids continued on isolated Negro homes until the blacks were, in the words of one commentator, "inspired . . . with a wholesome respect for the white population" and "encouraged to become useful citizens." [29]

In Hallettsville a band of masked men tried to force their way into the house of Jacob Oakman, a Negro. When Oakman successfully prevented their entrance, the interlopers fired shots into his home from all directions. The raiders returned again a week later with the same results. At Brenham a party of men rode about shooting at Negroes, hogs, dogs, and houses, creating much anxiety among the local blacks. Whites who attempted to organize Negroes politically were a favorite target of Klan groups. In Trinity County the church housing one such meeting was fired upon by unknown assailants, while in Belton a scalawag who had talked to Negroes was ducked in a nearby creek. Also in Belton, Klansmen regularly used cellars as places of punishment for recalcitrant blacks and their white allies. [30]

General Reynolds tried unsuccessfully to halt these raiders. The marauders were usually well mounted and easily outran infantry pursuit. One frustrated officer told headquarters that his foot soldiers were not worth "room in hell," and he had to have cavalry. He commonly had to move patrols over fifty miles to maintain order in his command area. [31] The army had too little cavalry to spare for the interior, although elements of the Sixth Regiment were used regularly in the interior to assist in upholding the law. Mounted infantry was also tried, with little result. Any mounted man was only as good as his horse, and the army seemed to have little but broken-down mounts. [32]

Besides the problem of ineffectual pursuit, the raiders' identities were well concealed by hoods and masks, and their victims were unable or unwilling to identify them. Reynolds ordered soldiers to arrest anyone wearing a mask or disguise. Troop commanders were to hold such suspects indefinitely. The arrested men were sent from post to post in the area in order to find witnesses who would identify them as Klansmen, but to little avail.

An exasperated General Reynolds informed Washington that civil law was dead east of the Trinity River. Law officers were Klan leaders, victims were regularly announced at public meetings, and the numbers of Negroes murdered was so high as to defy an accurate body count, said Reynolds. Federal soldiers sent to restore order were frequently ambushed and killed. [33]

The Klan was not the only force disrupting law and order in Texas. Cullen Baker, Benjamin F. Bickerstaff, and Bob Lee led major outlaw gangs that pillaged northeastern Texas. Baker, the "Swamp Fox of the

Sulphur," was typical of the bandit chieftains. He had a record of murder before the war and joined the Confederate army, only to desert in 1863 to the safety of the swamps east of Sulphur Springs. Here he began his career of plunder, which was spiced by numerous killings of Negroes and Freedmen's Bureau agents—a Baker specialty. He disdainfully referred to anyone who opposed him as an "abolitionist" who was marked for death.[34]

Soon Baker's name was known throughout the region because of his ability to make fools out of the soldiers sent to capture him. He rode singlehandedly up to one patrol, introduced himself, and, except for the misfiring of his revolver, would have shot the lieutenant in command. Another time, the lone Baker was credited with chasing a patrol into Boston, Texas, and then audaciously demanding that the twenty soldiers surrender to him.

Baker allegedly ran an outlaw's school in the swamp, where he taught his recruits the fine points of using a six-shooter and the virtues of shooting all prisoners or wounded soldiers in the head. His gang regularly ambushed the columns sent for it in the dense woodlands. If the army made things too risky in Texas, Baker would slip across the border to Indian Territory or Arkansas until the situation quieted. Then he would return and resume his raiding in Texas.[35]

Because of his success against the army and his convincing rationalization of thievery as a loyal Southern act, Baker became a kind of Robin Hood in northeastern Texas. He gained fame in spite of his frequent murders of Texans who dared to associate his name with any crime whatsoever. Baker's psychotic drive to kill finally became obvious even to the most ardent Confederate flag-wavers. It was evident that citizens were afraid of him and had rationalized their losses as aid to a persecuted son of the South, just as Baker hoped they would. On January 6, 1869, one of Baker's "abolitionist" enemies, Thomas Orr, fearful of his own life, rounded up a half dozen friends and gunned Baker down in his sleep.[36]

Within three months of Baker's death, Bickerstaff and Lee were both killed by troopers of the Sixth Cavalry. Like Baker, they had specialized in bushwhacking soldiers and stealing Army supplies. Bickerstaff's gang controlled the Sulphur Springs area so tightly that the local army garrison lived in a state of siege. In September, 1868, General Reynolds sent Captain A. R. Chaffee and Captain T. M. Tolman with two companies of the sixth Cavalry to Sulphur Springs to destroy the outlaws. Tolman took immediate charge of the town and imposed a brutal discipline on both his men and the townspeople which resulted in his eventual suspension from rank, confinement to his duty station, and reprimand in general orders.[37]

While Tolman secured the town, Chaffee hounded the Bickerstaff gang across northern Texas. His merciless tactics earned his unit the nickname "Chaffee's Guerrillas," but he, like Tolman, produced results. Several bandits were captured near Pilot Grove, and the gang was scattered. Bickerstaff managed to elude capture until April, 1869, when he and two accomplices were killed near Alvarado.[38] About the same time, Bob Lee was shot while resisting arrest outside Sherman. It had been a difficult victory for the army; one of the companies that helped bring the outlaws to bay had marched over a thousand miles in three months.[39]

Other smaller gangs of marauders plagued Texas, but few matched the impact of the Baker, Bickerstaff, or Lee bands. One group of bandits roamed the Trinity County region until, in a rare case of courage, a local resident sent the army a list of the outlaws' names. One audacious group of brigands disguised themselves in Yankee army uniforms and terrorized the citizens of Montgomery.

Another raider, Elisha Guest, intimidated the Clarksville area. When a patrol of soldiers looking for Guest rode into Mount Pleasant, the lieutenant in charge found the place "in a state of rebellion" and had to arrest three townsmen. The officer also reported that the whole country was in sympathy with Guest. Captain A. R. Chaffee, who participated in the destruction of the Bickerstaff gang, recommended offering the standard reward of one thousand dollars for Guest, dead or alive. Often such tactics failed to produce the desired results. Warnings by citizens in Bell County, for example, enabled a local gang to escape the patrol sent to capture them.[40]

Law enforcement was severely compromised by the frequent failure of local sheriffs to do their duty. The sheriff was very important to Reynolds and the Republicans. When soldiers arrived in a community, the officer in charge contacted the sheriff first. Troop commanders usually had orders to assist these men directly, to obtain their side of any problem first, and to follow their orders in quelling disturbances in the area.[41]

In cases where Democratic officials tended to ignore criminal activity against Negroes and Loyalists, a Unionist could complain about a matter to the army, and the army could respond by reporting it to the local Democratic sheriff, who could then act to frustrate rather than assist Republican objectives in an area with the assistance of army patrols. Reynolds never did remove all Democratic officeholders on the local level.[42]

In places where town and county officials were lax in their duties, conscientious Republican judges found it necessary to have soldiers guard their courtrooms. Judge Moses B. Walker of the Fourth Judicial District traveled his circuit with an escort of soldiers. Judge B. F. Barkley of Fort Worth took the same precaution. The fear of assassination, however, drove many a lesser man from office. Others became more selective about whom they arrested and tried for crimes. Officials who were lax in prosecuting criminals, however, were warned by the army "to use increased diligence" and were removed from office if they did not. Although it was an ineffective option, removal from office was the only threat the army had.[43]

The Conservative press fastened upon Reynolds's policy of removals and appointments as one of the prime causes of continued lawlessness. "If they have officials of their own choosing and an army of bayonets to back them, why do they not put a stop to the ungodly business at once?" cried the *Denton Monitor*. The *Monitor* asserted that "Radicals want the crime to continue, or else they are ignorant to know whose duty it is to suppress crime in a country." The newspaper concluded that the Republicans had to be "either knaves or fools" to plead such a "bad case" before the people of Texas. When the periodical received news that the Republican judges of several counties were absent from the bench attending the state convention, the *Monitor* hooted, "Radical lawlessness again!"[44]

Unfortunately the *Monitor* had a point, for the net effect of removals was often to frustrate the enforcement of the laws by eliminating the few men willing to serve as sheriff or county judge. A Refugio County judge, for instance, appealed for any kind of assistance available. He said the area was so disorganized that he could not hold court.[45]

When a local subaltern had tried to assist the civil officials by instituting a military court, headquarters ordered him to release his first convicted felon, a freedman involved in a robbery. An investigation into disturbances in Bowie County revealed that there had been no town government in Boston for years; the town charter had been misplaced in the resulting chaos.[46]

Even when civil authorities did their duty, people complained. A Houston man asked the army to send a stenographer to observe and take notes on a city murder trial, claiming that any civil trial in Texas was "a mockery and a farce." Reynolds tended to agree with this assessment. "I am decidedly opposed to Military Commissions in a time of peace, except in such extreme cases as are provided by the laws of Congress," said the general. But he believed that the legal climate in Texas was so unstable that the only way to achieve a fair, thorough trial was through a military court. Although the general treated the civil law as subordinate to military supervision, he ordered officers to follow state laws whenever possible, especially in noncriminal cases. No soldier, however, was to respect a civil writ unless specifically ordered by headquarters.[47]

White Texans severely criticized Reynolds for avoiding civil trials. Reynolds tried to temper this disapproval by inviting state district attorneys to attend civilian trials held by the army. He also tightly controlled military commissions by demanding lists of prisoners held, charges perferred, and action taken, in an attempt to maintain consistency. No officer was to issue an order affecting a civilian or civil law without prior approval by the commanding general.[48]

Throughout his tenure, Reynolds intervened in the court processes, bypassing less active jurists to order special court terms at the request of diligent judges, quashing indictments, and ordering defendants to appear in civil or military courts. The general also pardoned offenders or reduced sentences where he thought appropriate. To the army's credit, the courts generally did try to find justice.[49]

But the attempts of the Texas command to maintain fair trials did not mitigate the hostility whites exhibited toward military trials of civilians. At times the protest was quite violent. When Tyler officials refused to select blacks or Loyalists for jury duty, the local Freedmen's Bureau officer, Lieutenant Gregory Barrett, resorted to military trials. In one early case, violence erupted in the courtroom after Barrett sentenced a Tyler inhabitant who was found guilty of assault. Friends of the defendant drew concealed weapons and fired on the court from the gallery. Three soldiers were hit, and in the confusion the convicted man escaped with his liberators.[50]

The convention appointed its special committee on lawlessness and violence to analyze this deteriorating state of affairs throughout Texas. On July 2, 1868, the committee reported its findings to the convention. Admittedly drawing upon incomplete records, the committee cataloged 939 homicides from June, 1865, to June, 1868. The committee did not attempt to tabulate assaults with intent to kill, rapes, robberies, whippings of freedmen, and other outrages, because "such a summation would impose an endless task." The investigators confessed that many "of these homicides have doubtless been committed for the purpose of plunder and robbery." They found the highways filled with thieves, most of whom were former Confederate soldiers.

The convention's committee was also appalled at the large number of freedmen killed by whites. Deaths of blacks composed 429 of the total homicides. Of those, 379 had been committed by whites; but, said the committee, freedmen were responsible for killing only 10 whites. "The great disparity between the numbers of the two races killed, the one by the other," concluded the investigators, "shows conclusively that 'the war between the races' is all on the part of the whites against the blacks."

Furthermore, the committee insisted that most of the 470 whites who had met a violent death were Unionists, while their attackers, with few exceptions, were former rebels. "The obligations of the government and the citizens are mutual and correlative," said the report. "If the true allegiance is rendered by the latter, ample protection is due from the former." The report pleaded "that Congress may afford such relief as, in their wisdom, we may be entitled to."

The committee concluded that it was "not difficult to fix the responsibility of this crime" on General Hancock and his General Orders No. 40. They castigated General Buchanan because he had "turned a deaf ear to the cry of tried and persecuted loyalists." The investigators charged Buchanan with the deaths of hundreds of Union men, "a responsibility that should load his name with infamy, and hand his very memory to coming years as a curse and an execration." The convention voted an appropriation of twenty-five thousand dollars in reward money to assist civil officers in apprehending criminals. It stipulated, however, that none of the money would be paid unless the offenders were tried by military commissions.[51]

To impress upon Congress the critical nature of violence in Texas, the convention sent Morgan C. Hamilton and Colbert Caldwell to Washington with a copy of the report. The convention asked Congress to pass a law to guarantee the filling of state offices with competent and loyal men, authorize the creation of a state militia, and allow the convention to appoint new voting registrars for the upcoming election. When Hamilton and Caldwell arrived in Washington, they found Congress in haste to adjourn, so little was accomplished.[52]

Conservatives were angered at what they believed were gross falsifications in the report on violence in Texas. "His Honor(!), so-called, Hardin Hart of Greenville, and late Grand Cyclops of the 7th Judicial Kangaroo," complained one Conservative sheet, had reported twenty murders in Hunt County since General Hancock's "famous reb-hell order." Local sources of the journal, however, knew of only two crimes committed in Hunt County in 1868, and one of these was a murder committed by a Federal soldier.[53]

Army records support neither the Conservatives' contention that crime in Hunt County was minimal nor Judge Hart's assertion that there was mass violence. For the sixteen-month period prior to December, 1868, for example, a total of twelve crimes of violence were reported to the army from Hunt County. This ratio of criminal activity remained steady at just under one crime per month throughout the years to April, 1870, when the army stopped keeping such records.[54]

Conservatives blamed lawlessness like that in Hunt County on personal, not political, disputes, compounded by the wartime armies, the complex racial animosities created by Reconstruction, and the unpopularity of military government, which lacked the respect of the people. Conservatives in the convention endorsed the minority report of W. H. Mullins, which they claimed categorically refuted all Republican charges on the issue.[55]

Especially bitter was C. C. Gillespie, editor of the *Houston Telegraph*. After criticizing the convention report and denying its truthfulness, he attacked the character and integrity of the Republican delegates who issued it. "We may say it solemnly," he concluded, "such men ought to die." The convention responded by adopting a resolution asking General Reynolds to arrest Gillespie and suppress his newspaper.

The state Democratic party held its own convention at Bryan shortly after the release of the convention report on violence and soundly condemned the document. The Democrats admitted that a great deal of lawlessness existed but blamed it on Reconstruction, Republicans, carpetbagger agitators, and dictatorial military rule.[56] They condemned a convention plan to establish a loyal militia as likely to incite a race war, for they assumed that such a group would be composed of Negroes. The party called for the end of military rule and repeal of the black vote. Only Democratic success, they said, would pacify Texas.[57]

The contentions of the constitutional convention regarding violence against blacks received confirmation from numerous race riots that occurred in Washington, Falls, and Freestone counties, as well as in the towns of Houston, Hempstead, Waco, and Millican. The convention appropriated five hundred dollars to investigate the Millican incident but never issued a report.[58]

By August, 1868, pressure created by the convention debates and increased racial disorder forced General Reynolds to send Lieutenant Charles A. Vernon to investigate the disturbances. Vernon visited as many towns as possible and assured local authorities that the army would uphold the law without regard to political party. The lieutenant also insisted that the civil processes be used in all disputes. The local law officers were warned that they were expected to fulfill the demands of their positions and were promised all the military aid they needed to keep the peace. In support of Vernon, Reynolds obtained the Fifteenth Infantry and sent the regiment to Marshall and Jefferson to bolster the defense of that area.[59]

In categorizing the crime record of Texas during Reconstruction, one is dependent upon limited sources that were often haphazardly compiled.[60] The army kept six massive ledger books on crime, which were organized into two series of three volumes each. The books covered, often intermittently, the crime statistics of 129 counties for a fifty-two-month period from January, 1866, to April, 1870. Of the counties that the army surveyed for criminal activity, 107 (83%) averaged one crime or less per month during Reconstruction (from 0 to 54 total crimes). Another 13 counties averaged between one and two crimes per month (58–85 total), while 8 counties averaged between two and three crimes per month (99–131 total). Only 1 county, McLennan, whose county seat is Waco, averaged over four crimes per month (a total of 221) over the period surveyed by the army.[61]

Considered as a whole, these figures seem to indicate that, while crime was widespread in Reconstruction Texas, except for isolated areas, it was not as severe as Republicans maintained. The crimes committed centered in counties with large towns and cities, counties with large black populations, and counties along border areas like the Red River or the Rio Grande. Places like Brownsville combined all three factors. Undoubtedly some of this criminal activity was political in nature, but the prevalence of crime in larger towns suggests that much of it was brought about by the increasing urbanization of the state or from personal conflicts unrelated to Reconstruction issues.[62]

Although they were specifically charged with drawing up a new state constitution, the convention delegates seemed eager to assume responsibility for additional problems, as illustrated by their considering the issues of lawlessness and dividing the state. But the convention went even further and passed a resolution which endorsed their desire to assume broad legislative powers. The delegates rationalized this position by pointing out that Congress had given them power to draw up a constitution and establish a loyal civil government. Hence the

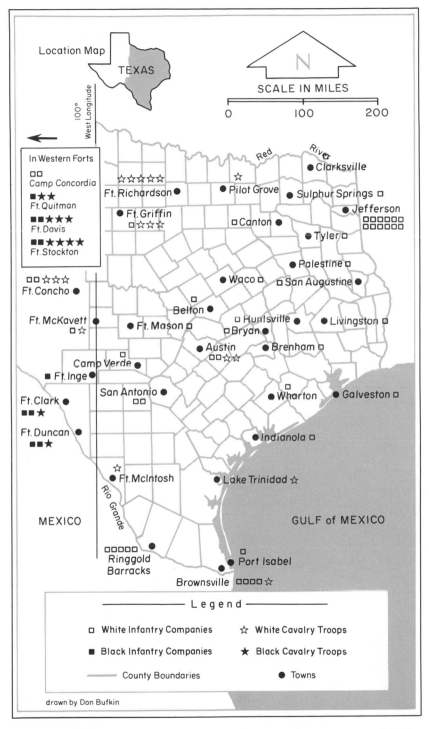

Map 7. Reynolds's Troop Assignments, November, 1868: Response to Ku Klux Klan
Activity in Northeast Texas

convention believed it ought to determine what ordinances and resolutions were necessary to carry out the will of Congress. Without
having had a legislative session in almost two years—and in any event
the Eleventh Legislature had been disloyal—the convention moved
forward into the legislative arena.[63]

The convention considered a multitude of legislative tasks, including newspaper patronage, state land sales, and internal improvements,
especially railroad relief and regulation. They also provided for the
chartering of towns, counties, and new business corporations. The
convention established funds for public education, benefits for Union
veterans, and monetary relief and stay laws to assist Loyalists. Then
they regulated the cattle trade. Finally, the body set up the state's election precincts and voter registration procedure and made appointments and removals in state government.[64]

By the end of August, 1868, the convention had been in session
eighty-five days and had failed to produce a constitution. Except for
the law and order issue, the Republican members were seriously divided over the questions of ab initio and the division of Texas. The
party also seemed ready to split over the question of white disfranchisement. The convention's $100,000 expense account was nearly ex-
hausted, and an irritated General Reynolds refused to authorize additional expenditures.[65]

In addition to the shortage of state funds and the inability of the
delegates to frame a constitution, the national political scene now assumed an important role in the Texas Reconstruction process. If General Grant, the Republican candidate, won the 1868 election, Military Reconstruction could be expected to continue in full force. The
Republican party in Texas would benefit from Federal patronage,
which could also help heal the party split. Should the Democrats win
the presidency and the House of Representatives, Texas might not be
pressured to comply with the Reconstruction Acts. In that event, the
Conservatives would be so strengthened that the convention's work
would become next to useless. Rather than hurry the framing of a constitution and risk defeat as a divided party, the Republicans recessed
the convention. There was no constitution, but Republicans hoped
that the party might strengthen itself during the interim period.[66]

Because the presidential race promised to be a close one, with a
possible deadlock developing in the electoral college, Conservatives
in Texas worked hard for a national Democratic victory. On July 20,
Congress had forbade counting electoral votes from the unrecon-

structed states of Texas, Mississippi, and Virginia, but the law did not expressly prohibit those states from holding an election.[67]

The Texas Democrats decided that their state should participate in the balloting just in case their electoral votes might be needed in a controversy. State law required the governor to order an election, but Pease refused to act. Rather than directly challenge Pease's authority by having Throckmorton (whom many considered the rightful governor) issue the proclamation, the Democratic state executive committee recommended an alternate course. All registered voters in each county would informally meet on November 3, appoint an election supervisor, cast their ballots, and send them to the committee. Reynolds, however, was taking no chances that Texas would appear in the Democratic column in any election. He immediately declared that no balloting for presidential electors would take place in any form at any time.[68]

Although supporting the Democrats' plan of action, some Conservatives, led by Lemuel D. Evans, who represented Marshall in the constitutional convention, realized that a national victory for the Democrats would require capturing more than just the presidency. For the party to alleviate the effects of the Reconstruction Acts, Democrats would have to carry one branch of Congress as well as the presidency, an event that seemed highly improbable to Evans.[69]

If the party installed only their own president, continued Evans, he would be as impotent as Andrew Johnson had been during the latter half of his administration. A Republican Congress still demanded full compliance with the Reconstruction Acts. Evans recommended that Texans of all political affiliations decide to accept any constitution framed by the second session of the convention, so long as it did not disfranchise whites.[70]

The nationwide victory of the Republican party in November bore out Evans's contentions. The only consolation to the Conservative forces was that President Johnson, disgusted with Reynolds's inability to supervise properly and to hasten the completion of Texas Reconstruction, removed the general from command of the Fifth Military District.[71]

In his stead, Johnson appointed Brevet Major General Edward R. S. Canby, who had been in charge of the Department of Louisiana immediately after the war. Canby had left Louisiana in 1866, and President Johnson used him as a troubleshooter in states with difficult Reconstruction problems. In this capacity, Canby had engineered successful constitution conventions in both of the Carolinas. Now Johnson hoped to utilize his services in Texas.[72]

Canby would need all the ability he could muster in dealing with the Texas problems. While the Texas Republican party had attained a new feeling of security in Grant's election and continued party control of Congress, critical issues still divided it. John L. Haynes, chairman of the Republican state executive committee, confessed his apprehensions shortly after the presidential contest was concluded. He realized that, if the Conservatives followed the Evans formula and accepted any constitution that promised to go no further than the Fourteenth Amendment in penalizing whites for the war, the Republican party was in trouble.[73]

As Haynes well knew, the breach in Republican ranks from the first session was not yet closed. A new debate on a controversial issue like disfranchisement could divide the party irreparably. "An attempt to build up Republican government in this state upon the basis of disfranchisement would be like positioning a pyramid upon its apex," said Haynes. "The first wind would topple it over and tumble it into ruins."[74]

A divided minority party had even less chance of ruling Texas. The impending party division made it necessary for Republicans to rely on some form of intervention from the Federal government through its active presence in the state, the United States Army.

9

The Army Writes a Constitution

O N NOVEMBER 20, 1868, shortly after Grant's election and just
prior to the reconvening of the state constitutional convention,
Governor Elisha M. Pease issued a Thanksgiving Day proclamation.
Although many presidents had declared days of prayer and thanksgiving, the holiday had been regularized in 1863 by President Lincoln
to celebrate Union victories in a momentous war year. In this same
vein, Governor Pease urged Texans to use the occasion to give thanks
to God for the "civil liberty we have enjoyed as a free people." But the
response to his declaration was not all he desired. Whimsically referring to the state executive as "Elishaphant M. Goober-Pease," the
Denton Monitor responded to his proclamation of the "Yankee holiday" with an irreverent "Amen! A-woman! Selah!"[1]

While the *Monitor* mirrored the disrespect toward the provisional
government felt by most citizens, the main obect of their scorn was
the convention itself. The attempt to draft a state fundamental law had
been a disorganized farce that cost the state's general fund $100,000.
Now the body had to reconvene, tackle its original purpose with vigor,
and tax the state for the new session, something the departed General
Reynolds had hoped to avoid. Yet, expectations of progress in the convention proved illusory, as the widening gap in Republican ranks rapidly demonstrated.[2]

Disappointed with the complications in the Texas readmission pro-
cess and blaming General Reynolds for incompetent coordination of
this effort, President Johnson had replaced Reynolds the day following
Grant's election. The new officer in charge of the Fifth Military Dis-
trict (Texas) was Brevet Major General Edward R. S. Canby.[3] Born in
Kentucky and appointed to the Military Academy from Indiana,
Canby had graduated second to last in the class of 1835. Surviving the
Second Seminole War with a commission in the Second Infantry,
Canby served in the Mexican conflict as regimental adjutant, earning
two brevets for heroism. He was transferred to the Tenth Infantry

as major in 1855 and appointed colonel of the Nineteenth Infantry in 1861.

During the Civil War Canby defended Union interests in New Mexico. He defeated the Texas invasion of that territory in 1862 and then came east as assistant adjutant general in the War Department.[4] In 1863, Canby was assigned the task of pacifying New York City after the draft riots and enforcing conscription there. Acquitting this job with his characteristic diplomacy, Canby went to Mississippi as general in charge. Severely wounded by guerrillas, the general recovered sufficiently to lead the charge upon Mobile, after which he took command of the Department of the Gulf. Here he received the surrender of Confederate troops under Richard Taylor and E. Kirby Smith. He also disagreed with Sheridan over command privileges, which led to Canby's eventual subordination to Sheridan as commander of the Department of Louisiana. Still unable to get along with Sheridan, Canby asked for reassignment for reasons of health in 1866.[5]

Although he lacked Sheridan's daring and Grant's sense of when to close in on the enemy, Canby displayed a cautiousness mixed with a great deal of common sense. These qualities made him a natural diplomat, and President Johnson so utilized him to produce constitutions and readmissions in the Carolinas. Now he was given the confusing and exasperating assignment of reconstructing Texas. Politicians in Washington agreed that Canby was the man for the job. The president liked him because the general exercised good judgment, foresight, and moderation in dealing with Southern whites. Rarely did he rely on a show of excessive strength. Congress also found Canby acceptable because he was insistent about protecting the rights of Negroes and Loyalists. He possessed the legendary ability of Kentuckians to cajole and compromise difficult issues between North and South.[6]

Canby's first task was to ensure that the Texas convention wrote a constitution. Then he was to call an election to ratify it and see that the voters chose a new government that would approve the Fourteenth Amendment and gain Congress's approval and thereby readmission to the Union.

Once again, however, the two Republican factions refused to cooperate with each other. Indeed the quarrel between the Radicals and the Moderates seemed to intensify. Although the ab initio issue had died out, the question of dividing Texas into several states persisted.[7]

To counter Radical demands that the state be divided, the Moderates began a prolonged filibuster. The basis of the delay was a heretofore unused rule, "the call of the house." Under this provision, all debate stopped until every delegate was present unless expressly excused by the convention. Since many delegates were absent who had not resigned or been excused, the call effectively paralyzed the proceedings.[8]

This tactic was due to A. J. Hamilton and irritated the Radicals considerably. Davis, Degener, and M. C. Hamilton threatened separate action through a rump convention. They and other divisionists even drew up a constitution for their so-called West Texas which they hoped to submit to Congress for approval. They accused A. J. Hamilton of being unduly influenced by railroad interests in his stand, a charge never proved. They also, with the aid of some conservatives, alleged that the Moderates wished to wreck the convention to delay the completion of Reconstruction and keep themselves in power as the provisional government with military assistance.[9]

Radicals' insistence on division revolved primarily around political issues. Republicans could never control Texas in an honest election with heavy voter participation. The white conservatives represented a large majority, and the Republicans knew it would only increase with the passage of time. Radicals preferred a three-way division of the state, which would give white Republicans control of western Texas and black Republicans control of eastern coastal districts and their estuaries, leaving the rest of northeastern and central Texas to the disloyal element. Barring division, the Radicals maintained that Texas was not ready for Reconstruction and the convention ought to adjourn and the delegates go home.[10]

Although the Moderates counseled delay until Congress indicated its approval of division, the Federal Constitution provided that no state could be divided against its own will. Statewide approval for division was therefore necessary sooner or later. The debates and delays over division lasted until late January, 1869, when the divisionists finally won. The measure authorizing division was passed only because of doubtful parliamentary measures, initiated by the convention president, E. J. Davis, which included voting without a quorum.[11]

After adopting the division resolution, the convention moved at last to the constitution and a final floor fight over a new topic: disfranchisement of former Confederates. The Moderates, led by A J Hamilton and Governor Pease, believed that the future of the Texas Republican party depended upon its attracting the "thinking element" of the opposition. To restrict their participation in politics beyond the officeholding restriction of the Fourteenth Amendment would alienate these potential voters from the party, which was still a minority in the state. The Moderate stand marked a modification of Governor Pease's earlier position as revealed in his address to the convention seven months before. The change was influenced by a series of factors, including possibly an unspoken deal with Conservatives.[12]

Radicals were dumbfounded at the Moderates' willingness to accommodate with the former rebels. Morgan C. Hamilton maintained that his brother's action was based on the false premise "that since the rebels cannot be governed, they must, therefore, be permitted to govern." He pointed out that the same principle had been adopted by Republicans in other Southern states, only to see the Conservatives turn on their Moderate Republican allies and throw them out of office. Compromise was out of the question on this issue, said the Radicals. They must divide the state into loyal and disloyal areas or at least disfranchise the disloyal men if the state were kept whole.[13]

Radicals therefore proposed that all voters be required to take an oath similar to the old ironclad oath of the war years. Each potential voter had to affirm (1) that he had not been disfranchised earlier for participation in rebellion, (2) that he had not held office under the Confederate or other disloyal state governments, (3) that he had not willingly aided the Confederacy in any way, (4) that he had not voted in any convention or legislative body for secession, (5) that he had not taken an oath to the state or Confederacy after taking a prior oath to the United States, and (6) that he belonged to no secret organizations hostile to the government of the United States.[14]

A. J. Hamilton and the Moderates successfully countered the proposed disfranchisement with a suggestion for universal male suffrage. (The convention considered the right of women to vote but eventually dropped the issue.) With the aid of four black Radicals who switched sides on this issue, Hamilton's Moderates carried the day. The result was a state fundamental law that recognized the supremacy of the Constitution, laws, and treaties of the United States, recognized the freedom of Negroes and their full and equal citizenship before the law, concentrated control of the state government in Austin by granting the governor extensive appointive powers, centralized the state school system and guaranteed blacks public education, provided for internal improvements, and allowed easier access to corporate charter. Most historians now see it as a fairly progressive document, especially in light of the bitterly divided convention.[15]

But because of the serious political infighting that preceded, few convention members were pleased with the new constitution. Moderates and Conservatives resigned themselves to accepting the document, but twenty-two Radicals introduced a resolution condemning it. They faulted the constitution for its failure to declare ab initio, disfranchise former Confederates, and truly safeguard equal political and civil rights for all persons. The signers of the Radical protest asked the voters to refuse to ratify the constitution.[16]

Although he communicated regularly with E. J. Davis by mail, Canby did his best to avoid interfering with the convention's business. He refused the seats offered him and his staff on the floor but promised to send regular observers to the proceedings. But by February, 1869, the convention was obviously deteriorating. Confusion reigned supreme; fist fights, insults, resignations, and lack of a quorum were common.[17]

When the body refused to provide for the preservation of records or to assemble and print the constitution, Canby intervened. The general warned the delegates that he would print the records if they did not. The convention was so divided by this time that each faction adjourned separately, which caused A. J. Hamilton to contact Canby and ask him to supervise the preparation of the convention's records.[18] Canby received the papers and ordered a three-man committee (M. C. Hamilton, a Radical; J. W. Thomas, a leading Moderate; and Major C. R. Layton of his staff) to supervise their preparation. Canby's action had been made possible only because A. J. Hamilton had confiscated the documents from an assistant secretary and Davis supporter, A. J. Bennett, in the closing hours of the convention.[19]

Having provided for the preservation of the convention's records, Canby then ordered the constitution submitted to the people in July. He believed the long delay was necessary because all of the registrars had been discharged after the last election and they still held the registration books. He feared that to locate them would take two or three months. The general also thought a semblance of law and order could be restored to Texas by summer, provided he could find civil officers for the thirty counties that had none.[20]

Canby's appointment policy was very flexible. He believed in filling offices with anyone, regardless of previous political record or present party label, who could carry out his duty as prescribed by state law.[21] He tended to be very meticulous in his orders, to the point of continually correcting misspelled names of his appointees, a degree of punctilio displayed by no other district commander. The Radicals distrusted Canby. Convention president Davis had asked the general to declare all absent delegates resigned and removed from office, but Canby had refused to act. Canby also refused to let Davis make such removals himself. His inaction had allowed the Moderates' "call of the house" strategy to succeed in blocking Radical goals.[22]

The general's policy with regular state offices was quite similar. Canby restricted himself to filling existing vacancies and appointed about two hundred men. Unlike his predecessors, he realized that continued removals for political reasons were self-defeating and removed only sixteen state officials during his four-month tenure.[23] This restraint frustrated all Republicans, and the convention accordingly sought to deny Canby the removal power and vest it in the provisional governor. Citing incessant disorder in the state, the convention wanted Congress to let Pease make all appointments without the necessity of military supervision. The attempt was unsuccessful and, with Canby's eventual replacement, unnecessary.[24]

Canby responded to convention complaints by issuing General Orders No. 4 in January, 1869. This proclamation was designed to secure prompt and exact execution of the laws, protect all persons in their rights and property, and suppress insurrection. All of these topics were of interest to the convention. The scope of the problem can be seen by the fact that 1,456 persons had forfeited bond or refused to appear in state courts since 1865.[25]

Canby told all post commanders to assume the powers of county officials and judges and to use the civil courts and Texas law to suppress the rampant lawlessness reported in the state. Canby hoped for the "moral support" of all "good citizens" to "avoid the necessity of military interference," but he authorized the use of military courts in criminal cases if civil officials refused to cooperate.[26]

He divided Texas into twenty-nine patrol areas and detailed soldiers to each zone. Troop commanders were to station their units as they saw fit, but a central reserve force was to be kept at each district headquarters. Canby hoped the assignments would allow the army to obtain more complete control by setting up a distinct chain of command and responsibilities.[27] When a fugitive fled from one zone to another, district commanders were authorized to continue pursuit, providing they notified the officer in charge of the next area. Unless the pursuit was immediate, however, Canby preferred commanders to signal the next zone officers to continue the chase.[28]

A few days later, Canby issued additional orders which included pertinent sections of the state code of criminal procedure. These directives described the duties of civil magistrates and peace officers in preventing and punishing crime and detailed the procedures for arresting fugitives and suppressing riots. Sheriffs and judges were ordered to

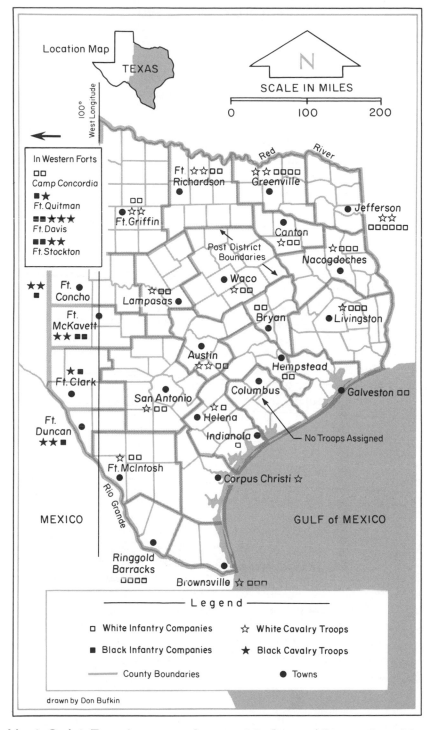

TEXAS

N

SCALE IN MILES

0   100   200

In Western Forts
□□ Camp Concordia
■★ Ft. Quitman
■■★★★ Ft. Davis
■■★★ Ft. Stockton

Red River

Ft. ☆☆□□ Richardson

☆☆□□□□ Greenville

Jefferson ☆☆ □□□□□□

● ☆☆ Ft. Griffin

Canton ☆□□

Post District Boundaries

☆□□□ Nacogdoches

★★ Ft. Concho ■

● Waco ☆□□

☆□□ Lampasas

☆□□□ Livingston

Ft. McKavett ★★ ■■

□□ Bryan

★ ■ Ft. Clark

Austin ☆☆□□

Hempstead □□

Columbus

Galveston □□

Ft. Duncan ★★■

San Antonio ☆□□

☆□ Helena

No Troops Assigned

☆□□ Ft. McIntosh

Indianola □

Corpus Christi ☆

Rio Grande

MEXICO

GULF of MEXICO

Ringgold Barracks □□□□

Brownsville ☆□□□

Legend

□ White Infantry Companies   ☆ White Cavalry Troops

■ Black Infantry Companies   ★ Black Cavalry Troops

——— County Boundaries   ● Towns

drawn by Don Bufkin

Map 8. Canby's Troop Assignments, January, 1869: Posts and Districts Created by General Orders No. 4

report anyone who threatened or obstructed them. All "combinations or conspiracies" were to be tried by military courts and punished according to Federal law. Each month sheriffs and marshals were to make consolidated reports of all crimes that occurred within their jurisdiction and to send them to the nearest post commander. Court clerks were to report immediately all persons charged with serious crimes who had forfeited their bail by not appearing in court. Garrison officers were expected to have a list of all the civil officers in their area and to recommend names to fill all vacancies. The civil officers were warned to enforce the laws, while army officers were instructed to render aid and to discipline their men strictly.[29]

Canby also called attention to the poor security of Texas jails. Prisoners that the army turned over to trustworthy civil authorities were very likely to escape. The jailhouses were in very poor condition and inadequately guarded. The locks could be picked easily, and in one town—Georgetown—hardware stores carried duplicate keys for jail locks.[30]

To solve the problem, the army constructed its own jails. These stockades, known as "bull pens," were generally small log forts with walls ten feet high and a guard walk near the top. There was rarely any permanent shelter, so prisoners took refuge from the weather in small A-tents. If the troopers were in an extremely hostile town, they spent the nights within the walls of the stockade for protection.[31]

The army also upgraded town jails. At Bryan, which had no jail, the soldiers supervised the construction of a structure fifteen feet off the ground on four uprights. Called the Bryan Sky Parlor, this imposing jailhouse could be reached only by means of a removable ladder. Life in these prisons was harsh. At Corpus Christi one prisoner complained of having been held in solitary confinement in an iron cage exposed to the elements. The prisoners at Brownsville claimed to be overworked and unsuitably housed.[32]

At times, military jails were not much more secure than their civilian counterparts. Sentries were bribed by prisoners to desert and help them to escape. At Jefferson, inmates escaped so regularly that Brevet Brigadier General George P. Buell, commander of the Fifteenth Infantry, threatened to bring charges of negligence against any officer of the day who had a prisoner escape on his watch. Buell had to assign control of the jail to his executive officer, restrict keys to the sergeant of the guard, and curtail visiting privileges to stop the rash of escapes.[33]

As Canby correctly observed, the "moral support of all good citizens," and the "timely exercize of the powers" with which the peace officers were invested would "generally preserve the peace and prevent the commission of crimes." At the same time, he warned military officers against "harshly or oppressively" executing the Reconstruction Acts. They were to see "that arrests are not made without sufficient cause; that the manner of arrest shall, as far as practicable, be the same as is prescribed by the laws of the State." He warned local authorities against using posses composed of men from one political party. Justice was to be impartial, said Canby, and all able-bodied volunteers were to be accepted, regardless of political sympathy.[34]

To facilitate the use of civil courts where possible, Canby ordered certain state judges to hold immediate special court sessions to clear the dockets of existing cases. It took a brave man to follow this edict, as Judge B. F. Barkley of Tarrant County proved. He complained of informers on sheriffs' posses preventing arrests and threatening letters signed with the ominous "K. K. K." His courthouse was often fired on by what Barkley described as "rebel elements." Still he carried on.[35]

While Canby was attacking the problem of civil affairs in Texas, both Republican factions sent committees to Washington to confer with Grant and Congress, in an effort to convince the national government that they represented the true loyal party. Each faction had its own state executive committee, impressive leadership, and program. Led by Morgan C. Hamilton, the Radicals presented their petition to Congress. The Radicals stressed the violence and lawlessness prevalent in the state and the defects they saw in the proposed state constitution, especially the lack of disfranchisement, and called for a delay in the July election. The Radicals' solution to Reconstruction in Texas was a three-way division of the state. The loyal area to the west of the Colorado River could be admitted to the Union without fear, while the two states east of the Colorado ought to remain under government supervision until a later date.[36]

The Moderates simultaneously introduced their memorial in Washington. In the document they attacked the Radicals as opportunists and impractical seekers of office, who had obstructed and hindered Reconstruction through nonsense doctrines like ab initio, state division, and disfranchisement. They defended the constitution as a liberal and fair solution to Texas readmission and maintained that the July election would hasten the return of order and decorum to the state's political scene and would hence further the goals of the party and Congress.[37]

Although the president-elect chose to remain noncommittal and informed the two Texas factions that patronage would be divided between them, the Moderates actually received the majority of Federal appointments in the state. The key figure in the Moderate success was General Reynolds, an old classmate of Grant and now his informal advisor on the Texas situation. Reynolds opposed dividing Texas into several states or prolonging Reconstruction as desired by the Radicals. He brought A. J. Hamilton and John L. Haynes to see Grant days before the inauguration, while the Radicals had to wait until a week later to see the president.[38]

While in Washington the Moderates managed to obtain another favor from Grant. Most Texas Republicans believed that General Reynolds had been treated unfairly when President Johnson removed him from the command of the Fifth Military District in November. There were continued references at the state convention to "the faithful and impartial manner" in which Reynolds acted to enforce the Reconstruction laws. One party member even tried to amend the convention's welcome to Canby by prefacing it with the statement, "While regretting the removal of Bvt. Maj. Gen. Reynolds. . . ."[39] They had no real quarrel with Canby's policies, but he was much too judicial and nonpartisan to suit party members. They needed someone reliable should an emergency situation develop as the Reconstruction process came to an end. In response to this worry, the day after his inauguration, Grant reassigned Reynolds to the Fifth Military District.[40]

Meanwhile Andrew J. Hamilton had announced his candidacy for the governorship. His method of securing the nomination was highly unusual and invited a Radical challenge. Hamilton simply told the people of Texas in a telegram sent from Washington that he would run for the office.

Endorsing his candidacy, John L. Haynes called on the Moderate Republican executive committee to meet in Austin on April 20 to plan strategy and approve of candidates or call a nominating convention. When Haynes's group met they endorsed Hamilton's candidacy, which later became his main claim to party regularity. Few members of the committee had been present, however, which led to cries that the "Austin Ring" had forced his nomination upon the party undemocratically.

Hamilton's failure to call for a statewide nominating convention after his May 6 return to Texas proved later to be a great mistake, for it helped deny him the national party recognition and support he needed to install a legitimate regime.[41] But these problems were far from Hamilton's thoughts in the spring of 1869. Ever the practical politician, he had long sought to expand the base of the Moderates by attracting Conservative support. He defended this appeal by maintaining that he limited his approach to the thinking element of the Conservatives and excluded staunch Secessionists.

The Conservatives welcomed Hamilton's approach. His stand in the convention against disfranchisement had mitigated much of the hostility his unionism had once aroused. "It is deeply gratifying to witness everywhere I go," he wrote his son-in-law, "so complete a change of feelings, sentiments, and purposes on the part of those who have been in hostility to the Government."[42]

As early as March, 1869, in response to Hamilton's appeal, the Conservatives adopted a "new departure" program. They would, at least grudgingly, accept the constitution, elect A. J. Hamilton as the new state governor, place former Democrats in the numerous local elective offices, and choose Conservative candidates for the state legislature. The capstone of the Conservative program would be the nomination and election of a "safe" lieutenant governor, something the party never realized. Then they could offer A. J. Hamilton a U.S. Senate seat and take over the executive post by default.

Conservative leaders saw that it was futile to oppose Congressional Reconstruction any longer. Led by men like John Reagan and Ashbel Smith, the Conservatives decided to work quietly behind the scenes for a Moderate Republican–Conservative victory. Their ultimate goal was simply the restoration of the old prewar Democratic ascendancy in Texas, albeit under a different name.

Although he did not openly endorse Hamilton's maneuvers in conjunction with the Conservatives, Pease took a stand very similar to Hamilton's in a letter to General Reynolds. Already promised a seat in the U.S. Senate by Moderates, Pease stayed somewhat aloof in case a compromise candidate was later needed to seal the gap between Republican factions. In his letter, Pease asked the general to call for an early election. Such a move would deny Radicals time to organize and would also lessen the chance for a disagreement that would wreck the tenuous Moderate Republican–Conservative alliance.[43]

Then, to enhance his appeal to Conservatives for the proffered Senate position, Pease contradicted his prior stand on lawlessness. He told Reynolds that the state was quiet for the first time since his assuming the provisional governorship, which made an early election feasible.[44]

Before Congress had adjourned that spring, it conferred upon President Grant the power to call the Texas election at a time of his own choosing.[45] Responding to the provisional governor's communiqué,

Reynolds wrote Washington and suggested an election in late May. Grant, however, did not answer the appeal, refusing to commit himself to any particular date.[46] Grant's hesitation reflected his doubts as to Hamilton's status among Texas Republicans. Grant feared that the Conservative strategy might prove successful and that the disloyal Democrats might again control Texas. He also responded to the able politicking of the Radical faction in Texas.

Disappointed at the Moderate victory in securing the Federal patronage, the Radical leaders had returned to the state executive committee and proposed a state party convention in Galveston on May 10. The Galveston meeting drew few delegates and conducted little business. Recognizing the abortive nature of the meeting, the presiding officer, George T. Ruby, asked the party to reassemble at Houston the following month. The Moderates decided to boycott the session and denounced the new convention as a Radical plot to commit the party to oppose the pending state constitution.

The Radical Republicans saw that the Moderate boycott would guarantee their success. They worked furiously to make the Houston convention appear to be representative of the people's wishes. An entire Radical slate of "truly loyal" men was put forward, headed by Edmund J. Davis as the gubernatorial nominee. In addition the Radicals adopted an astonishing program. Declining to mention ab initio, state division, or disfranchisement, the party platform instead treated these issues as settled by the constitutional convention. The Houston platform endorsed the state constitution for the first time and supported the Fourteenth Amendment, the proposed Fifteenth Amendment, the Reconstruction Acts, and the funding of the national debt.

Texans were amazed. The Radicals had dropped their heretofore uncompromisable principles. The Houston platform was so close to the Moderate statement, against which Davis had led the original revolt a year earlier, that Morgan C. Hamilton and his associates called it a clear surrender to the Moderate side. A. J. Hamilton accused the Davis-led Radicals of the foulest duplicity and cheap politics.[47]

The Radical switch in policy has puzzled historians ever since. One group of writers believes that Republicans in Washington encouraged the Texas Radicals to abandon their principles as the price for national party support.[48] Other analysts contend that Davis finally understood that there was no white voter support in Texas, regardless of party, for the Radical stand on ab initio, division, and disfranchisement. The U.S. Supreme Court's recent decision against ab initio merely served to emphasize the futility of the Radicals' adherence to these principles.

Davis thus decided to recognize reality. Although ideologues like Morgan Hamilton were angered, they would never vote for A. J. Hamilton or support an independent candidate who would assure a Moderate victory. Davis gave up his principles to gain the votes of as many whites as possible in the upcoming elections. He could worry about principle later.[49]

Unlike Davis, historians generally have failed to recognize that General Reynolds was the key to victory in Texas. Reynolds had arrived in Galveston on April 6 with James H. Bell, a Moderate leader.[50] Two days later in Austin, Reynolds formally reassumed command. Upon his appearance at the capitol, Reynolds had indicated to the warring Republican factions the displeasure of the national party and the Grant administration with their quarrel. Should they be unable to compromise on the issues dividing them, said Reynolds, he would find it necessary to "put aside" the now recognized party leaders (like the Hamiltons, Davis, Pease, Haynes, and Bell) and "organize on the basis of new men," including himself.[51]

The Moderates responded to the general's pressure first. Knowing it was "certainly not impossible for him to have political asperations himself" and believing that Reynolds "might not dispise a seat in the U.S. Senate," Moderate leaders approached Reynolds and offered the Senate seat in exchange for his support prior to the election. "I think he should be industriously manipulated," wrote A. P. McCormick to Bell, "and you and Haynes and Governor Pease will have to do this for Gov. Hamilton wont do that kind of work."[52]

While the Moderate leadership was courting Reynolds, the general was diligently preparing a registration procedure designed to assure a large white Democratic, or at least Moderate, turnout. He used for this purpose an order issued the previous October just before Canby replaced him. Under these provisions any white not covered by the officeholding limitations of the Fourteenth Amendment could register to vote. Reynolds supported the proposal of universal male suffrage in the new state constitution, once he arrived in Austin.[53]

Reynolds also made critical changes in local officeholders. In February, Congress had passed a law compelling the removal from office of anyone who could not take the ironclad oath. The Fifth Military District headquarters had issued an order confirming this law just before Reynolds's return to the state. All Texas officials unable to take the ironclad oath were to surrender their positions by April 25, 1869. Full compliance with this procedure would have suspended all civil business in much of Texas.[54] A loophole in the order, however, allowed existing officials to retain their offices without taking the oath until they actually received a copy of their dismissal notice. So Reynolds contented himself with ordering local commanders to prepare lists of those officials who had not taken the ironclad oath and possible replacements, but he did not fully enforce congressional desires unless the offices were held by anti-Hamilton men.[55]

Rumors abounded in Texas and Washington about Reynolds's deal with the Moderates. No one was sure of the terms, but a senatorial seat was most frequently mentioned. In due time A. J. Hamilton learned the truth from his backers. Hamilton had never liked military interference with the state government under the Reconstruction Acts. He had attacked Military Reconstruction at its inception, maintaining that loyal men "crave no such boon." He stated that soldiers should fight wars and let politicians and the people rule state government. He admitted that military men were "good and honest but they are tyrants by education and practice." Even George Washington, as a military officer, would be an unfit supervisor for a civilian government. Hamilton said that any military government threatened the republican nature of American institutions.[56]

Given these personal convictions, Hamilton was so incensed at the negotiations that had gone on behind his back that he publicly repudiated the whole agreement. Hamilton's desire for an honest, open election, his dslike of military rule, and his fear of alienating the Conservatives through army influence had put him at a great disadvantage. Reynolds was greatly embarrassed and angered. He incorrectly thought the whole theoretical diatribe was in direct reference to him and his conduct in Texas.[57]

Although he acted much later than the opportunistic Moderates, Edmund J. Davis knew that his Radicals would have to respond to Reynolds's demands. The general's activities on A. J. Hamilton's behalf would guarantee a Moderate sweep of the election. At first the Davis group tried to have Reynolds ousted, but they failed to shake Grant's confidence in him.[58]

Then, in Houston, they changed the Radical platform. "Reynolds still has the confidence of General Grant," said Davis to Radical dissenter James P. Newcomb, "and we better get along with him." Davis complained that the general's biased Moderate stance "sometimes seems to be very unfair." But at all costs, emphasized Davis, "don't let us enter into a quarrel with him."[59]

Davis therefore had to change their original program so that, as Reynolds had insisted, the Radicals could appear outwardly coopera-

tive with the Moderates. By refusing to attend the Houston convention, the Moderates appeared unwilling to get along with other loyal
elements in the state.

Yet at the same time Davis cleverly refused to join the Moderates
openly, because of A. J. Hamilton's blatant appeal to rebel votes.
Davis thus hoped to woo Reynolds and, through him, Grant, members
of the cabinet, and Republican congressmen to the side of what Davis
saw as the legitimate, loyal, anti-Democrat, truly Republican party
faction.[60]

10

The Army Installs a Government

In Washington in the spring of 1869, Andrew J. Hamilton had a "fierce interview" with Grant's attorney general, E. Rockwood Hoar. The two men quarreled over a justice department appointee in Texas, Hamilton disliking the suggested applicant because he was too Radical. In return, Hoar disgustedly called Hamilton a copperhead, alluding to his affinity for the Texas Conservatives over loyal Republicans of the Radical stripe. Hamilton, who had already caned one Washington critic, leaped up and shook his fist at Hoar. "G——d d——n you, or any man, who impugns my political motives," he shouted. Hamilton had risked his life in defense of Union principles—had Hoar done the same? Hamilton then took the patronage problem directly to the president, who replaced Hoar's choice for the job with Hamilton's. "It is said Jack is pretty certain to be elected Governor of Texas," wrote the recorder of this incident, "and this interview will not set him back much."[1]

With the "thinking element" of the Conservative party and the "practical" Republicans voting for him, and with the patronage and support of the army in the person of General Reynolds buttressing his efforts, it did seem as if A. J. Hamilton's Moderate Republican–Conservative coalition simply could not lose an honestly conducted election in Texas.

Yet there were flaws in this nearly perfect equation. General Reynolds knew that elections in Texas might not be honestly conducted, and he had already indicated his willingness to support the most conciliatory section of the Republican party. And although the Davis committee had failed to secure Grant's support in March, the Texas Radicals did make a favorable impression in Congress as well as in Grant's cabinet. Hamilton, on the other hand, had offended some important party men, as the Hoar incident illustrated, which would eventually hinder him.[2]

Republican leaders in Washington disliked Hamilton's ties with the

Conservatives. In the state convention he was responsible for guaranteeing them the right to vote, and now he appeared ready to use the white majority for his own advancement. Hamilton seemed to oppose Republican Reconstruction goals; he looked shifty, dishonest—even corrupt. Congress reflected this distrust in March, when it rejected a list that Hamilton submitted of Texans who should have all political disabilities removed. Just prior to adjournment, however, Congress endorsed a similar list drawn up by Davis and his backers.

Then in July, Governor William Claflin of Massachusetts, the national Republican party chairman, recognized the Radical state committee as the official party representatives in Texas. Claflin, as Davis hoped he would, looked behind the records of party leaders to their bases of support. Only Davis and the Radicals could show loyal white and black support untainted by suspicious rebel associations.[3]

General Reynolds, rebuffed by the Moderates in his attempt to gain political position, calmly turned to the Radicals with a similar proposal. For the senatorial seat, Reynolds offered the Radicals time to organize their party on the local level and the state patronage with which to accomplish this task, personal influence with the president as well as confirmation of the national party's recognition, and control of the state election machinery.

Reynolds first contacted Grant and asked him to postpone the scheduled July election until further notice. Time was on the Radicals' side; the longer they could wait, the more tenuous the alliance between Hamilton and the Conservatives would become. Time would also give Davis and Reynolds an opportunity to replace local officeholders who supported Hamilton. Grant responded with a proclamation delaying the Texas election until the end of November. Radicals unsuccessfully sought a longer reprieve, at least until December.[4]

The Radicals had wanted a further delay in the election to allow for time to organize the party at the grass-roots level through political appointments. Governor Pease, a Moderate, had largely controlled the state patronage through the army for nearly two years. The Radicals also had to undo the damage caused earlier in the spring of 1869, when General Reynolds and Pease had replaced Davis officeholders with Moderates.

Reynolds now reversed the process and began to replace Hamilton men with Radicals. The procedure was made easy because of Canby's policy of appointing anyone who would enforce the law, regardless of his political antecedents, and because of Hamilton's earlier insistence that the state government be organized with men who qualified under the proposed constitution, rather than requiring the ironclad oath as Congress required in February, 1869.[5]

Reynolds rigidly enforced the congressional sanction, which he promulgated earlier as General Orders No. 60. Hundreds of office-holders found themselves disqualified. Morgan Hamilton estimated that at least half of the three thousand Pease appointees needed to be removed.[6] Between January, 1869, and January, 1870, the army issued 300 orders in Texas, of which 196 concerned removals and appointments. Seventy percent of these decrees were Reynolds's, and the rest were Canby's. Nearly every Reynolds order after Special Orders No. 95, April 22, 1869, was filled with politically motivated removals and appointments. By insisting on the ironclad oath, Reynolds was able to fill nearly two thousand political openings in local government with new men, most of whom were allegedly Radicals.[7]

As soon as the news of Grant's postponement of the election to November arrived in Texas, Davis Radicals organized a new committee to visit Washington and lobby for "proper" Federal patronage.[8] Reynolds's influence was decisive in securing this objective for the Radicals. Because the Republican party in Texas was split, the president turned to Reynolds, his old West Point classmate, for the truth about events there and for advice on all appointments. In the summer of 1869, Reynolds recommended Radicals, just as he had earlier suggested Moderates. Appropriately, the first Moderate to lose his Federal office was the customs collector at El Paso, W. W. Mills, Hamilton's son-in-law.[9]

Queried about the change in policy, Reynolds told the president that he had tried to use the best men of both Republican factions but found that he could not. A. J. Hamilton had many men on his ticket who could not qualify for office under the Reconstruction Acts; he had refused to cooperate with the Radicals in the Houston convention; and the Moderates were allied with the Democrats. A Hamilton victory "will put the State in the hands of the very men who, during the entire period of the rebellion, have exerted every nerve to destroy the Union, and who have uniformly opposed the reconstruction laws."[10]

Reynolds's use of the Federal patronage and his letter to Grant brought about an unexpected dividend—Governor Pease's resignation. Pease had never liked being governor and had reluctantly assumed the job "to aid in carrying out the laws of Congress for equal rights for all." He believed the only way to achieve this objective was to ratify the new constitution and elect Hamilton.[11]

Pease disliked the manner in which "the influence and patronage of the military Commander of this State, and of the Administration at Washington" was being used "in behalf of those Republicans who have exerted themselves to delay and defeat reconstruction of the State." Hamilton was supported by "eight-tenths" of the Texas Republican party, said Pease. He refused to have his name connected with Reynolds's actions and therefore resigned.[12]

After Pease's departure Reynolds disappointed the Radicals by refusing to appoint one of their own men governor. Some Radicals panicked. They feared that Reynolds was flirting with the idea of selecting another Hamilton man. They also doubted that Reynolds fully comprehended the attempts of Moderates to manipulate him. "Reynolds is an honest amiable man," declared one Radical, "but he is no more fit for a Military commander in Texas than a child." They thought that the general was so nervous over his letter to Grant announcing his support of the Radicals that he would back down and compromise.[13]

Morgan C. Hamilton quelled these worries, at the same time showing some contempt for the new Radical ally. Leave Reynolds alone, he said; the general was already frightened to death over what he had done for the Radical cause. M. C. Hamilton suspected that Reynolds would not fill the gubernatorial vacancy but handle the functions himself. It would be a clever move. He would not openly commit himself to the Radical cause and thus refuse to give substance to the reasons for Pease's resignation. The governor's position also gave Reynolds a direct form of control over the election, appointment, and removal policies of the state that no commander had ever had before. By December he indicated to M. C. Hamilton that he would not appoint a new governor unless compelled to do so by the president. He never was.[14]

Nothing guaranteed administration support for Reynolds's alliance with the Radicals better than the unreconstructed audacity of the "Democratic Editors' Convention," which met in Brenham at the end of September. The editors criticized any alliance with A. J. Hamilton, the man who had begun the disastrous Reconstruction process the state was about to complete. They found the new state constitution to be abominable and the proposed Fifteenth Amendment to the United States Constitution to be unbelievable. The editors concluded that continued military rule was far better than the election of either Hamilton or Davis.

To give Texans a real choice in the upcoming election, the editors recommended a state ticket led by one of their number, Hamilton

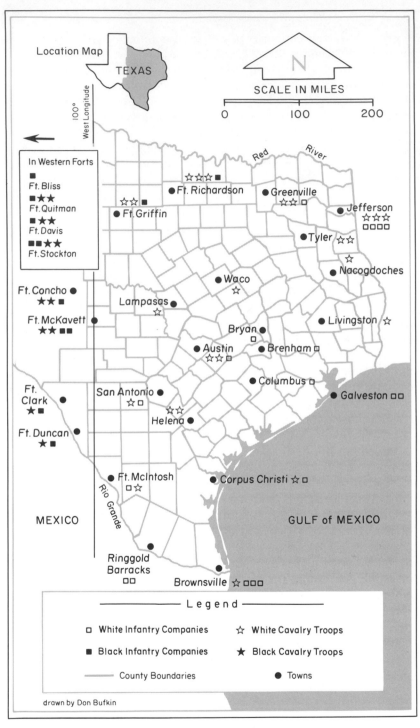

Map 9. Reynolds's Troop Assignments, September, 1869: Reynolds
Assumes Governorship

Stuart. This unusual position directly challenged Congressional Reconstruction, a stance that most Southern states had sought to avoid by working within "Conservative" parties. A. J. Hamilton knew that an unreconstructed Democratic ticket would only aid the Radicals and urged Stuart to withdraw. Fourteen prominent Democrats issued a statement repudiating Stuart and endorsing Hamilton and the Conservative approach. The Democratic state executive committee did not formally declare for Hamilton, but they did ask party members to take a conservative approach. Stuart refused to back down, which meant now that tickets headed by him, A. J. Hamilton, and Davis would be available on election day. With the Democratic party so obviously unreconstructed and many of its leaders backing Hamilton, Davis more than ever appeared the only loyal man in the race.[15]

Concurrently with the political problems he faced, General Reynolds had to cope with other Reconstruction questions, including newspaper censorship. The majority of the state's journals were openly disloyal in their editorial comments. Except in the larger cities like Galveston, Houston, Austin, and San Antonio, few Republican sheets existed.[16]

An early troublesome periodical was the *Brownsville Daily Ranchero*. A rabidly anti-Negro, pro-Democratic organ that regularly lambasted the black soldiers of the Army of Occupation during the first years of Reconstruction, the *Ranchero* commonly used the "basest language" when referring to Federal authority and openly supported Maximilian in Mexico. The black soldiers stationed in the Rio Grande valley hated the paper's sentiments and had to be closely watched by their officers to prevent them from rioting and destroying the newspaper plant. Such an incident would only have helped the former Confederates.[17]

Because of the *Ranchero* and other such papers in Texas and the South, the War Department asked commanders to keep a close watch on editorial policy. The district commanders required Texas editors to send a copy of each issue to Galveston, where it was perused for disloyal articles. By August, 1866, Congress considered Federal control in the state strong enough and canceled the order.[18] The repeal of censorship did not free the editors from the army's yoke, although editors soon realized that some military persecution had its advantages. An offensive article was a sure way for a publisher to sell his product. If he was arrested, he became an instant martyr, and sales fairly boomed.

Such an incident occurred at Jefferson during Canby's tenure, the aftermath of which affected General Reynolds. Four freedmen and a white radical named George W. Smith were arrested by civil authorities on charges that were obviously false. They appealed to the local commander for protection, and the army succeeded in having them transferred to its stockade.

Upon the request of civil authorities, who maintained that they could protect the accused until trial was held, the army remanded the prisoners to city control and provided an armed guard of soldiers to assist the sheriff. That night, however, a noisy mob of over one hundred men disguised in Ku Klux Klan regalia forced the jail entrance and murdered the accused. Smith had been a convention delegate of some influence, so something had to be done. The army cracked down and arrested thirty-five suspects, who were held without the privilege of the writ of habeas corpus.[19]

In response, R. W. Loughery, editor of both the *Jefferson Times* and the nearby *Marshall Texas Republican,* wrote an impassioned plea denouncing the army's action as arbitrary, despotic, and unnecessary four years after the war. Loughery pointed out that he had made numerous appeals to the Northern press to speak out but was met by silence. He asserted that the arrested citizens had been dragged from their beds at night "by an armed soldiery, who paid no respect to the feelings of families or the delicacy which belongs to domestic relations." He saw "no excuse or apology for these atrocious measures." Jefferson now had a military mayor, and it was overrun by spies and detectives who were "extorting" testimony through offering bribes and intimidation. "There is no telling to what extent, if not checked, this despotism will be carried."[20]

Loughery's impassioned appeal came to the attention of William T. Sherman, the commanding general of the army. Sherman asked Reynolds to investigate and report on Loughery's charges.[21] Reynolds replied that he had little to add to prior reports regularly submitted to headquarters on the affair. He outlined the principal facts of the case, noting that many prominent persons in Jefferson had left town recently for "no apparent cause," including the district judge. He implied that those who had fled were involved in the murder. Reynolds also promised a military trial of the prisoners at an early date. Continued outbursts by Loughery led to his arrest two months later, and like other editors before him, he became an instant hero.[22]

Editor Loughery's criticism of the use of military commissions to try civilians raised an issue that was a constant sore point between the army and Texans throughout Reconstruction. As of October 20, Reynolds reported that fifty-nine cases had been tried by military tribunals in 1869 alone; all of them involved criminal charges brought against civilians. Reynolds convened nine military commissions in 1869 and nine more in 1870. Canby, however, had less frequent military trials, preferring to rely first upon the civil courts.[23]

Unlike Canby, General Reynolds utilized state courts consistently only when private wrongs were involved.[24] In any judicial conflict involving the public peace or a crime, the general reserved the right of intervention, usually before civil authorities could act. Reynolds authorized the arrest and incarceration of prisoners without charges and ordered them held until he approved of their release. He regularly requested information on specific cases and demanded lists of all civilian prisoners held, along with the charges placed against them. Reynolds also sent lists to local posts, naming those who would be tried by military commissions, who should be released on bail, and who could be represented by which attorney and specifying when a local judge could officiate.[25]

In spite of Reynolds's close supervision of state law enforcement, crime continued unabated, murders alone averaging one a day state-wide.[26] Trial by military commission did not help either. Through careless procedure and a lack of witnesses, military tribunals in 1869 had a conviction rate of 36 percent.

The murder case involving George W. Smith and the four blacks in Jefferson, which editor Loughery had so harshly criticized, illustrates the problem. The army arrested thirty-six persons in connection with the incident, but brought only twenty-four to trial. In a tortuous session, during which one of the military judges was arrested by the army and another was withdrawn from the bench for acting more like a prosecutor than a judge, six of the original defendants were convicted. These men received relatively short jail sentences, at a time when murder was punishable by death.[27]

The following year a Brownsville newspaper explained this "leniency." Even if a murderer was sentenced to death, "There is considerable doubt about the death penalty ever being inflicted by virtue of a trial by a military commission in times of profound peace. It involves other questions," said the periodical, "the responsibility of which careful men are cautious not to incur."

The criminal procedure in a military commission was too different from a traditional criminal court trial to be palatable even to many army officers. Canby had realized this discrepancy and acted to enforce state law through state courts and procedure. But Reynolds refused to alter his course in this regard. Rather, he increased the frequency of military trials of civilians until the army's role in Reconstruction ended in April, 1870.[28]

Another complication that faced General Reynolds in the fall of 1869 was the reorganization of the regiments under his command. On March 3, 1869, Congress reduced the size of the United States Army to twenty-five regiments of infantry, which resulted in a complicated series of troop movements across Texas to facilitate the reduction. The first step in the reorganization in the Fifth Military District was the transfer of the Seventeenth Infantry to the Atlantic coast. Since many of the Seventeenth's companies were in frontier garrisons, the Fifteenth and Thirty-fifth regiments were sent to relieve it. In the process, these latter two outfits were consolidated as the new Fifteenth Infantry, which involved a reduction in strength of each by 50 percent.[29]

The vacancies opened in east Texas by this maneuver were filled by the arrival of the companies of the Eleventh Infantry, which entered Texas via the Red River and Galveston. At the same time, the Twenty-sixth Infantry was renumbered and combined with the Tenth Infantry, which arrived along the coast from Indianola to Brownsville. The Forty-first (Colored) Infantry was consolidated with another black regiment to form the Twenty-fourth (Colored) Infantry, which remained in the far west of Texas. The cavalry was not affected by the new law, leaving Texas with the Fourth and Sixth regiments as before. The net result was that by November, 1869, Reynolds lost over eight hundred men who had previously guarded the interior.[30]

The new men assigned to Texas soon found that military-civilian relations had not changed since the first troops had arrived there in the summer of 1865. A few lucky detachments, like Company G, Seventeenth Infantry, could point with pride to their stay in Texas. Upon receiving news of the departure of the Seventeenth for Virginia, the *Dallas Herald* commented on the sterling conduct of Company G and its commander, Captain Henry Norton. "We parted from him with regret," said the pro-Democratic newspaper, "but commend him to our friends in the Old Dominion as a gentleman, a good officer, and beloved by our citizens." The *Herald* called the unit's conduct "high toned in the extreme."[31]

The enlisted men of most companies were usually not as well regarded as those in Captain Norton's command. Federal soldiers, in one incident, rode into Pilot Grove and victimized a local storekeeper for rations. They had just come from a neighborhood farm where they forced the farmer's wife to cook a free meal for the detachment.[32] Civilians and officers continually complained of drunkenness among the ranks. Officers blamed civilians for selling liquor, while the citizenry castigated the army for its lack of discipline.

Brevet Major Lynde Catlin, irritated at the "frequent and protracted intoxication" of his unit, suggested that General Reynolds prohibit the sale of liquor to troopers on the penalty of confiscation of goods. Nothing came of the suggestion.[33] One harried officer reported that he had ten enlisted men awaiting courts-martial which had not yet been convened by the proper authorities.[34]

Violence against bluecoats continued as before. Two infantrymen from the Seventeenth Infantry were murdered in Brenham. Townspeople shielded the killers from authorities, a common occurrence in that village. Unknown parties killed a troop commander at Bryan Station. The army posted a one-thousand-dollar reward for information leading to arrest and conviction, but no one collected.[35]

When a discharged Federal soldier had the temerity to attend a dance in Tarrant County in the company of a local belle, he encountered immediate hostility. He had paid the entrance fee, but Federal soldiers were not wanted there, especially native Texans like himself (he had enlisted in 1865). Several men offered to fight him for the privilege of entering. The rebuffed former soldier retired from the scene with his partner and later returned to the dance alone, where unidentified parties fired on him.[36]

Other harassment was still common. A lieutenant of the Eleventh Infantry was attacked by citizens as he traveled harmlessly along the highway to a new duty station. He reported that such occurrences were not out of the ordinary. The post commander at Jefferson ruled him nonnegligent in shooting his attackers. In Lampasas a sergeant made a complaint against a local citizen who allegedly assaulted him on the street. The citizen filed a countersuit asserting that the sergeant began the altercation.[37]

Soldiers were still incarcerated on false charges, like the Fourth Cavalry bugler who spent several months in a Waco jail until his commander forced his release. Usually the army tried to ignore specious civil accusations, as in the refusal to cooperate in the case of a San Antonio man against Brevet Brigadier General James Oakes. But such tactics proved so frustrating to one officer that his colonel had to remove him from command for displaying "personal hatred wholly unworthy a gentleman and a soldier."[38]

In his new capacity as both military commander and provisional governor, General Reynolds faced a multitude of miscellaneous tasks not envisioned in the scope of the Reconstruction Acts. He acted as an advisor in municipal government and was involved with such matters as incorporating towns.[39] In a typical case, Reynolds received two petitions; the first asked that a county seat be removed to a new location, while the other begged that it be allowed to remain where it was. The general tried to avoid the issue by refusing to consider either request, thus deciding by default in favor of the second petition.[40]

Even stranger requests were made of the general. A Fort Worth resident asked him to intervene and evict squatters from his land because there was "no telling when there will be any Court held in Denton district." Another man asked Reynolds to decide who owned all the rails, timber, and property deposited on his land by a flash flood. The exasperated general decreed that everything belonged to the man on whose property they lodged, unless the original owner laid claim to them. If the contending parties could not reach an agreement, they could resort to the state courts.[41]

Still more picayune problems rolled into headquarters. A letter from Weatherford asked the army to provide more and better mail service. Reynolds accordingly ordered all males between seventeen and fifty to report to the county courts to repair the public roads, which were in an abysmal condition. Army headquarters ordered the post commandant at Waco to enforce the ordinance on the removal of hogs from the city streets until the law had been ruled on by the state supreme court.[42]

With Reynolds acting as military commander and governor, the Radicals now controlled all of the election machinery in the state. Before Reynolds joined their cause, the Radicals had had only one advantage over the Moderates. Because he had presided over the convention, Davis saw to it that the election returns for each district would be sent to "safe" collection points, and counted by "reliable" men.[43] Now Davis and Reynolds would show A. J. Hamilton that victory was guaranteed not necessarily to whoever had the most votes but to whoever counted them.

At Reynolds's suggestion, President Grant ordered the Texas election to be held from November 30 to December 3, six months later than originally planned by the Moderates. In compliance with this edict from Grant, Reynolds issued General Orders No. 174. The voters were to take part in two actual elections: a vote on the constitution's ratification and a selection of state and local officials, should the constitution be approved. To facilitate the proper registration of electors, a board of registrars would sit at the county seat of each county for ten days beginning November 16.[44]

All registrars had to subscribe to the ironclad oath; two white and two black persons could be selected to challenge registrants before each board. Such challenges could be appealed to the district commander. Registrars were to conduct themselves in accordance with General Orders No. 92, which was a comprehensive listing of the four Reconstruction Acts, the ironclad oath, the oath of future loyalty (for those pardoned by Congress), the act requiring all state officials to take the ironclad oath or resign, and the Thirteenth, Fourteenth, and proposed Fifteenth Amendments to the Federal Constitution. Should a registrar be absent, the remaining members of the board could appoint a replacement.[45]

The registrars were also to conduct the election in each county. Voting would take place only at the county seat. Each black voter would have his ballot marked "colored" before it was deposited in the ballot box. Two registered voters could act as challengers. No intoxicating liquors were to be dispensed during the election period. The sheriff of each county and two deputies were to enforce the abstinence rule and preserve the peace during registration and the election. Any disturbance was to be reported to the nearest army officer. During the election, disturbances that threatened anyone's right to vote would automatically close the polls until the army reopened the voting there.[46]

A week later Reynolds issued new instructions which established the members of registration boards in 125 counties. Each board had three members, and in sixty-four cases, one of the members was an officer of the United States Army. Ten days later, Reynolds ordered one officer and ten soldiers to accompany each registration team to assist the sheriff and his deputies in maintaining a proper decorum during registration and the ensuing election. The troops were not to appear physically at the polls, however, unless a breach of the peace occurred. The troop assignment was effected, although some officers complained that, because of the troop consolidations and reductions coming to a close simultaneously with the election process, they had too few men to meet all of the requirements.[47]

The result of the registration was a large increase in potential white voters. Seventy-two percent of those added to the lists were white, which gave the Conservatives an overall advantage in the registration figures. By election day there were 81,960 whites and 53,593 blacks registered to vote. Although some historians have suggested that the

Radicals used this opportunity to enroll unqualified men, neither side protested the new registration nor its administration.[48]

Like registration, the election was remarkably quiet and without incident. The constitution was overwhelmingly approved. Because a large number of whites stayed home, however, Hamilton's vote was much smaller than expected. Numerous cases of fraud were reported. Radicals accused their opponents of turning rural blacks away from the polls; Moderates maintained the army confused the voters by not properly informing them of their correct precincts at registration.[49]

Both sides claimed that ballot boxes had been stuffed, lost, or rigged in some mysterious fashion by the opposition. One disappointed Radical candidate protested that he had been defeated by black voters who could neither read nor write and that his Conservative opponent had tricked them into voting the wrong way. The army told him simply to run a tighter campaign next time.[50]

Moderates and Conservatives were adamant that Reynolds investigate the election irregularities in Navarro and Milam counties, for the winner in these counties would take the election for governor. Without them Davis had a slight lead; with them Hamilton would probably win. Hamilton's side suggested a new election there, to be fair to both contenders. Reynolds, however, simply refused to count the vote in these counties and declared Davis elected by about 800 votes statewide.[51]

Reynolds's services to the Radicals were not yet completed. In December, Morgan C. Hamilton wrote the district commander and complained that the oath of office in the new Texas constitution was excessively lenient and easily falsified. He asked the general to require that the oath be administered by a Federal official and that the penalties for perjury be attached to it.[52]

Reynolds went further than Hamilton had asked. On February 5, 1870, the general ordered all members-elect of the state legislature to subscribe to the ironclad oath. Reynolds reasoned that, since he had appointed them to office in January by special order, these men were serving provisionally until Congress approved of the new constitution and government. Hence they were technically Federal rather than state officials.[53]

At the suggestion of local commanders and politicians, Reynolds then issued over fifty special orders appointing elected officials on all levels to the offices they had won. Local commanders were to notify all men they were elected and appointed.[54] Those who could not take the

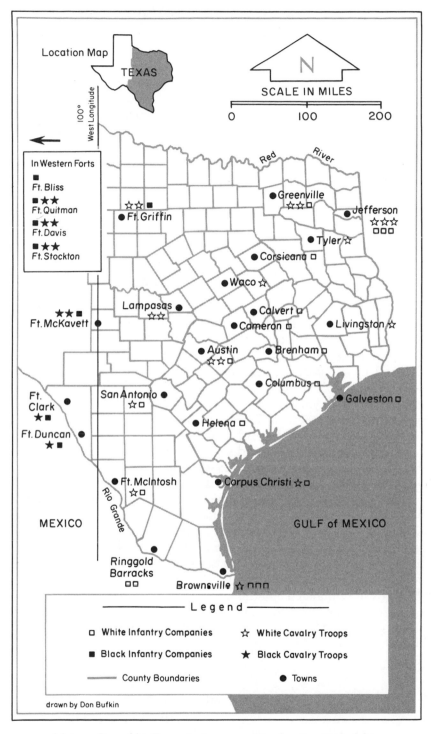

Map 10. Reynolds's Troop Assignments, March, 1870: End of the
Fifth Military District

ironclad oath were replaced by men who could, thus contradicting the people's election choices.[55]

After requiring the ironclad oath of all state officials, Reynolds appointed a board of military officers to hear disputes over eligibility questions concerning contested state legislature seats. The board was to rule on a candidate's ability to take the ironclad oath, but such a ruling had to be accepted by the respective house of the state legislature before the winner in question could take or be denied a seat. Naturally, with their Democratic, Confederate antecedents, Hamilton candidates would have more difficulty in taking the ironclad oath.[56]

In February the provisional legislature met in Austin. It quickly ratified the Fourteenth and Fifteenth amendments and proceeded to the election of United States Senators. As expected, Reynolds was among the leading contenders. Opposition developed, however, within the Radical party, and state newspapers castigated him for becoming a candidate before a body which he had largely manipulated into office.[57]

Faced by mounting opposition, the general announced that he would not seek any office, out of "convictions of right and propriety." The *Brownsville Daily Ranchero* chuckled that Reynolds's note had "the ring of 'sour grapes' about it," remembering that the general had not declined until "after the legislature had been in session for several days." The *Ranchero* surmised that Reynolds had a sudden attack "of great pride. He loves to be a reconstructing General, but to be known as a carpetbag Senator, it is quite evident, was more than his pride would permit him to bear." Although his disavowal of public office impressed the *Ranchero* editor and some historians as sincere, Reynolds's persistent attempts to become Texas's United States Senator in later years belies his alleged lack of political ambition.[58]

With Reynolds out of the Senate race, the state legislature elected Morgan C. Hamilton and J. W. Flanagan to represent Texas in the upper house of Congress.[59] Their election, the seating of the Davis legislature, and the ratification of the Fourteenth and Fifteenth amendments meant that Texas had at last complied fully with the Reconstruction Acts. On March 31, the jurisdiction of the Fifth Military District was terminated and the state became the Military Department of Texas, commanded by Reynolds. Civil government was fully restored on April 16, 1870. Nine years after she had left it, Texas was back in the Union.[60]

Conclusion:
The Role of the Army in Texas
Reconstruction

How few men there are who are really fit to be
entrusted with such power.

—Brig. Gen. Neal Dow to his wife,
September 30, 1862

In analyzing the army's effect on Texas Reconstruction, it is helpful to conceive of the era in three periods, corresponding to the tenure of the officers who exercised the most influence on the state and military organizations. The first of these periods roughly corresponds to so-called Presidential Reconstruction, encompassing the eighteen months from May, 1865, when General Philip Sheridan assumed command and engineered the initial invasion, to December, 1866, when General Charles Griffin took over the Texas command, according to Sheridan's orders. The second time period corresponds to Griffin's tenure as commander of the District of Texas in the first nine months of 1867, when the transition was made from Presidential Reconstruction to Congressional Reconstruction. During most of the third period, which culminated in the election of a loyal government and the state's readmission to the Union, General Joseph J. Reynolds exercised control of the Texas Command.

Because of the latitude of the Reconstruction Acts, the personality of each commander heavily influenced the character of Military Reconstruction in his district. The army alone was responsible for the Radical success in 1869, and every knowledgeable Texan knew it.[1] Typical of its crucial role in determining who was elected was the request of the Indianola board of registrars for advice on the 1869 election. The board forwarded ten doubtful ballots with the comment that, if they were counted, a Republican sheriff would be elected; if not, a Democrat would win. We cannot simply say that the board was trying to avoid its responsibility. The important factor was that the army, in this case General Reynolds, was willing to assume an active part in the electoral decision.[2]

187

Conclusion

We may see the political interference of Texas commanders more clearly by comparing Reynolds's administration with that of Major General John Schofield in Virginia. Schofield believed that the 1867 congressional acts were a terrible oppression, yet he ruled Virginia with an iron hand and showed favor to neither black nor white. He divided the state into fifty-five districts and placed an officer in charge of civil affairs in each area. Schofield refused to make wholesale removals and allowed local citizens to assist in choosing qualified men. He disliked extremists and preferred any moderate person, Republican or Democrat, who could take the oath.

All registration boards had one military representative, who was to guarantee fairness, and troops patrolled all election sites to ensure an orderly process and an honest count of the ballots. Schofield threatened to use military courts whenever necessary, but he rarely resorted to them. His impartiality in Virginia politics was praised throughout the state, in obvious contrast to the criticism voiced in Texas, even by Republicans, for army political interference.[3] Schofield admittedly encountered no frontier problem, ruled a smaller geographic area, and had an uninterrupted tenure of more than a year. Still, one wonders if Reynolds could not have done better.

The army's role in Texas clearly demonstrates the ease with which sweeping military power can lead to arbitrary rule, despite the military and civil controls built into the American system of government. As one Civil War general belatedly realized, military government was "a terrible machine, capital, like fire when under good control, . . . but awful as a conflagration when it escapes beyond the bounds of truth and right." He lamented, "How few men there are who are really fit to be entrusted with such power."[4]

Texans frequently concurred in this less than attractive assessment of military supervision. "I look for serious troble all over the South," wrote a planter, "when the incendiary scoundrels now overrunning the country . . . learn of the wiping out of all civil law & the placing [of] us under Military Govt."[5] A Houston woman complained to a friend about "the blue-coated dogs of despotism in & around our town. There seems to be no end to these & their congeries—the free niggers. Devil take them all say I."[6]

Political manipulation and private citizens' criticism notwithstanding, the army generally conducted itself well in Texas. It defended the frontier as well as might be expected with its limited resources, suppressed hostile groups of brigands, held reasonably fair trials of civilians accused of wrongdoing, and even administered minor governmental affairs at the county and municipal levels.[7]

A listing of military functions like these raises the disputed question of just how much control the army exercised in Texas. Some writers have argued that the relatively small numbers of soldiers stationed in the south shows how weak military influence really was.[8] One chronicler, Robert Shook, has defended this point with regard to Texas in particular.[9] Other historians maintain that the army's power, influence, and activity cannot be measured in numbers alone because the blue uniform had a great psychological effect on Southern whites. Rarely would whites attack a Federal troop contingent or openly challenge federally backed governments, these historians say, because they feared the severe repercussions that would follow such action. The series of Enforcement Acts passed by Congress in 1870 and 1871 illustrate this potential power available to army units stationed in the South.[10]

In Texas, except in selected areas and situations, the army's physical strength was usually minimal. Although there were exceptions, in situations of potential violence the blue uniform seemed generally to provoke, not to restrain, armed resistance.[11] All too often, Texas citizens were more than willing to challenge the army's authority in the state. "*Blue* was as enraging to secesh eyes . . . as *red* is to the eyes of a turkey gobbler," said one Unionist. Loyal men commonly reported that "occasional visits from soldiers only exasperates lawlessness."[12]

In spite of minimal numbers, the army did exercise great political influence in Texas, as demonstrated by the very scope of its involvement in civil affairs and by Griffin's and Reynolds's political manipulations and the manner in which each political faction sought the army's approval and support for its programs. Reynolds's willingness to bargain with politicians particularly helped delay Reconstruction and intensify the lawlessness and disorder prevalent in the state during the period. The general's removal of Democrats in 1867 and 1868, Radicals the following spring, and Moderate Republicans in the autumn of 1869 led to much confusion over who legally held various state and local positions.[13]

Even headquarters at Austin could not keep up with the constant changes in personnel that Reynolds made. The general's bewildered adjutant once wrote the post commander at Indianola inquiring who had appointed a man named Hayes Yarrington as hide inspector, who had removed him, and who currently held the position.[14] The constant turnover of offices also resulted in a shortage of personnel. Many appointees refused to serve or could not take the oath,[15] which continually forced Reynolds to reappoint men to various positions or to place soldiers in others.[16]

Perhaps the major reason for the prolonged nature of Texas Reconstruction and the army's political manipulations concerned the role of the Negro and scalawag in the process. The heavy registration of blacks, the election of some blacks to state office, and the large numbers of freedmen enrolled in the state militia and later the state police caused many Conservatives and historians to claim that Texas suffered from "Negro rule."[17] These assertions are highly inaccurate. Although the army encouraged blacks to register and vote,[18] their political influence was kept at an absolute minimum by the racist attitudes of the scalawags who composed a majority of the Republican party infrastructure and the Davis regime. Frustrating black aspirations, the scalawags refused to elect a black as United States Senator, to nominate or appoint blacks to any important state office (a policy the army acquiesced in), or to protect adequately their political and civil rights.[19]

Most Texas Republicans supported the black vote for purely political not moral, reasons—the Negro vote offered them power. For the same reason, Republicans relied upon the army, and later the state police, to protect the blacks from attacks by white terrorists. Undoubtedly a few Texas party leaders wished to guarantee blacks' rights; most Republicans, however, were more concerned with preserving blacks' access to the polls. This access largely disappeared when Reconstruction collapsed in the early 1870s, after the army physically withdrew from the interior counties, which demonstrates the army's critical role in this area.[20] With the exception of Griffin's token declaration of black rights to use freely all public facilities, the army followed the racial policy of Texas scalawags without a murmur.

National Republican leaders clearly expected the black population throughout the South to provide a large base of loyal Republican support in the process of Reconstruction. They did not anticipate, however, that in Texas, as well as in Georgia and Virginia (states which also delayed their readmission to the Union through their hesitation to include blacks in government and to exclude certain whites), white Republicans and Negroes together would still remain a minority.[21] More was needed to assure the Republicans of a majority at the polls. The need for additional support in order to gain control of the state and local governments led to army involvement in state politics, which resulted in a split in the Republican party.

The scope of the problem had been revealed dramatically at the end of A. J. Hamilton's fourteen-month provisional regime, when, in spite of determined efforts on the part of Loyalists, Throckmorton and the Conservatives handily gained control of most state offices. There were just not enough white loyal men in Texas to hold the state for the Union party. The addition of freedmen to the ranks of the newly formed Republican party in 1867 helped but still did not achieve the needed majority for Texas Loyalists. To hold the line temporarily, Griffin and Reynolds utilized the army and the patronage powers granted the district commanders under the Reconstruction Acts to assist the Republicans in building the necessary grass-roots organization.

Unfortunately for the Republicans, the army would not supervise Texas government forever. Sooner or later, on their own merits, the Republicans would have to face the Texas electorate alone. A. J. Hamilton, E. M. Pease, John L. Haynes, and others decided to broaden their support in the traditional manner, namely, by compromising with the main source of voter strength in Texas, the old Democratic party. To maintain their position as loyal men, these Moderate Republicans rationalized that they were appealing merely to the thinking element of educated, respectable men among the Conservative forces. To attract these men to their standard, Hamilton and the Moderates refused to disfranchise former Confederates, opposed an ab initio declaration, and refused to divide the state in pieces. Hamilton, after all, if he desired their support, could not disfranchise the thinking element, pillory their everyday administration of the state during the war, or exclude them from a loyal Texas.

The Moderates' opponents within the party—the Radicals, led by E. J. Davis, M. C. Hamilton, James P. Newcomb, and their adherents—refused to make any compromise with the Secessionists. They preferred to disfranchise much of the Conservative majority, deny their ability to rule the state, and exclude them from loyal areas of Texas by dividing the state into three new political areas controlled by white Republicans, black Republicans, and Secessionists administered by Congress through the army. Failing to achieve any of their principles, the Radicals had to seek other ways to nullify the apparent success of A. J. Hamilton's plans.

Davis grasped the proper course of action when the national Republican party and the Grant administration indicated that they desired party harmony and unification in Texas. Davis temporarily abandoned principle and shrewdly adopted a platform very similar to that of the Moderates. This position gave him the appearance of being reasonable

and implied that, if A. J. Hamilton would drop his support from disloyal voters in Texas, the two Republican factions could at last work
together to purify the state of the taint of secession.

When Hamilton refused to make concessions to Davis or to keep
the deals promised to General Reynolds by his cronies for fear of losing
the Conservative vote, the Radicals rapidly seized upon this opportunity to secure Reynolds's decisive influence in their behalf. After
all, the Radicals could not remake Texas society according to their
dictates or moral authority unless they could obtain office first. The
Radicals resorted to the army for support and, in so doing, sealed the
fate of the Republican party in Texas for a century.[22] The Republicans'
tragedy was that, no matter which road they took in 1869, they were
doomed to ultimate disaster at the hands of the hostile white voting
majority.

The readmission of Texas to the Union in the spring of 1870 legally
completed Military Reconstruction. The blacks were registered to
vote and guaranteed their political and civil rights, and a loyal administration had taken over the state. Theoretically the need for the
army's services in civil affairs had ended, and the troops were rapidly
shifted to frontier posts.[23] Elements of military rule lingered on, however, because the Davis government could never command sufficient
votes to stay in power.

The Radicals' fear of submitting to another election after their nar-
row victory in 1869 was evident when the legislature granted Governor Davis vast appointive powers to fill local offices and bypass the
need for interim elections. The usefulness of the power of appointment had already been well demonstrated by Reynolds. The legislature also postponed for one year the state election scheduled for November, 1871, which further isolated the Radicals from the white
electorate. The legislature then further guaranteed the voters' hatred
by passing numerous controversial state-funded programs, which sent
taxes to a new high.[24]

The Radicals compounded their electoral vulnerability by arguing
among themselves. The two U.S. Senators, M. C. Hamilton and
Flanagan, condemned state legislature policies and Davis's support of
them. Hamilton's remarks were especially biting, which led to a lack
of political and economic support of the regime from Washington.
Angered by the effects of Hamilton's defection, party leaders in Texas
decided to replace him with a more reliable man. Arguing that Hamilton had not been legally elected because he had been chosen before

Congress actually readmitted Texas as a state in March, 1870, the state legislature certified the election of the obsequious General Reynolds instead. It was quite natural to turn to Reynolds. He wanted the job, and he had insured Radical control of the state in the first place. But Congress thwarted this plan by refusing to unseat Hamilton.[25]

The two senators had severely criticized the Radicals for their creation of the Texas State Police and the state militia as institutions not only to combat lawlessness and protect loyal men but to ensure Radical control of state government. Established in 1870, the state police had the authority to make searches and arrests without warrants and to exercise a statewide jurisdiction in criminal matters. The governor appointed all of the members, who were responsible to him alone. The governor could also suspend the writ of habeas corpus to assist their investigations.[26]

Early state historians condemned the state police as one of the greatest evils of Reconstruction, while more modern scholars defend it by stressing its great contribution in assuring law and order.[27] Both of these analyses overlook the fundamental role of the state police. It was not primarily designed to preserve order or to replace the defunct, rebellion-tainted Texas Rangers, although it may have performed creditably in that task. Its basic purpose in replacing the army was to handle not merely the soldiers' police duties but their political functions as well, including policing the polls and protecting Republican voters, blacks, and loyal men in general from coercion and intimidation. It may not have been successful in this goal,[28] but the analogy with the army is valid nonetheless.

Because of the similarity in function among the state police, the state militia, and the army, there was some confusion even among contemporaries as to when Military Reconstruction ended and the army turned over the policing of state elections to the state organizations. Numerous accounts report that, during Reconstruction, voters had to pass between two lines of black soldiers armed with rifles and bayonets. These same sources erroneously refer to these blue-uniformed men as Federal soldiers. Because the army did not use Negro troops in the interior after 1866, they were likely members of the state police and state militia. The racial composition of these units was about 40 percent black; they were the "soldiers" raised by the Davis administration to watch elections in the early 1870s, after the army no longer interfered in civil affairs.[29]

The United States faced a quandary in Texas. It had to subject the democratic process of self-government to military regulation and take equal rights from the majority to protect a deserving minority. The alternative was to allow the whites to rule as before the war and re-serve second-class citizenship for the freedmen. According to the first Texas state constitution, written in 1845, "All political power is inher-ent in the people, and all free governments are founded on their au-thority and instituted for their benefit." Most white Texans believed that the Reconstruction policy of the national government, in par-ticular, the army's role in enforcing that policy, denied this basic truth.

The impassioned hostile editorials of the *Brownsville Daily Ranchero* perhaps best expressed the attitude of white Texans toward military supervision of state government. In the spring of 1867, this anti-Reconstruction sheet confessed to be tired of the vile abuse the "man-acled" south had received from "Radicals," particularly their use of the words "traitors" and "rebels" in reference to Southerners. "But the most despicable means of the conquerors, and the one that sinks its perpetrators deep, deep down into the lowest depths of ineffable in-famy," spat the newspaper, "consists in attempting to muzzle the South, throttle it, choke it down and strangle it by means of the mili-tary arm into the silent, passive object of ignominious insult, degrada-tion and unparalleled outrage."[30]

A year later, after Griffin and Reynolds had installed the Republicans in power, and in spite of Hancock's moderating influence, the *Ranchero* expanded on its never-ending critique of the army's role in the state. "Under the head of Military Necessity various and sundry things have been done. Under this plea, which is a perfect bar to all answers," continued the *Ranchero*'s complaint, "a nation has well nigh parted with her liberties. Under this claim, which is superior to law, equity, [and] justice, strange things have been done and still stranger things are going to be done," predicted the journal. "What has not been done," challenged the newspaper, "under a military necessity plea?"[31]

Ultimately Texans were not alone in their questioning of military government. There was always a painful uncertainty present in the Civil War and Reconstruction era, a feeling that, despite the war, the nation had never been truly shattered in twain, that the South had never truly seceded.[32] President Lincoln fought the war in large part with this idea uppermost in his mind—and the conflict was officially entitled the War of the Rebellion.[33] The South had accepted defeat in the same mode, adhering to a so-called Southern Theory of Reconstruction, whereby the attempted secession had been crushed by the war and the Union remained whole. The South surrendered honorably, went this viewpoint, agreeing to the authority of the Constitution as it stood in 1860 and automatically reassuming the rights guaranteed to the states in that document. There were individuals perhaps who were guilty of treason, but the vast majority of the citizens and the individual states were not.[34]

Determining the status of the conflict was important, because it made a difference whether the army had occupied an enemy nation (an understandable action, for which there was some precedent) or a section of the United States (a unique and heretofore unparalleled deed).[35] Even General Sheridan came to realize that a forced military occupation was harder on a wayward fragment of your own nationality than on an enemy country.[36] With seven years of the readmission of Texas to the Union in 1870, this questioning of and distaste for forced military occupation would become fairly universal North and South and hallowed in the Compromise of 1877.

The only real compromise Texans were willing to make with their prewar principles in 1865 was to become states' rights nationalists like their Northern Democratic brethren who had opposed Lincoln's "unconstitutional" war measures. This position was the one Governor Throckmorton adopted before Sheridan removed him from office as an "impediment to reconstruction."[37] But in Texas, states' rights meant far more than state authority versus that of the central government. Within the state itself, the doctrine of decentralization was also used to support an exaggerated localism that denied the authority of the state government to compel counties and municipalities to follow its wishes. Even Governor Throckmorton, the only popularly supported governor, found that he could not convince local authorities of the need for minimum compliance with the results of the war.[38] This principle of the rights of local governments was so pervasive that Texans incorporated it into their state constitution in the 1876 revision, which still remains the state's fundamental law today.[39]

In the final analysis, the imposition of military government in Texas and the South went a long way toward compromising the promises of Union victory in the War of the Rebellion. It provided a convenient excuse for the denial of justice and equality to blacks without forcing whites to face up to the racism which made these goals unpalatable.[40]

Although the South lost its War for Southern Independence, it won much of the peace. The concept of equality and the idea of democracy were enshrined in white supremacy. The notion of republicanism was hallowed as states' rights. And the army marched off to the frontier, where its presence would be epitomized as heroic rather than a despicable interference with civil government. But the conflict would be back: the Second Reconstruction was less than a century away.

Abbreviations Used in Notes

AAAG	Acting Assistant Adjutant General
AAG	Assistant Adjutant General
AG	Adjutant General
AGO	Adjutant General's Office, Washington, D.C.
APL	Austin History Center, Austin Public Library
ASCA	Acting Secretary of Civil Affairs
CA	Office of Civil Affairs
Circ.	Circular Orders
CO	Commanding Officer
DG	Division (later Department) of the Gulf Records
DT	District of Texas Records
FB	Records of the Bureau of Refugees, Freedmen, and Abandoned Lands
FMD	Fifth Military District Records
FRC, FW	Federal Records Center, Fort Worth, Texas
GCMO	General Court Martial Orders
GO	General Orders
LC	Archives Division, Library of Congress
LR	Letters Received
LS	Letters Sent
LSU	Department of Archives and Manuscripts, Louisiana State University
MDSW	Military Division (later Department) of the Southwest Records
NA	National Archives
RG	Record Group
SCA	Secretary of Civil Affairs
SO	Special Orders
TAGO	Texas Adjutant General's Office Papers
TR	Telegrams Received

Abbreviations

TS	Telegrams Sent
TSL	Archives, Texas State Library
USA	United States Army
USCI	United States Colored Infantry
UT	Barker Texas History Center, University of Texas

Notes

INTRODUCTION

1. Frank E. Vandiver, "Some Problems Involved in Writing Confederate History," *Journal of Southern History* 36 (1970): 410; C. Vann Woodward, "The Irony of Southern History," ibid. (1953):3–5.

2. Ralph A. Wooster, "Texas," in *The Confederate Governors*, ed. W. Buck Yearns (Athens: University of Georgia Press, 1985), p. 215; David E. Engdahl, "Soldiers, Riots, and Revolutions: The Law of Military Troops in Civil Disorders," *Iowa Law Review* 57 (1971): 53–61.

3. Seymour V. Connor and Odie B. Faulk, *North America Divided: The Mexican War* (New York: Oxford University Press, 1971), pp. 9–11; Justo Sierra, *The Political Evolution of the Mexican People* (Austin: University of Texas Press, 1969), pp. 213–14.

4. Engdahl, "Soldiers, Riots, and Revolutions," pp. 1–70; see also James E. Sefton, *The United States Army and Reconstruction, 1865–1877* (Baton Rouge: Louisiana State University Press, 1967), pp. 253–54; William A. Dunning, *Essays on Civil War and Reconstruction* (New York: Macmillan Company, 1904), pp. 251–52; Henry W. Ballentine, "Unconstitutional Claims of Military Authority," *Yale Law Journal* 24 (1914–15): 201–202.

5. Clarence I. Meek III, "Illegal Law Enforcement: Aiding Civil Authorities in Violation of the Posse Comitatus Act," *Military Law Review* 70 (1975): 83–136; W. S. Holdsworth, "Martial Law Historically Considered," *Law Quarterly Review* 18 (1902): 117–32; George W. Dennison, "Martial Law: The Development of a Theory of Emergency Powers, 1776–1861," *American Journal of Legal History* 18 (1974): 52–54.

6. Bernard Bailyn, *Ideological Origins of the American Revolution* (Cambridge, Mass.: Harvard University Press, 1967), pp. 112–19; John Shy, *Toward Lexington: The Role of the British Army in the Coming of the American Revolution* (Princeton, N.J.: Princeton University Press, 1965); John Phillip Reid, *In Defiance of the Law* (Chapel Hill: University of North Carolina Press, 1981).

7. Merrill Jensen, *The New Nation: A History of the United States during the Confederation, 1781–1789* (New York: Alfred A. Knopf, 1950), pp. 28–30; Jackson Turner Main, *The Anti-Federalists: Critics of the Constitution, 1781–1788* (Chicago: Quadrangle Books, 1964), pp. 146–48.

8. Russell F. Weigley, *History of the United States Army* (New York: Macmillan Co., 1967), pp. 74–94; and his *The American Way of War: A History of United States Military and Strategic Policy* (New York: Macmillan Co., 1973), pp. 40–56.

9. On democracy in the South, see Ralph A. Wooster, *The People in Power: Courthouse and Statehouse in the Lower South* (Knoxville: University of Tennessee Press, 1969), pp. 24–26, 91, 105–107, 113–14, 116–17. See also Fletcher M. Green, "Democracy in the Old South," *Journal of Southern History* 12 (1946): 3–23.

10. Alvy L. King, *Louis T. Wigfall: Southern Fire-Eater* (Baton Rouge: Louisiana State University Press, 1970); Philip J. Avillo, Jr., "John H. Reagan: Unionist or Secessionist?" *East Texas Historical Journal* 13 (1975): 23–33; Alwyn Barr, "The Making of a Secessionist: The Ante-Bellum Career of Roger Q. Mills," *Southwest Historical Quarterly* 79 (1975–76): 129–44.

11. Wooster, "Texas," pp. 195–98; Nancy Head Bowen, "A Political Labyrinth: Texas in the Civil War—Questions in Continuity" (Ph.D. diss., Rice University, 1974), pp. 2–45; and her "A Political Labyrinth: Texas in the Civil War," *East Texas Historical Journal* 11 (1973): 3–11. All further citations from Bowen will be from her dissertation. See also Fredericka Ann Meiners, "The Texas Governorship, 1861–1865: Biography of an Office" (Ph.D. diss., Rice University, 1975), pp. 20–79, 389.

12. Wooster, "Texas," pp. 199–208; Bowen, "Political Labyrinth," pp. 49–118; Meiners, "Texas Governorship," pp. 80–256, 389–91; Robert P. Felgar, "Texas in the War for Southern Independence" (Ph.D. diss., University of Texas, 1935), p. 458. For GO 45, May 30, 1862, DT, which declares the suspension of habeas corpus in selected areas of Texas, see *The War of the Rebellion: The Official Records of the Union and Confederate Armies*, 128 vols. (Washington, 1880–1901), series 1, IX, 715–16 (hereafter cited as *O.R.*, with all references to series 1, unless otherwise noted). For the actions of the military tribunal at San Antonio, see Alwyn Barr, ed., "Records of the Confederate Military Commission in San Antonio, July 2–October 10, 1862," *Southwestern Historical Quarterly* 70 (1966–67): 93–107, 289–313, 623–44, and 71 (1967–68): 247–78.

13. Meiners, "Texas Governorship," 231–55; Florence Elizabeth Holliday, "The Extraordinary Powers and Functions of the General Commanding the Trans-Mississippi Department of the Southern Confederacy" (M.A. thesis,

University of Texas, 1914), p. 14–100; Robert L. Kerby, *Kirby Smith's Confederacy: The Trans-Mississippi South, 1863–1865* (New York: Columbia University Press, 1972), pp. 136–49. See also Lt. Gen. E. Kirby Smith to President Jefferson Davis, September 11, 1863, and Secretary of War James Seddon to Kirby Smith, October 10, 1863, *O.R.*, XXII, pt. 2, pp. 1003–10, 1038–42.

14. Bowen, "Political Labyrinth," pp. 128–37.

15. Ila Mae Myers, "The Relation of Governor Pendleton Murrah of Texas with the Confederate Military Authorities" (M.A. thesis, University of Texas, 1929); Wooster, "Texas," pp. 208–15; Bowen, "Political Labyrinth," pp. 163–254; Meiners, "Texas Governorship," pp. 258–382, 391–92. Most of Kirby-Smith's policies were enforced by his provost marshals; see Allan C. Ashcraft, "Role of the Confederate Provost Marshals in Texas," *Texana* 6 (1968): 390–92.

16. Bowen, "Political Labyrinth," pp. 185–218, 241–43; Meiners, "Texas Governorship," pp. 260–318; quotation from James W. Throckmorton to Benjamin H. Epperson, June 18, 1864, Epperson Papers, UT.

17. Bowen, "Political Labyrinth," p. 247 n. 27, 319; Meiners, "Texas Governorship," pp. 6–7. The law is in James M. Matthews, ed., *Statutes at Large of the Confederate States of America, Commencing with the First Session of the First Congress* (Richmond, Va.: R. M. Smith, 1862–64), 1st. Cong., 4th sess., pp. 187–89.

18. Bowen, "Political Labyrinth," pp. 261–63; 26 *Texas Reports* at 387, especially pp. 406–407, 410, 412, 413–14, 415–16.

19. The cases are outlined in Charles L. Robards, *Synopses of the Decisions of the Supreme Court of the State of Texas . . . for Writs of Habeas Corpus* (Austin: Brown & Foster, 1865), an important volume, as of the twenty-five cases extant, only five of them are in *Texas Reports*. See 26 ibid. at p. 385, and 27 ibid. at pp. 105, 705, 715, 731. See also Bowen, "Political Labyrinth," p. 235.

20. Quotation from Bowen, "Political Labyrinth," p. 243; see also p. 253 n. 98; Meiners, "Texas Governorship," pp. 366–68.

21. Bowen, "Political Labyrinth," p. 288; Meiners, "Texas Governorship," p. 319. For Texans' resentment of Confederate military rule, see Lois Ellsworth, "San Antonio during the Civil War" (M.A. thesis, University of Texas, 1938), pp. 48–59.

22. C. Vann Woodward, "Seeds of Failure in Radical Race Policy," in *New Frontiers of the American Reconstruction*, ed. Harold Hyman (Urbana: University of Illinois Press, 1966), pp. 124–47; Dunning, *Civil War and Reconstruction*, pp. 251–52; Avery O. Craven, *Reconstruction: The Ending of the Civil War* (New York: Holt, Rinehart & Winston, 1969), pp. 304–307; Barry

A. Crouch and L. J. Schultz, "Crisis in Color: Racial Separation in Texas Reconstruction," *Civil War History* 16 (1969): 37–49; Philip J. Avillo, Jr., "Phantom Radicals: Texas Republicans in Congress, 1870–1873," *Southwestern Historical Quarterly* 77 (1973–74): 431–44.

23. The conclusion in William John Ulrich, "The Northern Military Mind in Regard to Reconstruction, 1865–1872; The Attitudes of Ten Leading Union Generals" (Ph.D. diss., Ohio State University, 1959), pp. 368–74, that Reconstruction would have been different if run by soldiers alone, overlooks this problem. See Engdahl, "Soldiers, Riots, and Revolutions," p. 56.

24. Engdahl, "Soldiers, Riots, and Revolutions," pp. 56, 61, 65 n. 318, 67, 70. On continued use of the army to maintain civil order, see Meek, "Illegal Law Enforcement," pp. 83–136; H. W. C. Furman, "Restrictions upon the Use of the Army Imposed by the Posse Comitatus Act," *Military Law Review* 79 (1959): 85–129; Paul Jackson Rice, "New Laws and Insights Encircle the Posse Comitatus Act," ibid. 104 (1984): 109–38.

25. Frank L. Owsley, *State Rights in the Confederacy* (Chicago, University of Chicago Press, 1925); David Donald, "Died of Democracy," in *Why the North Won the Civil War*, ed. Donald (New York: Macmillan Co., pp. 79–90.

26. Meiners, "Texas Governorship," pp. 383, 392.

27. See, for example, Alma Dexta King, "The Political Career of Williamson Simpson Oldham" (M.A. thesis, University of Texas, 1929), p. 185. Oldham, who served in the Confederate Senate alongside Louis T. Wigfall, believed that the Confederacy was defeated by too much, not by too little, centralism.

1: THE OCCUPATION OF TEXAS

1. Francis B. Heitman, *Historical Register and Dictionary of the United States Army . . .* , 2 vols. (Washington, D.C.: Government Printing Office, 1903), I, 881; C. W. Denison, *Illustrated Life, Campaigns, and Public Services of Philip H. Sheridan* (Philadelphia: T. B. Peterson & Bros., 1865), 25–29, 33, 35; *Proceedings of the State Assembly of the State of New York, on the Life and Services of Gen. Philip H. Sheridan, as Held at the Capitol, April 9, 1889* (Albany: J. B. Lyon, 1890), 13–22, 29–30; Carl Coke Rister, *Border Command: General Phil Sheridan in the West* (Norman: University of Oklahoma Press, 1944), p. 7; Ezra J. Warner, *Generals in Blue: Lives of the Union Commanders* (Baton Rouge: Louisiana State University Press, 1964), pp. 437–39; Mark M. Boatner III, *The Civil War Dictionary* (New York: David McKay Company, 1959), pp. 747–48. An interesting analysis of Sheridan is in Russell F. Weigley, "Philip H. Sheridan: A Personality Profile," *Civil War Times Illus-*

trated 7 (1968–69): 46–47. The most recent biography of Sheridan is Paul Andrew Hutton, *Phil Sheridan and His Army* (Lincoln: University of Nebraska Press, 1985). Hutton emphasizes Sheridan's Indian fighting days and, in discussing Sheridan's Reconstruction policy, finds that he "executed the laws of Congress with the same vigor with which he charged up Missionary Ridge, treating civil officials as if they were subordinates in his army" (p. 27).

2. Philip H. Sheridan, *Personal Memoirs of Philip H. Sheridan*, 2 vols. (New York: Charles L. Webster, 1888), II, 209, 210–11.

3. Grant to Sheridan, May 17, 1865; Sheridan to Grant, May 29, 1865, Grant Papers, LC.

4. The command area included all territory west of the Mississippi and south of Arkansas to Mexico. See GO 1, May 29, 1865, MDSW, RG 94, NA; Sheridan to Grant, May 29, 1865, Grant Papers, LC.

5. Canby's command area included Louisiana, Mississippi, Alabama, and Florida. It overlapped Sheridan's zone in western Louisiana, where both officers had independent and conflicting authority. The surrender negotiations are in O.R. XLVIII, pt. 2, pp. 591, 600–602, 604, 606, 692; *Official Records of the Union and Confederate Navies in the War of Rebellion*, 26 vols. (Washington, D.C.: Government Printing Office, 1894–1922), series 1, XXII, pp. 196–97, 198, 199, 202, 206, 273 (hereafter cited as O.R.N., with all citations to series 1, unless otherwise noted). See also Charles W. Ramsdell, *Reconstruction in Texas* (New York: Columbia University Press, 1910), pp. 27–40.

6. Ramsdell, *Reconstruction in Texas*, pp. 33–41; Robert W. Shook, "Federal Occupation and Administration of Texas, 1865–1870" (Ph.D. diss., North Texas State University, 1970), pp. 20–24; Edmund Thornton Miller, *A Financial History of Texas* (Austin: University of Texas Press, 1916), p. 155; Louis J. Wortham, *A History of Texas from Wilderness to Commonwealth*, 5 vols. (Fort Worth: Wortham-Molyneaux Co., 1924), IV, 364–65; *Appleton's Annual Cyclopaedia* (1865), p. 786. Confederate officers tried to control their men but failed. Others, in their haste to reach Mexico, abandoned their commands or were abandoned by them. See Thomas Affleck to John Andrews, May 23, 1865, Affleck Papers, LSU. See also William L. Richter, "'It Is Best to Go in Strong-Handed': Army Occupation of Texas, 1865–1866," *Arizona and the West* 27 (1985): 113–42.

7. Thatcher to Maj. Gen. N. P. Banks, May 31, 1865; Canby to Thatcher, May 31, 1865; Thatcher to Canby, May 31, 1865; Gustava Vasa Fox to secretary of the navy, June 8, 1865, O.R.N. XXII, 209–11, 216–17.

8. "Army of Observation" was the official title of the invasion force and not as Shook implies, a phrase coined by later commentators. See his "Federal Occupation," p. 143, and also his "Custer's Texas Command," *Military History of Texas and the Southwest* 9 (1971): 49, 54 n. 4. Sheridan used the

XIII Corps from Alabama and Louisiana with elements already in the Rio Grande valley, the IV corps from Tennessee, and the XXV (Colored) Corps from Virginia. The VII Corps from Arkansas was originally to be used, but Sheridan cancelled its participation. See SO 4, June 7, 1865, MDSW, RG 94, NA; Sheridan to Bvt. Maj. Gen. John A. Rawlins, June 4, 1865, *O.R.*, XLVIII, pt. 2, p. 767.

9. Heitman, *Historical Register*, I, 469; Warner, *Generals in Blue*, p. 181; Boatner, *Civil War Dictionary*, pp. 351–52.

10. GO 3, June 19, 1865, DT, RG 94, NA.

11. GO 4, June 19, 1865, ibid.

12. Granger to Sheridan, June 19, 1865, *O.R.*, XLVIII, pt. 2, pp. 927–28. See also AAG to Col. W. F. Moore, June 19, 1865, AAG to Col. John Kelly, June 28, 1865, AAG to Maj. Gen. C. C. Andrews, July 11, 1865, Andrews to AAG, July 11, 1865, all in ibid., pp. 931, 1017–18, 1078; Frank MacD. Spindler, "The History of Hempstead and the Formation of Waller County," *Southwestern Historical Quarterly* 63 (1959–60): 419; Mrs. R. E. Chapman to Thomas Affleck, August 7, 1865, Affleck Papers, LSU.

13. Maj. Gen. N. P. Banks to AAG, May 30, 1865, Maj. Gen. Francis Herron to AAG, June 16, 18, 1865, *O.R.*, LXVIII, pt. 2, pp. 677–78, 903, 918; Max S. Lale, "Military Occupation of Marshall, Texas, by the Eighth Illinois Volunteer Infantry, U.S.A., 1865," *Military History of Texas and the Southwest* 13 (1976): 39–47; *Flake's Daily Bulletin* (Galveston), June 28, 1865.

14. See various communiqués between Grant, Sheridan, Granger, and Steele, *O.R.*, XLVIII, pt. 2, pp. 601–602, 716–17, 927–28, 930, 931; Steele to Sheridan, June 20, 1865, Sheridan Papers, LC; Sheridan to Grant, August 1, 1865, Grant Papers, LC.

15. See various letters between Rawlins, Grant, Weitzel, Halleck, *O.R.*, XLVI, pt. 3, pp. 1125, 1130, 1168, 1193; Sheridan to Weitzel, June 2, 1865, Sheridan Papers, LC; Granger to Brig. Gen. R. H. Jackson, June 8, 1865, *O.R.*, XLVIII, pt. 2, p. 819; Col. C. G. Sawtell to Maj. Gen. Montgomery Meigs, December 13, 1865, ibid., LIII, 607.

16. See IV Corps correspondence in *O.R.*, XLIX, pt. 2, pp. 537, 1023, LIII, 605–609; Grant to Sheridan, May 31, 1865, Sheridan to Rawlins, June 13, 1865, Grant Papers, LC; Sheridan to Grant, June 28, 1865, box 9, RG 108, NA.

17. Maj. Gen. D. S. Stanley to Prov. Gov. A. J. Hamilton, August 8, 1865, Governor's Papers (Hamilton), TSL.

18. GO 1, Second Brigade, Third Division, IV Corps, September 10, 1865, *O.R.*, XLVIII, pt. 2, pp. 1223–24.

19. For the command structure, see SO 249, May 22, 1865, AGO, ibid., XLVI, pt. 3, pp. 1193, 1195; GO 4, June 9, 1865, MDSW, RG 94, NA. Sheridan assembled the columns in northern Louisiana because the lower part of the state was too swampy. See Sheridan to Grant, June 5, 1865, Grant Papers, NA.

20. Sheridan to Maj. Gen. Wesley Merritt, July 5, 1865, Sheridan Papers, LC. Information on Merritt's column is in Samuel A. Fletcher and D. H. Fletcher, *History of Co. "A", Second [Illinois] Cavalry* (Chicago, 1912), pp. 165–66; Sheridan to Granger, June 29, 1865, O.R., XLVIII, pt. 2, p. 1026; *Flake's Daily Bulletin* (Galveston), July 13, 15, 31, 1865; *Dallas Herald*, August 5, 1865; *Galveston Daily News*, August 11, 1865. Merritt was about ten days behind his anticipated schedule. See A. R. Roessler to A. J. Hamilton, June 21, 1865, Governor's Papers (Hamilton), TSL.

21. Charles Henry Lothrop, *A History of the First Regiment Iowa Cavalry* . . . (Lyons, Iowa: Beers & Eaton, 1890), p. 216. J. Monaghan, *Custer: The Life of General George Armstrong Custer* (Boston: Little Brown & Co., 1959), pp. 251–52.

22. See particularly Grierson to his wife, June 21, 1875, Benjamin H. Grierson Papers, Southwest Collection, Texas Tech University, Lubbock. The best study of Grierson, who emerged from Sheridan's exile to enjoy a long military career in the colored cavalry service, is Bruce J. Dinges, "The Making of a Cavalryman: Benjamin H. Grierson and the Civil War along the Mississippi, 1861–1865" (Ph.D. diss., Rice University, 1978); see also William H. Leckie and Shirley Leckie, *Unlikely Warriors: General Benjamin Grierson and His Family* (Norman: University of Oklahoma Press, 1984), especially p. 132.

23. Thomas Sydenham Cogley, *History of the Seventh Indiana Cavalry Volunteers* . . . (Laporte, Ind., 1876), pp. 167–74, 182; Lothrop, *First Iowa Cavalry*, p. 239. The detailed orders of march for the columns are given in Lothrop, pp. 220–22. See also *Flake's Daily Bulletin* (Galveston), July 15, 1865. For more on Custer, see William L. Richter, "'A Better Time Is in Store for Us': An Analysis of the Reconstruction Attitudes of George Armstrong Custer," *Military History of Texas and the Southwest* 11 (1973): 31–50; Shook, "Custer's Texas Command," pp. 49–50.

24. GO 95, May 17, 1865, AGO, RG 94, NA.

25. Sheridan to Rawlins, July 3, 7, 1865, Sheridan to Grant, July 4, 1865, Grant to Sheridan, July 6, 1865, Grant Papers, LC.

26. GO 1, July 17, GO 4, July 20, 1865, MDSW, RG 94, NA.

27. Granger to Johnson, May 29, 1865, Andrew Johnson Papers, LC; Grant to Sheridan, July 13, 1865, Sheridan to Grant, July 15, 1865, Grant

Papers, LC; GO 5, June 30, 1865, AAG to [Maj. Gen. T. J. Wood], August 6, 1865, in *O.R.*, XLVIII, pt. 2, pp. 1031–32, 1169–70; *Standard* (Clarksville), August 5, 1865; *Flake's Tri-Weekly Bulletin* (Galveston), June 17, 1865.

28. Sheridan to Grant, July 15, 1865 (original spelling retained). See also Bvt. Brig. Gen. George A. Forsyth to Granger, July 19, 1865, and SO 2, July 15, 1865, MDSW, in *O.R.*, XLVIII, pt. 2, pp. 1081, 1093.

29. Heitman, *Historical Register*, I, 1062; Warner, *Generals in Blue*, pp. 170–71; Boatner, *Civil War Dictionary*, pp. 949–50.

30. John L. Waller, *Colossal Hamilton of Texas: A Biography of Andrew Jackson Hamilton* (El Paso: Texas Western Press, 1968), pp. ix, 3–55; John Robert Adkins, "The Public Career of A. J. Hamilton" (M.A. thesis, University of Texas, 1947), p. 146; Homer Thrall, *A Pictorial History of Texas from the Earliest Visits of European Adventures to A.D. 1879* (St. Louis: N. D. Thompson & Co., 1879), pp. 549–50.

31. Maj. Gen. C. C. Andrews to President A. Johnson, July 28, 1865, Johnson Papers, LC; Waller, *Colossal Hamilton*, pp. 58–61; Wortham, *History of Texas* V, 2; Ernest Wallace, *Texas in Turmoil, 1849–1875* (Austin: Steck-Vaughn Co., 1965), p. 163; Ramsdell, *Reconstruction in Texas*, pp. 55–58; Allan C. Ashcraft, "Texas in Defeat: The Early Phase of A. J. Hamilton's Provisional Governorship, June 17, 1865, to February 7, 1866," *Texas Military History* 8 (1970): 203.

32. Undated Speech, 1865, A. J. Hamilton Papers, UT (original spelling retained). See also Waller, *Colossal Hamilton*, p. 62. Gideon Welles, *Diary of Gideon Welles*, ed. Howard K. Beale, 3 vols. (New York: Houghton, Mifflin Co., 1911), II, 315–16, mentions that Pease was nearly chosen as provisional governor over Hamilton. Shook's ironic comment in "Federal Occupation," p. 148, is in error. Pease was never a Radical Republican choice for governor. See Roger A. Griffin, "A Connecticut Yankee in Texas: A Biography of Elisha Marshall Pease" (Ph.D. diss., University of Texas, 1973), pp. 185–89.

33. Hamilton to Johnson, July 24, 1865, Hamilton Papers, UT; Hamilton to Johnson, August 30, 1865, Johnson Papers, LC; Ashcraft, "Texas in Defeat," pp. 202–203; Waller, *Colossal Hamilton*, pp. 62–63; Griffin, "Pease," p. 187.

34. Hamilton to Wright, October 4, 1865, RG 307, TSL.

35. Hamilton to Johnson, August 30, 1865, James H. Bell and others to Johnson, August 30, 1865, Johnson Papers, LC.

36. For troop figures in August, 1865, see Sheridan to AAG, August 8, 1865, *O.R.*, XLVIII, pt. 2, p. 1171.

37. Kathryn Abbey Hanna, "The Role of the South in the French Intervention in Mexico," *Journal of Southern History* 20 (1954): 16–18; Thomas

Schoonover, "Confederate Diplomacy and the Texas-Mexican Border, 1861–
1866," *East Texas Historical Journal* 11 (1973): 33–39. See also Grant to
Sheridan, May 17, 1865, *O.R.*, XLVIII, pt. 2, p. 746; Grant to Sheridan,
July 25, 1865, in *Proceedings of the State Assembly*, pp. 50–51.

38. Sheridan to Grant, December 16, 1865, Sheridan Papers. LC. This
attitude was probably caused by the extreme nervousness of the French over
the presence of so many American soldiers. See Sheridan to Grant, June 28,
November 20, 1865, Grant Papers, LC.

39. Seward's desire to bluff the French into withdrawing from Mexico is
emphasized in Dexter Perkins, *The Monroe Doctrine, 1826–1867* (Baltimore:
Johns Hopkins University Press, 1933), pp. 467, 476, 502, 504; and Thomas
D. Schoonover, "Mexican–United States Relations, 1861–1867" (Ph.D.
diss., University of Minnesota, 1970), pp. 156–77. For the order restricting
local initiative, see Grant to Sheridan, June 19, 1865, Grant Papers, LC. For
the reprimand of General Brown for undue friendliness toward the French,
see Sheridan to Steele, June 29, 1865, Sheridan Papers, LC. Also Grant to
Sheridan, July 1, December 1, 19, 1865, Grant Papers, LC; Sheridan to
Granger, July 5, 1865, Sheridan Papers, LC; Grant to Sheridan, July 25,
1865, in *Proceedings of the State Assembly*, pp. 50–51.

40. *Flake's Daily Bulletin* (Galveston), January 4, 1866; Sheridan to
Wright, January 7, 1866, Sheridan Papers, LC; Sheridan to Grant, November 20, 1865, January 12, 1866, Grant Papers, LC.

41. E. H. Saulnier to Seward, January 13, 1867, E. H. Plumb to Seward,
March 7, 1867, Seward to Campbell, April 6, June 1, 1867, Campbell to
Seward, May 15, 28, 30, 1867, *House Executive Documents*, 40th Cong.,
1st sess., no. 30, pp. 39, 42, 58, 63, 69, 70; Sheridan to Grant, April 18,
May 27, 1867, Grant Papers, LC. The *Brownsville Daily Ranchero* sold out its
issues of June 28 and 29, 1867, in which it announced Maximilian's death.

42. The theme of a connection between the American Civil War and the
French intervention was constantly expressed, not only by Sheridan, but
by Grant and Matías Romero, the Juarista minister to Washington. See
Sheridan to Rawlins, November 14, 1866, *O.R.*, XLVIII, pt. 1, p. 300;
Sheridan to Grant, June 29, 1867, Grant Papers, LC; Sheridan, *Personal
Memoirs*, II, 227–28; Robert Ryal Miller, "Matías Romero: Mexican Minister
to the United States during the Juárez-Maximilian Era," *Hispanic-American
Historical Review* 45 (1965): 231. On the reasons for French withdrawal, see
C. A. Duniway, "Reasons for the Withdrawal of the French from Mexico,"
American Historical Association, *Annual Report* (1902), I, 317, 319, 321,
327–28. Albert Guerard, in his *Napoleon III: A Great Life in Brief* (New York:
Alfred A. Knopf, 1955), pp. 162–63, 329–40, contrasts the halfhearted
support the French gave Maximilian with their conquest of Morocco, where

it took millions of francs, forty years of occupation, and a standing army of between sixty thousand and eighty-five thousand men to subdue that part of Africa alone. For a modern version of Secretary Seward's decisive influence on the French retreat from Mexico, see Perkins, *Monroe Doctrine*, pp. 514–21; and Alfred Jackson Hanna and Kathryn Abbey Hanna, *Napoleon III and Mexico: American Triumph over Monarchy* (Chapel Hill: University of North Carolina Press, 1971). Also of interest is Lynn M. Case, ed., *French Opinion on the United States and Mexico, 1860–1867* (New York: D. Appleton-Century Co., 1936), pp. 402–36. A thorough discussion of U.S. assistance appears in Robert B. Brown, "Guns over the Boarder: American Aid to the Juárez Government during the French Intervention" (Ph.D. diss., University of Michigan, 1951).

43. Even brigades that had served together during the war were broken up, and only a part of their regiments was sent to Texas, all of which angered and dismayed the men. For examples of partial musters-out, see Fletcher and Fletcher, *Second [Illinois] Cavalry*, p. 163; Asbury L. Kerwood, *Annals of the Fifty-seventh Regiment Indiana Volunteers . . .* (Dayton, Ohio: W. J. Shuey, 1868), p. 316; Charles T. Clark, *Opdyke Tigers, 125th Ohio Volunteer Infantry . . .* (Columbus: Spahr & Glenn, 1895), pp. 389, 391; SO 25, July 18, 1865, DT, RG 94, NA.

44. *Flake's Daily Bulletin* (Galveston), January 12, 1866. The record of the battalion is in Frederick H. Dyer, *A Compendium of the War of the Rebellion*, 3 vols. (New York: Thomas Yoseloff, 1959), III, 15–19. See also AAG to CO, Post of Galveston, February 26, 1866, LS, Central DT, RG 393, NA; *Flake's Daily Bulletin* (Galveston), March 20, 22, 1866; Grant to Sheridan, April 10, 1866, Grant Papers, LC; Sheridan to Wright, April 10, 1866, Sheridan Papers, LC. The mutiny of the Forty-eighth Ohio Battalion is not reported in Sefton, *Army and Reconstruction*, p. 51.

45. *Bellville Countryman*, August 18, 1865.

46. Sheridan to Rawlins, June 21, 1866, Sheridan to Brig. Gen. E. D. Townsend, August 24, 1866, Sheridan Papers, LC. See also post rosters, MSS, RG 94, NA.

47. The last nine regiments and one battalion left in May, 1866. Hamilton's letter was prompted by the muster-out of twenty-three infantry regiments, four cavalry regiments, a cavalry battalion, and two artillery batteries in November and December, 1865. See Hamilton to Sheridan, January 17, 1866, Andrew Johnson Papers, LC. Sheridan initially agreed with Governor Hamilton.

48. Sheridan to Grant, October 7, 1865, January 20, 1866, Grant to Sheridan, January 22, 1866, Grant Papers, LC.

49. May 1, 1866. The only volunteer regiment known to have expressed a desire to stay in the service was the First Texas (Union) Cavalry. One Unionist, John L. Haynes, wrote to Governor Hamilton that their muster-out would be a blow to loyalism and would invite atrocities from former Confederates (Haynes to Hamilton, August 25, 1865, Governor's Papers [Hamilton], TSL). Nonetheless, the regiment was mustered out a month later (Sheridan to Merritt, September 20, 1865, Sheridan Papers, LC).

50. Sheridan to Rawlins, November 15, 1865, Grant Papers, LC.

51. James Larson, "Memoirs," p. 217, MS in James Larson Papers, UT.

52. Fletcher and Fletcher, *Second [Illinois] Cavalry*, p. 168; Larson, "Memoirs," pp. 218–19.

53. Lothrop, *First Iowa Cavalry*, pp. 294–97. One company of the Sixth U.S. Cavalry was sent to New Orleans for orderly service with Sheridan's headquarters. See W. H. Carter, *From Yorktown to Santiago with the Sixth U.S. Cavalry* (Baltimore: Lord Baltimore Press, 1900), p. 36.

54. Heitman, *Historical Register*, I, 113–15.

55. C. St. Chubb, "The Seventeenth Regiment of Infantry," in *The Army of the United States*, ed. Theodore F. Rodenbough and William L. Haskin (New York: Maynard, Merrill & Co., 1896), p. 637; Aubrey A. Wilson, "A Soldier of the Texas Frontier: Brevet Major Robert Patterson Wilson, United States Army," West Texas Historical Association *Year Book* 34 (1958): 86.

56. *Flake's Daily Bulletin* (Galveston), February 25, 27, 28, April 25, 26, 27, May 3, 17, 19, June 5, 22, 1866; *Galveston Daily News*, March 29, April 26, May 17, 19, 1866. For more on this incident and others involving the army and the civilian population, see William L. Richter, "Spread-Eagle Eccentricities: Military-Civilian Relations in Reconstruction Texas," *Texana* 7 (1970): 311–27.

57. Wright to AAG, July 21, 1866, *House Reports*, 39th Cong., 2d sess., no. 61, p. 4.

58. St. Chubb, "Seventeenth Regiment," 637. It took months to fill out the complements of each new regiment. See Bvt. Maj. Gen. S. P. Heintzelman to AAG, November 23, 1866, TR, DG, RG 393, NA; Sheridan to AG, USA, January 31, 1867, LS, FMD, RG 393, NA; Grant to Secretary of War Stanton, April 10, 1867, Grant Papers, LC.

59. See *Appleton's Annual Cyclopaedia* (1866), 30–33; Sheridan to Brig. Gen. E. D. Townsend, October 24, 1866, Sheridan Papers, LC. Brief sketches of each regiment are in Heitman, *Historical Register*, I, 113–15, 125–26, 133.

60. Sheridan to Rawlins, November 14, 1866, O.R., XLVIII, pt. 1, pp. 300, 301.

1. Sheridan to Rawlins, November 14, 1866, O.R., XLVIII, pt. 1, p. 301.
2. Sheridan to Rawlins, October 1, 1866, Sheridan Papers, LC.
3. Sheridan to Rawlins, November 14, 1866, O.R., XLVIII, pt. 1, p. 301.
4. C. Vann Woodward, "Equality: The Deferred Commitment," *American Scholar* 27 (1958): 459–72. See also his "Seeds of Failure," pp. 124–47.
5. These figures are estimates. See Hubert Howe Bancroft, *History of the North Mexican States and Texas*, 2 vols. (San Francisco: H. H. Bancroft, 1889), II, 480. Wallace's figures of 200,000 for 1861 and 400,000 for 1865 (*Texas in Turmoil*, p. 153) are closer to the 1860 census, which lists 182,566 slaves. See Joseph C. G. Kennedy, comp., *Population of the United States in 1860* . . . (Washington, D.C.: Government Printing Office, 1864), pp. 479, 483. The historian of Matagorda County claims that so many Negroes were sent there from the rest of the South during the war that whites in the county remained in the minority until 1910. See John Columbus Marr, "The History of Matagorda County, Texas" (M.A. thesis, University of Texas, 1928), p. 163. The 1870 census, however, shows a substantial decrease in black population in comparison with the 1865 estimates. See Francis A Walker, comp., *The Statistics of the Population of the United States* . . . (Washington, D.C.: Government Printing Office, 1872), p. 65.
6. U.S., *Statutes at Large*, XIII, 507–509. General works on the bureau include Oliver Otis Howard, *Autobiography*, 2 vols. (New York: Baker & Taylor, 1908); Paul Skeels Pierce, *The Freedmen's Bureau: A Chapter in the History of Reconstruction* (Iowa City: University of Iowa Press, 1904); W. E. Burghardt DuBois, "The Freedmen's Bureau," *Atlantic Monthly* 87 (1901): 354–65; John Cox and La Wanda Cox, "General Howard and the 'Misrepresented Bureau,'" *Journal of Southern History* 19 (1953): 427–56; George R. Bentley, *A History of the Freedmen's Bureau* (Philadelphia: University of Pennsylvania Press, 1955); John A. Carpenter, *Sword and Olive Branch: Oliver Otis Howard* (Pittsburgh: University of Pittsburgh Press, 1964); William S. McFeely, *Yankee Stepfather: General O. O. Howard and the Freedmen* (New Haven: Yale University Press, 1968). On Texas, the standard study of the bureau is still Claude Elliott, "The Freedmen's Bureau in Texas," *Southwestern Historical Quarterly* 56 (1952–53): 1–24. An excellent analysis of the bureau personnel in Texas is Lonnie Sinclair, "The Freedmen's Bureau and Texas: The Assistant Commissioners and the Negro" (Paper submitted to the Institute of Southern History, Johns Hopkins University, Baltimore, July 22, 1969; I thank Edward Rademaker for drawing my attention to this paper). The most recent comprehensive study is James Smallwood, *Time of Hope*,

Time of Despair: Black Texans during Reconstruction (Port Washington, N.Y.: National University Publications, 1981). For a survey of the literature and problems of the bureau in Texas, see Barry A. Crouch, "Hidden Sources of Black History: The Texas Freedmen's Bureau Records as a Case Study," *Southwestern Historical Quarterly* 83 (1979–80): 211–26; and his "Freedmen's Bureau Records: Texas, a Case Study," in *Afro-American History: Sources for Research,* ed. Robert L. Clarke (Washington, D.C.: Howard University Press, 1981), pp. 74–94.

7. Elliott, "Freedmen's Bureau in Texas," p. 3.

8. This policy was informal at first and later made mandatory. See Capt. ———— Abert to AAG, June 9, 1866, LR, FB, RG 105, NA.

9. See Nat Hart Davis to Hamilton, August [?], 1865, Governor's Papers (Hamilton), TSL; and testimony of Bvt. Maj. Gen. Davis S. Stanley, *House Reports,* 39th Cong., 1st sess., no. 39, p. 39, for the belief that former slaveholders would be compensated for the loss of their slaves. For an excellent analysis of the postwar movement of blacks, see James Smallwood, "Black Texans during Reconstruction: First Freedom," *East Texas Historical Journal* 14 (1976): 11–23.

10. See, for example, Thomas Ford and others to Hamilton, September 6, 1865, W. Longworth to Hamilton, October 9, 10, 1865, T. S. Richardson to Hamilton, September [?], 1865, Governor's Papers (Hamilton), TSL; Maurine Mattie O'Bannion, "The History of Caldwell County" (M.A. thesis, University of Texas, 1931), pp. 45–46.

11. John E. Thompson to Hamilton, October 8, 1865, D. J. Baldwin to Hamilton, November 7, 1865, Governor's Papers (Hamilton), TSL.

12. C. W. Buckley to Hamilton, August 22, 1865, ibid.; John William Rogers, *The Lusty Texans of Dallas* (New York: E. P. Dutton & Co., 1951), pp. 101, 102.

13. Fred C. Cole, "The Texas Career of Thomas Affleck" (Ph.D. diss., Louisiana State University, 1942), pp. 227–46; Alonzo Bettis Cox, "The Economic History of Texas during the Period of Reconstruction" (M.A. thesis, University of Texas, 1948), p. 428; Berta Lowman, "The Cotton Industry in Texas during the Reconstruction Period" (M.A. thesis, University of Texas, 1927), pp. 55, 69, 73, 124.

14. The source of this myth is hard to identify. There were no abandoned lands in Texas, as in other Southern states, to give to the freedmen. The army, the bureau, and the executive branch have all been blamed. See, for example, Ramsdell, *Reconstruction in Texas,* p. 72; Theodore B. Wilson, *The Black Codes of the South* (University, Ala.: University of Alabama Press, 1965), pp. 55–56; La Wanda Cox, "The Promise of Land for the Freedmen,"

Mississippi Valley Historical Review 45 (1958–59): 413–40; Martin Abbott, "Free Land, Free Labor, and the Freedmen's Bureau," *Agricultural History* 30 (1956): 150–56.

15. Pierce, *Freedmen's Bureau*, p. 53; A. Cox, "Economic History of Texas," p. 35.

16. J. O. Thally to Hamilton, November 6, 1865, Charles P. Stuart to Hamilton, November 27, 1865, citizens of Liberty County to Hamilton, November ———, 1865, Governor's Papers (Hamilton), TSL.

17. W. B. Price to Hamilton, December 23, 1865, F. W. Grossmeyer to Hamilton, November 22, 1865, ibid.; 1st Lt. C. C. Hardenbrook to AAG, June 18, 1866, LR, FB, RG 105, NA. For more on the insurrection panic of 1865, see Dan T. Carter, "The Anatomy of Fear: The Christmas Day Insurrection Scare of 1865," *Journal of Southern History* 42 (1976): 345–64.

18. Elliott, "Freedmen's Bureau in Texas," pp. 1–3; Bentley, *History of the Freedmen's Bureau*, pp. 60, 121; Howard, *Autobiography*, II, 217–18; McFeely, *Yankee Stepfather*, pp. 72–73; Pierce, *Freedmen's Bureau*, pp. 47–48.

19. Circ. 1, October 12, 1865, FB, RG 105, NA.

20. Proclamation to the people, September 11, 1865, and Proclamation to the freedmen, November 17, 1865, RG 307, TSL. See also Hamilton to President Johnson, Johnson Papers, LC.

21. See, for example, Mrs. C. Forshey to AAG, December 9, 1865, LR, FB, RG 105, NA; Ramsdell, *Reconstruction in Texas*, p. 73 n. 2; Elliott, "Freedmen's Bureau in Texas," p. 3; Wallace, *Texas in Turmoil*, p. 154.

22. Gregory to Howard, December 9, 1865, *House Executive Documents*, 39th Cong., 1st sess., no. 70, pp. 374–77.

23. Elliott, "Freedmen's Bureau in Texas," pp. 5–6, portrays the two men as differing in attitudes. He confuses, however, the journey that Gregory and Strong made together with the one taken by Gregory alone. See McFeely, *Yankee Stepfather*, pp. 68–70; Strong to Howard, January 1, 1866, *House Executive Documents*, 39th Cong., 1st sess., no. 70, pp. 308–12.

24. Gregory to Howard, January 31, 1866, *House Executive Documents*, 39th Cong., 1st sess., no. 70, pp. 304–305.

25. Mintzer to Gregory, January 31, 1866, ibid., p. 307.

26. Gregory to Howard, October 12, 1865, LS, FB, RG 105, NA. See, for example, Sam L. Earle to James H. Bell, October 13, 1865, James H. Bell Papers, UT; G. M. Martin to Hamilton, August 1, 1865, Governor's Papers (Hamilton), TSL.

27. Circ. 2, December 5, 1865, Circ. 4, December 29, 1865, FB, RG 105, NA. See also Shook, "Federal Occupation," p. 247.

28. Gregory to Howard, September 21, 1865, LS, FB, RG 105, NA;

Gregory to Howard, January 31, 1866, Strong to Howard, January 1, 1866, *House Executive Documents,* 39th Cong., 1st sess., no. 70, pp. 306, 313.

29. Gregory's policies are found in his circular letter, October 17, 1865, LS, FB, RG 105, NA; Circ. 2, December 5, Circ. 3, December 9, 1865, FB, RG 105, NA; Gregory to Benjamin G. Harris, January 20, 1866, LS, FB, RG 105, NA. For tax policies, see *Flake's Daily Bulletin* (Galveston), January 6, 1866. The daily efforts of a local agency are revealed in Barry A. Crouch, "The Freedmen's Bureau of the 30th Sub-District in Texas: Smith County and Its Environs during Reconstruction," *Chronicles of Smith County, Texas* 11 (1972): 17–20.

30. A. P. McCormick to Hamilton, November 13, 1865, Governor's Papers (Hamilton), TSL.

31. Thomas Affleck to Alexander Hannay, July 14, 1865, Affleck Papers, LSU.

32. Circ. 4, March 6, 1866, FB, RG 105, NA.

33. Sinclair, "Freedmen's Bureau and Texas," pp. 4–6.

34. *Galveston Daily News,* January 21, 1866.

35. Circ. 12, March 30, 1866, FB, RG 105, NA. Before leaving Texas, Gregory made another tour of inspection. He later took over bureau operations in Maryland. See Elliott, "Freedmen's Bureau in Texas," pp. 10–14; Bentley, *History of the Freedmen's Bureau,* p. 121; McFeely, *Yankee Stepfather,* pp. 68–70; *Galveston Daily News,* June 20, 1866.

36. Circ. 13, 1866, April 2, 1866, FB, RG 105, NA; Heitman, *Historical Register,* I, 596; Boatner, *Civil War Dictionary,* pp. 458–59; Elizabeth B. Custer, *Tenting on the Plains; or, General Custer in Kansas and Texas* (New York: Charles L. Webster, 1887), p. 305; McFeely, *Yankee Stepfather,* pp. 92–93.

37. Circ. 14, May 15, 1866, FB, RG 105, NA.

38. Circ. 17, June 19, 1866, ibid.

39. Circ. 20, August 31, 1866, ibid. For Howard's commitment to education, see *Autobiography,* II, 330; a lengthy list of sponsoring missionary groups is in ibid., p. 196; Elliott, "Freedmen's Bureau in Texas," pp. 7–14. See also James Smallwood, "Black Education in Reconstruction: The Contribution of the Freedmen's Bureau and Benevolent Societies," *East Texas Historical Journal* 19 (1981): 17–40.

40. Howard, *Autobiography,* II, 384–85. Texans, had they paused to listen, might have been amazed at the doubts many teachers voiced regarding the concept of equality; see Sandra E. Small, "The Yankee Schoolmarm in Freedmen's Schools: An Analysis of Attitudes," *Journal of Southern History* 45 (1979): 381–402.

41. Claude H. Nolan, *The Negroes' Image in the South: The Anatomy*

of White Supremacy (Lexington: University of Kentucky Press, 1967), pp. 104–109.

42. A. M. Bryant to AAG, May 14, 1867, D. T. Allen to AAG, August 16, 1867, AAAG to DeWitt C. Brown, May 15, 1867, LR, FB, RG 105, NA.

43. Howard, *Autobiography*, II, 377; Henry Lee Swint, *The Northern Teacher in the South, 1862–1870* (Nashville: Vanderbilt University Press, 1941), pp. 130–31.

44. D. J. Baldwin to Hamilton, November 7, 1865, Governor's Papers (Hamilton), TSL.

45. Elliott, "Freedmen's Bureau in Texas," pp. 16–18, 21–24. See also Alton J. Hornsby, Jr., "The Freedmen's Bureau Schools in Texas, 1865–1870," *Southwestern Historical Quarterly* 76 (1972–73): 397–417, for a general survey of the bureau's education efforts.

46. Capt. H. P. Spaulding to AAG, April 26, 1866, *House Executive Documents*, 40th Cong., 2d sess., no. 57, p. 113. A good survey of the problem is Barry A. Crouch, "Black Dreams and White Justice," *Prologue* 6 (1974): 255–65.

47. Testimony of Thomas J. Mackey, "Report of the Joint Committee on Reconstruction," *House Reports*, 39th Cong., 1st sess., IV, 30.

48. Testimony of Lt. H. S. Hall, ibid., pp. 46–47, 50; William Boneby (free man of color) to AAG, August 4, 1866, LR, FB, RG 105, NA; Dudley Richard Dobie, "History of Hays County, Texas" (M.A. thesis, University of Texas, 1932), p. 78; W. S. Mills, *History of Van Zandt County* (N.p., 1950), pp. 235–36.

49. See, for example, Edward Austin to AAG, March 21, 1866, Champ Carter, Jr. to AAG, June 2, 1866, LR, FB, RG 105, NA; Hiram Christian to Hamilton, October 21, 1865, Governor's Papers (Hamilton), TSL.

50. Ramsdell, *Reconstruction in Texas*, 60 n. 1.

51. Elliott, "Freedmen's Bureau in Texas," p. 12.

52. Ramsdell, *Reconstruction in Texas*, pp. 77–78.

53. See, for example, Capt. H. P. Spaulding to AAG, April 24, 1866, *House Executive Documents*, 40th Cong., 2d sess., no. 57, p. 113; GCMO 51, August 11, 1866, DT, RG 94, NA. The rules under which military commissions operated are set forth in U.S. Judge Advocate General, *Digest of Opinions . . . 1862–1868* (Washington, D.C., 1868), pp. 222–35; Wright to Hamilton, September 22, 1866, Governor's Papers (Hamilton), TSL.

54. J. R. Burns to Hamilton, November 15, 1865, Governor's Papers (Hamilton), TSL.

55. Hamilton to Brig. Gen. N. J. T. Dana, December 20, 1863, Hamilton Papers, UT.

56. Hamilton to President Johnson, August 30, 1865, James H. Bell and others to President Johnson, August 30, 1865, Johnson Papers, LC; Hamilton to Maj. Gen. C. C. Andrews, August 17, 1865, RG 307, TSL.

57. Hamilton to Wright, September 27, 1865, Governor's Papers (Hamilton), TSL. While Hamilton condoned the use of military tribunals in the state's legal processes, he never admitted to total military supremacy, contrary to Richard Moore's implication in "Radical Reconstruction: The Texas Choice," *East Texas Historical Journal* 16 (1978): 17.

3: THE RETURN OF REBEL RULE

1. Sheridan to Rawlins, October 7, 1865, Grant Papers, LC.

2. Wright to Hamilton, October 10, 1865, Stanton to Sheridan, October 10, 1865, Governor's Papers (Hamilton), TSL; Wright to AAG, November 20, 1865, *House Reports*, 39th Cong., 2d sess., no. 61, p. 1; Wright to Sheridan, October 16, 1865, Sheridan Papers, LC. Quite a few soldiers had Wright's attitude; see William L. Richter, "'Outside . . . My Profession': The Army and Civil Affairs in Texas Reconstruction," *Military History of Texas and the Southwest* 9 (1971): 5–21.

3. GO 5, January 5, 1866, AGO, RG 94, NA; GO 5, January 27, 1866, DT, ibid.

4. James D. Richardson, comp., *A Compilation of the Messages and Papers of the Presidents, 1789–1897*, 10 vols. (Washington, 1897), VI, 429–32; Circ. 3, April 17, 1866, DT, RG 94, NA; Benjamin Thomas and Harold M. Hyman, *Stanton: The Life and Times of Lincoln's Secretary of War* (New York: Alfred A. Knopf, 1962), p. 478.

5. GO 26, May 1, 1866, AGO, RG 94, NA; GO 19, May 19, 1866, DT, ibid.; GO 20, May 26, 1866, ibid.

6. GO 21, May 28, 1866, ibid.; GO 44, July 3, 1866, AGO, ibid.; Sefton, *Army and Reconstruction*, p. 73. See also Donald G. Nieman, "Andrew Johnson, the Freedmen's Bureau, and the Problem of Equal Rights," *Journal of Southern History* 44 (1978): 399–420.

7. Proclamation of the governor, September 11, 1865, RG 307, TSL.

8. Waller, *Colossal Hamilton*, pp. 85–86.

9. "Truman Report," *Senate Executive Documents*, 39th Cong., 1st sess., no. 43, p. 6; "Report of the Joint Committee on Reconstruction," *House Reports*, 39th Cong., 1st sess., no. 30, pp. 72–76; Hamilton to Johnson, February 11, 1866, Johnson Papers, LC.

10. Waller, *Colossal Hamilton*, pp. 89–90.

11. Richardson, *Papers of the Presidents*, VI, 321–23.

12. The actual debates may be followed in *Journal of the State Convention . . . 1866* (Austin: Southern Intelligencer, 1866). For a good synopsis of the proceedings, see Ramsdell, *Reconstruction in Texas*, pp. 99–102; John P. Carrier, "A Political History of Texas during the Reconstruction, 1865–1874" (Ph.D. diss., Vanderbilt University, 1971), pp. 40–43. The definitive analysis of the proceedings is John Conger McGraw, "The Texas Constitution of 1866" (Ph.D. diss., Texas Tech University, 1959). The best look at issues from a loyal point of view is Ronald N. Gray, "Edmund J. Davis: Radical Republican and Reconstruction Governor of Texas" (Ph.D. diss., Texas Tech University, 1976), pp. 72–95.

13. Ramsdell, *Reconstruction in Texas*, pp. 94–96, 103–104.

14. Ibid., pp. 106–108; Thrall, *Pictorial History of Texas*, p. 598; Benjamin Hillon Miller, "Elisha Marshall Pease, a Biography" (M.A. thesis, University of Texas, 1927), pp. 121–22; Griffin, "Pease," pp. 1–185. See also Robert J. Franzetti, "Elisha Marshall Pease and Reconstruction" (M.A. thesis, Southwest Texas State University, 1970). For numerous letters urging Pease's candidacy, see Pease-Graham-Niles Papers, APL, April and May, 1866.

15. Pease to Carrie [his daughter], May 8, 18, 1866, Pease Papers, APL. The terms "Radical" and "Conservative" as used by Texas historians for this period are often misleading. See, for example, Ramsdell, *Reconstruction in Texas*, p. 106; and Wallace, *Texas in Turmoil*, pp. 179–80. The election of 1866 had one issue—unionism. The Republican party was not organized until a year later. Even then, there was no real "Radical" party in Texas until the Republicans split over the issues of the 1868–69 convention. Radicals were always present, but not until 1869 could the majority of the opposition to the Democratic-Conservative coalition be called Radical. Men like A. J. Hamilton or Pease were never really in the Radical camp. See Carrier, "Texas during the Reconstruction," pp. 84–105, for a more accurate treatment of parties and factions in the 1866 contest; and Griffin, "Pease," pp. 185–204, especially pp. 195–96, who finds Pease to be a Radical only in the sense that he supported continued military Reconstruction. Also of interest is Jane Lynn Scarborough, "George W. Paschal: Texas Unionist and Scalawag Jurisprudent" (Ph.D. diss., Rice University, 1972), p. 158 n. 15.

16. Ramsdell, *Reconstruction in Texas*, pp. 111–12; Griffin, "Pease," pp. 190–96.

17. Alexander Rossy to Pease, May 8, 1866, Pease to Carrie, June 30, 1866, Pease Papers, APL.

18. See Kenneth Stamp, *The Era of Reconstruction* (New York: Alfred A. Knopf, 1965), pp. 71–73, for this analogy used on the national level.

19. Waller, *Colossal Hamilton*, p. 93. Ramsdell errs when he calls the

Johnson-Throckmorton alliance "natural" (*Reconstruction in Texas*, p. 111). Johnson was maneuvered into the alliance by forces he could not control.

20. E. J. Davis to Pease, July 14, 1866, Pease Papers, APL (italics original). Lack of popular support was the crux of the party's inability to govern without outside help throughout Reconstruction. See James Alex Baggett, "Birth of the Texas Republican Party," *Southwestern Historical Quarterly* 78 (1974–75): 20.

21. Throckmorton to Johnson, July 24, 1866, Johnson Papers, LC; Circ. of James H. Bell, secretary of state, Texas, August 13, 1866, RG 307, TSL.

22. Thrall, *Pictorial History of Texas*, pp. 625–26; Claude Elliott, *Leathercoat: The Life History of a Texas Patriot* (San Antonio: Standard Printing Co., 1938), is the standard work on Throckmorton. See also Ruby Crawford Holbert, "The Public Career of James Webb Throckmorton, 1851–1867" (M.A. thesis, University of Texas, 1932); Moore, "Radical Reconstruction," pp. 15–23; and William L. Richter, "Texas Politics and the United States Army, 1866–1867," *Military History of Texas and the Southwest* 10 (1972): 159–86.

23. Richardson, *Papers of the Presidents*, VI, 438.

24. Sheridan tried to skirt the president's proclamations, maintaining that he had never been properly notified, but Grant cut him short in this effort. See Sefton, *Army and Reconstruction*, pp. 80–81. Sefton's criticism of Thomas and Hyman, *Stanton*, pp. 498–99, is well taken.

25. Elliott, *Leathercoat*, pp. 137–39, 166–67; Holbert, "Throckmorton," pp. 82–92; Wortham, *History of Texas*, V, 49. See also John L. Haynes, "Scrapbook," pp. 92–93, MS in John L. Haynes Papers, UT; and Wallace, *Texas in Turmoil*, pp. 186–89.

26. Throckmorton to Wright, August 17, 1866, RG 307, TSL.

27. Wright to AAG, July 21, 1866, *House Reports*, 39th Cong., 2d sess., no. 61, p. 4; Sheridan to Throckmorton, September 3, 1866, Sheridan Papers, LC.

28. GO 59, August 6, 1866, copy in Sheridan Papers, LC.

29. Sheridan to Grant, August 22, 1866, ibid.

30. Wright to AAG, August 18, 1866, TR, DG, RG 393, NA; Heitman, *Historical Register*, I, 1062; George W. Cullum, *Biographical Register of the Officers and Graduates of the U.S. Military Academy . . .* , 2 vols. (New York: D. Van Nostrand, 1868), II, 5–6.

31. Getty's career is presented in Heitman, *Historical Register*, I, 452; Cullum, *Biographical Register*, I, 603–604; Warner, *Generals in Blue*, pp. 170–71; Boatner, *Civil War Dictionary*, pp. 229–30. For questions on his assumption of command, see AAG Texas to AAG DG, September 3, 1866, TR,

DG, RG 393, NA; Kiddoo to AAG, September 16, 1866, ibid. For confirmation of his assumption of command, see GO 2, September 24, 1866, DT, RG 94, NA.

32. Ramsdell, *Reconstruction in Texas*, p. 114; Elliott, *Leathercoat*, p. 296.

33. Ramsdell, *Reconstruction in Texas*, pp. 114–15; Wallace, *Texas in Turmoil*, pp. 184–85; Wortham, *History of Texas*, V, 16. Burnet's biographer, Mary Whatley Clarke, *David G. Burnet* (Austin: Pemberton Press, 1969), pp. 240–41, points out that Burnet was actually a Unionist in 1861, which suggests the quarrel, although expressed in ideological terms, was actually one of personalities.

34. Ramsdell, *Reconstruction in Texas*, pp. 99–101.

35. Resolution of March 15, 1866, in *Journal of the State Convention*.

36. Bentley, *History of the Freedmen's Bureau*, p. 139.

37. John Corbett to Hamilton, December 7, 1865, Col. Edward Colyer to J. L. Cunningham, March 5, 1866, Cunningham to Hamilton, March 8, 1866, Governor's Papers (Hamilton), TSL; Throckmorton to Kiddoo, November 7, 1866, J. W. Throckmorton Papers, UT; R. H. Watlington, "Memoirs," pp. 64–65, MS in R. H. Watlington Papers, UT.

38. Elliott, "Freedmen's Bureau in Texas," pp. 19–20; Throckmorton to Kiddoo, November 16, 1866, Throckmorton Papers, UT; M. C. Hamilton to Pease, November 9, 1866, Pease papers, APL.

39. W. Longworth to AAG, November 12, 1866, L. P. Hughes and others to AAG, May 21, 1866, LR, FB, RG 105, NA.

40. 1st Lt. C. C. Hardenbrook to AAG, November 13, 1866, 1st Lt. I. M. Beebe to AAG, May 26, 1866, LR, DT, RG 393, NA; J. C. Devine to AAG, October 24, 1866, LR, FB, RG 105, NA.

41. Frances Jane Leathers, *Through the Years: A Historical Sketch of Leon County and the Town of Oakwood* (Oakwood, 1946), p. 53.

42. Throckmorton to Kiddoo, October 25, 1866, Throckmorton Papers, UT. Frank Brown, "Annals of Travis County," chap. 26, p. 15, MS in Frank Brown Papers, UT; John J. Linn, *Reminiscences of Fifty Years in Texas* (New York: D. & J. Sadlier & Co., 1883), p. 358.

43. J. M. Alexander to AAG, September 17, 1866, LR, FB, RG 105, NA; Thomas Affleck to Alexander Hannay, July 14, 1865, Affleck to Capt. T. S. Post, September 5, 1865, Affleck Papers, LSU.

44. Affleck to Lt. B. I. Arnold, November 12, 1865, Affleck Papers, LSU (emphasis in original). For an example of such a fine, see W. H. Brown to AAG, April 1, 1865, LR, FB, RG 105, NA.

45. Ramsdell, *Reconstruction in Texas*, p. 122; W. E. Burghardt DuBois, *Black Reconstruction* (New York, 1935), p. 143.

46. Cole, "Texas Career of Thomas Affleck," pp. 360–61, 361 n. 33; Sefton, *Army and Reconstruction,* pp. 42–43; Wilson, *Black Codes of the South,* pp. 57–60. Cf. Joe M. Richardson, "The Florida Black Codes," *Florida Historical Quarterly* 47 (1968–69): 369–70.

47. H. N. P. Gammell, comp., *The Laws of Texas, 1822–1897,* 10 vols. (Austin: Gammel Book Co., 1898), V, 998–99; Circ. 14, May 15, 1866, FB, RG 105, NA. Circ. 17, June 19, 1866, ibid., ordered bureau agents to read Circ. 14 to the Negroes in their areas and to ensure that the circular was strictly enforced. For the "general apprentice law," which had similar penalties, see Gammel, *Laws of Texas,* V, 979–81. Some civil rights were given to blacks (the right to sue, "to have and to enjoy the rights of personal security, liberty, and private property"), and certain slave codes were repealed at the same legislative session; see ibid., pp. 976, 1049–50.

48. Ibid., V, 982; Circ. 25, December 21, 1865, FB, RG 105, NA; A. Cox, "Economic History of Texas," p. 41.

49. The provost marshal of Galveston had placed "all idle negroes" to work on the city streets within two weeks of the army's arrival (*Galveston Daily News,* June 28, 1865). See also Gammel, *Laws of Texas,* V, 1020–22; Circular Letter, October 17, 1865, Gregory to Benjamin G. Harris, August 20, 1865, LS, FB, RG 105, NA. Local communities followed the state legislature's lead and established strict vagrancy laws. See Dobie, "History of Hays County," p. 77; Egon Richard Tausch, "Southern Sentiment among Texas Germans during the Civil War and Reconstruction" (M.A. thesis, University of Texas, 1965), p. 81.

50. Cole, "Texas Career of Thomas Affleck," pp. 360–61, maintains that the men who introduced the labor laws were also interested in attracting immigrant laborers to the state. These laws were designed to safeguard the employer's rights when these laborers arrived. Cole believes that, as a secondary consideration, the laws received little opposition because it was recognized that they could be used against Negro labor. The sponsors of the acts thought free black labor would never be successful and were looking for a practical alternative. Cole's thesis contradicts that of Ramsdell, *Reconstruction in Texas,* p. 125, and DuBois, *Black Reconstruction,* p. 143.

51. The law is in Gammel, *Laws of Texas,* V, 994–97. Similar statements by the bureau are in Circular Letter, October 17, 1865, LS, FB, RG 105, NA.

52. Gammel, *Laws of Texas,* V, 994–97. Ramsdell, *Reconstruction in Texas,* p. 122, sees the Black Codes as an honest attempt by the legislature to provide the "constant watchfulness and semi-coercion" that the bureau used to keep the blacks at work by providing "a system of regulation more permanent than that of the Bureau professed to be." The labor act went consider-

ably further, however, than the bureau directives. See Ramsdell's discussion, pp. 120–21, 125–26. For the cumulative effect of Federal and state policies toward black laborers, see James Smallwood, "Perpetuation of Caste: Black Agricultural Workers in Reconstruction Texas," *Mid-America* 61 (1979): 5–24.

53. Wilson, *Black Codes of the South*, pp. 138–52; Cole, "Texas Career of Thomas Affleck," pp. 360–61.

54. J. L. Haynes to Pease, October 4, 1866, Pease Papers, APL; Circ. 23, November 1, 1866, FB, RG 105, NA.

4: PRIDE IN REBELLION

1. For the governor's reluctance to relinquish his office and leadership, see Elliott, *Leathercoat*, pp. 75–76.

2. Sheridan to Rawlins, November 14, 1866, Grant Papers, LC; Sheridan, *Personal Memoirs*, II, 232–33; Holbert, "Throckmorton," p. 105.

3. L. B. Camp to Pease, January 3, 1867, Pease to Carrie, May 26, 1866, F. H. Duval to Pease, October 18, 1866, Pease Papers, APL. On Pease's vacation and continued political activity, see Griffin, "Pease," pp. 196–99.

4. Throckmorton to Epperson, January 21, 1866, Throckmorton Papers, UT.

5. See clippings from *Galveston Tri-Weekly News*, September 28, 1866, in "Scrapbook," Pease Papers, APL.

6. J. L. Haynes to Pease, October 1, 1866, ibid.

7. Throckmorton to Heintzelman, September 8, 1866, Throckmorton to [James P. Kean, mayor of Victoria], September 24, 1866, RG 307, TSL; Throckmorton to Heintzelman, September 25, 27, 1866, Throckmorton Papers, UT.

8. Throckmorton to Sheridan, November 8, 1866, Sheridan to Throckmorton, November 19, 1866, Capt. Charles W. Peters to AAG, November 29, 1866, AAAG to Throckmorton, December 15, 1866, Governor's Papers (Throckmorton), TSL.

9. Elliott, *Leathercoat*, pp. 150–52; Holbert, "Throckmorton," p. 99. Davis's name is usually spelled "Daws" by historians (the problem is Throckmorton's handwriting). But see Maj. S. H. Starr to Throckmorton, September 16, 1867, Throckmorton Papers, UT.

10. Elliott, *Leathercoat*, p. 152; Sefton, *Army and Reconstruction*, p. 95.

11. Custer, *Tenting on the Plains*, p. 266; Edwin Bohne, "History of the Brenham Banner Press" (M.A. thesis, Sam Houston State University, 1950), p. 2.

12. See communiqués between Craig and AAG FB headquarters, August, 1866, FB, RG 105, NA; Testimony in "Burning of Brenham, Texas, 1866," *House Executive Documents*, 40th Cong., 3d sess., no. 145.

13. The Brenham matter is discussed in detail in William L. Richter, "The Brenham Fire of 1866: A Texas Reconstruction Atrocity," *Louisiana Studies* 14 (1975): 286–314.

14. Throckmorton to Kiddoo, October 13, 1866, Throckmorton to Sheridan, October 30, 1866, Throckmorton Papers, UT; GO 101, May 18, 1869, FMD, RG 94, NA.

15. Guards were sent with all recruits to prevent desertion before the men could be assigned to an actual unit. See, for example, SO 12, September 30, 1866, DT, RG 94, NA.

16. Affidavit of Capt. George Everett, n.d., Lt. Col. S. D. Sturgis to Throckmorton, January 3, 1867, "Transcript of Records, 1838–1869," TAGO, UT, Throckmorton to Sturgis, January 4, 1867, Throckmorton Papers, UT.

17. Throckmorton to Wright, August 17, 1866, RG 307, TSL; Throckmorton to Heintzelman, September 25, 1866, Throckmorton Papers, UT; Throckmorton to Johnson, September 26, 1866, Stanton to Throckmorton, September 28, 1866, *House Executive Documents*, 40th Cong., 2d sess., no. 57, pp. 40–43. Throckmorton also wrote Johnson on August 25, 1866, Throckmorton Papers, UT.

18. Sheridan to Rawlins, April 26, 1866, *House Executive Documents*, 40th Cong., 2d sess., no. 57, p. 35; Sheridan to Throckmorton, September 3, 1866, Throckmorton to Sheridan, September 18, 1866, Sheridan Papers, LC. These units may not have arrived at Camp Verde or Fort Martin Scott until October, 1866.

19. Sheridan to Grant, October 11, 1866, Grant to Sheridan, October 11, 1866, *House Executive Documents*, 40th Cong., 2d sess., no. 57, pp. 40–41, 43.

20. Sheridan to Heintzelman, October 15, 1866, Sheridan to Rawlins, October 15, 1866, Sheridan Papers, LC; Sheridan to Rawlins, October 16, 1866, Grant Papers, LC. See also Throckmorton to David G. Burnet and Oran M. Roberts, November 16, 1866, Epperson Papers, UT; Sheridan to Throckmorton, November 3, 1866, Governor's Papers (Throckmorton), TSL.

21. Sheridan to Throckmorton, October 16, 1866, Heintzelman to Throckmorton, October 26, November 13, 1866, Governor's Papers (Throckmorton), TSL; Throckmorton to Sheridan, November 22, December 11, 1866, Throckmorton to Maj. George A. Forsyth, October 29, 1866, Throckmorton to Heintzelman, November 19, 1866, Throckmorton Papers, UT;

Sheridan to Throckmorton, January 18, 1867, "Transcript of Records, 1838–1869," TAGO, UT; C. B. Comstock to Sheridan, January 21, 1867, Grant Papers, LC; Sheridan to Rawlins, November 14, 1866, *O.R.*, XLVIII, pt. 1, pp. 301–302.

22. Throckmorton to Getty, October 3, 1866; Throckmorton to Heintzelman, October 22, 1866; Throckmorton to CO, DT, December 6, 1866; Throckmorton to Griffin, December 11, 1866, Throckmorton Papers, UT. Sheridan to Rawlins, October 15, September 6, 1866; Sheridan to Grant, October 12, 1866, January 25, 1867, *House Executive Documents*, 40th Cong., 2d sess., no. 57, pp. 34, 36, 43–44. Sheridan to Rawlins, September 8, 1866, Sheridan Papers, LC. Sheridan's Report, November 14, 1866, *O.R.*, XLVIII, pt. 1, p. 301.

23. Throckmorton and Hamilton attempted separately to negotiate for the release of goods captured by Indians. See letters between R. W. Black and Throckmorton, R. W. Black Papers, UT. The army attempted to return all recaptured property to its original owners. See Circ. 8, March 25, 1867, DT, RG 94, NA.

24. T. S. Lyons and others to Hamilton, August 5, 1865, Charles Jordan to Hamilton, September 5, 1865, Hamilton to Frank Carter, October 5, 1865, Governor's Papers (Hamilton), TSL.

25. Throckmorton to Sheridan, September 18, 1866, Sheridan to Grant, October 3, 1866, Sheridan Papers, LC; Throckmorton to Sheridan and Johnson, September 26, 1866, Throckmorton to Stanton, September 29, 1866, *House Executive Documents*, 40th Cong., 2d sess., no. 57, pp. 40–42; Throckmorton to Sheridan, September 29, 1866, Throckmorton Papers, UT; Sheridan to Throckmorton, October 1, 1866, Governor's Papers (Throckmorton), TSL.

26. Throckmorton to Sheridan and Grant, October 6, 1866, Throckmorton Papers, UT; Grant to Sheridan, October 8, 1866, Grant Papers, LC; Grant to Throckmorton, October 20, 1866, *House Executive Documents*, 40th Cong., 2d sess., no. 57, pp. 40–45.

27. GO 5, October 9, 1866, DT, RG 94, NA.

28. Heitman, *Historical Register*, I, 521; Cullum, *Biographical Register*, I, 295–96; Warner, *Generals in Blue*, pp. 227–28; Boatner, *Civil War Dictionary*, p. 392.

29. GO 6, October 24, 1866, DT, RG 94, NA. Heintzelman was delayed by an assignment on a military board. See Heintzelman to AAG, October 23, 1866, TR, DG, RG 393, NA.

30. Barry M. Cohen, "The Texas-Mexican Border, 1858–1868 . . . ," *Texana* 6 (1968): 154–61.

31. Heintzelman to AAG, October 25, 1866, TR, DG, RG 393, NA;

Sheridan to Grant, October 29, 1866, Grant Papers, LC; Sheridan to Throckmorton, November 11, 1866, *House Executive Documents,* 40th Cong., 2d sess., no. 57, p. 129.

32. Perhaps, as subordinates sometimes do, Forsyth wrote what he believed Sheridan wanted to hear rather than describe the actual situation. See Sheridan to Rawlins, October 20, November 11, 1866, Forsyth to Sheridan, November 2, 1866, *House Executive Documents,* 40th Cong., 2d sess., no. 57, pp. 44, 129–30; Throckmorton to ——, October 29, 1866, Throckmorton Papers, UT.

33. Carl Coke Rister, *The Southwest Frontier, 1865–1881* . . . (Cleveland: Arthur H. Clark & Co., 1928), 102 n. 101, asserts that Forsyth went only to Waco. In his report, Forsyth said he went to Weatherford. See Forsyth to AAG, December 16, 1866, *House Executive Documents,* 40th Cong., 2d sess., no. 57, p. 46.

34. Fort Belknap was not garrisoned by Federal troops at the time of Forsyth's journey. It was one of a series of civilian forts where settlers had gathered for mutual protection.

35. See Forsyth's Report, December 16, 1866, *House Executive Documents,* 40th Cong., 2d sess., no. 57, pp. 46–48.

36. Ibid.

37. Printed form in Throckmorton Papers, UT.

38. Throckmorton to Stanton, August 5, 1866, ibid.; AAG DT to AAG FMD, August 24, 1867, LR, FMD, RG 393, NA. See also W. C. Holden, "Frontier Defense, 1865–1889," *Panhandle-Plains Historical Review* 2 (1929): 46–48; Joseph I. Lambert, "The Defense of the Indian Frontier of Texas by the U.S. Army" (M.A. thesis, St. Mary's University, San Antonio, 1948), pp. 93–95.

39. M. C. Hamilton to Pease, November 28, 1866, Pease Papers, APL.

40. AAG to Sheridan, November 1, 1866, *House Executive Documents,* 40th Cong., 2d sess., no. 57, pp. 18–19; Stanbery to Throckmorton, November 6, 1866, Governor's Papers (Throckmorton), TSL; Throckmorton to AAG, November 7, 1866, LR, FB, RG 105, NA.

41. Wortham, *History of Texas,* V, 17.

42. C. E. Pratt to AAG, September 15, 1866, LR, FB, RG 105, NA.

43. W. C. Rives to Pease, November 13, 1866, Pease Papers, APL.

44. J. L. Haynes to Pease, November 28, 1866, ibid.

45. Sheridan to Grant, October 6, 1866, *House Executive Documents,* 40th Cong., 2d sess., no. 57, p. 18; Sheridan to Rawlins, November 14, 1866, *O.R.,* XLVIII, pt. 1, pp. 297–303; Holbert, "Throckmorton," p. 105; Ramsdell, *Reconstruction in Texas,* p. 134.

46. *San Antonio Express,* December 13, 1866.

47. Sheridan to Grant, November 10, 1866, Grant to Sheridan, October 3, November 10, 1866, Grant Papers, LC.

48. Throckmorton to Heintzelman, December 5, 1866, Throckmorton Papers, UT; *Dallas Herald,* December 19, 1866.

49. GO 10, December 1, GO 11, December 11, 1866, DT, RG 94, NA. Griffin's character is described in William A. Russ, Jr., "Radical Disfranchisement in Texas, 1867–1870," *Southwest Historical Quarterly* 38 (1934–35): 40; Bruce Catton, *A Stillness at Appomattox* (New York: Doubleday, 1953), pp. 63–66. See also Heitman, *Historical Register,* I, 478; Cullum, *Biographical Register,* II, 196–97; Warner, *Generals in Blue,* pp. 190–91; Boatner, *Civil War Dictionary,* pp. 360–61. For more on Griffin, his Civil War career, and his Reconstruction policies, see William L. Richter, "Tyrant and Reformer: General Griffin Reconstructs Texas, 1866–1867," *Prologue* 10 (1978): 225–41.

50. R. B. Hayes to Guy M. Bryan, February 15, October 1, 1866, in E. W. Winkler, ed., "Bryan-Hayes Correspondence," *Southwestern Historical Quarterly* 25 (1921–22): 288.

51. John H. Reagan, *Memoirs, with Special Reference to Secession and the Civil War* (Austin: Pemberton Press, 1968), p. 240.

52. Throckmorton to Hamilton, October 29, 1866, Johnson to Throckmorton, October 30, 1866, Johnson Papers, LC.

53. Reagan, *Memoirs,* pp. 240–41.

54. Craven, *Reconstruction,* pp. 51–52.

5: THE POLITICAL GENERAL

1. D. J. Baldwin to Hamilton, May 28, 1865; Hamilton to James Speed, June 19, 1865, box 680, RG 60, NA.

2. Baldwin to Maj. [Barnes] Lathrop, December [?], 1866, Heintzelman Papers, LC.

3. 21 How. at 523 (1859). This decision maintained that the individual states lost their inherent sovereignty once they joined the Union. See Arthur Bestor, "State Sovereignty and Slavery: A Reinterpretation of the Pro-Slavery Constitutional Doctrine, 1846–1860," Illinois State Historical Society, *Journal* 54 (1961): 117–80.

4. D. J. Baldwin to Heintzelman, December 29, 1866, RG 21, FRC, FW.

5.. W. C. Philips to Pease, December 18, 1866, William Alexander to Pease, February 8, 1867, E. Degener to Pease, December 30, 1866, Pease Papers, APL.

6. L. B. Camp to Pease, January 3, 1867, M. H. Beatty to Pease, January 12, 1867, ibid.

7. F. H. Duval to Pease, January 25, 1867, ibid.; C. Caldwell to Hamilton, January 23, 1867, M. C. Hamilton to A. J. Hamilton, January 8, 1867, Hamilton Papers, UT. William Clarke Quantrill led a group of Confederate guerrillas, most noted for destroying the Union town of Lawrence, Kansas, in 1863. His band spawned many members of the later Jesse James gang.

8. *Galveston Daily News*, February 7, March 19, 1867.

9. Throckmorton to Griffin, March 5, 1867, RG 307, TSL; Throckmorton to Oran Roberts, David G. Burnet, and B. H. Epperson, December 20, 1866, Epperson Papers, UT.

10. Throckmorton to Griffin, February 7, 22, 1867, RG 307, TSL; Throckmorton to AAG, February 22, 1867, LR, FB, RG 105, NA.

11. *Galveston Daily News*, January 8, 1867.

12. *Brownsville Daily Ranchero*, April 9, 1867.

13. Ibid., June 6, 1867.

14. C. E. Culver to AAG, August 2, 1867, LR, FB, RG 105, NA.

15. Sheridan to Grant, May 10, 1867, Grant Papers, LC.

16. 1st Lt. Stanton Weaver to AAG, May 24, 1867, *House Executive Documents*, 40th Cong., 1st sess., no. 20, pp. 100–101.

17. See, for example, Col. James Oakes to Gov. E. M. Pease, August 29, 1867, and 2d Lt. J. P. Richardson to AAG, September 3, 1867, Governor's Papers (Pease), TSL.

18. D. A. Barzizi to AAG, December 6, 1866, H. S. Bennett to AAG, n.d. [1867], LR, FB, RG 105, NA.

19. Bvt. Col. J. C. De Gress to AAG, December 15, 1866, Throckmorton to AAG, December 22, 1866, ibid.; Throckmorton to E. M. Stanton, February 18, 1867, Throckmorton Papers, UT.

20. Throckmorton to Griffin, December 18, 1866, Throckmorton Papers, UT; Throckmorton to President Johnson, December 22, 1866, Throckmorton to Brig. Gen. E. D. Townsend, January 8, 1867, Johnson Papers, LC.

21. Shook, "Federal Occupation," p. 249.

22. Throckmorton to AAG, October 29, 1866, LR, FB, RG 105, NA.

23. Lt. Col. William H. Sinclair to Throckmorton, January 17, 1867, "Transcript of Records, 1838–1869," TAGO, UT.

24. Report of prisoners at Huntsville, February 26, 1867, box 21, FB, RG 105, NA.

25. Throckmorton to Bvt. Brig. Gen. James Oakes, March 18, 1867, Governor's Papers (Throckmorton), TSL; Throckmorton to AAG, December 29, 1866, LR, FB, RG 105, NA.

26. Sheridan to Charles Leonard, January 29, 1867, Johnson Papers, LC.

27. *Galveston Daily News*, January 25, 1867.

28. Sheridan to Grant, January 25, 1867, Johnson Papers, LC.

29. James A. McKee to Pease, February 5, 1867, Pease Papers, APL.

30. W. C. Philips to Pease, January 10, 1867, ibid.

31. Circ. 1, January 12, 1867, DT, RG 94, NA.

32. Bvt. Col. J. C. De Gress to AAG, December 4, 1866, LR, FB, RG 105, NA; Capt. N. F. Randlett to AAG, February 16, 1867, "Transcript of Records, 1838–1869," TAGO, UT; Throckmorton to Griffin, January 1, 1867, Throckmorton Papers, UT.

33. Circ. 3, December 9, 1866, Circ. 25, December 25, 1866, FB, RG 105, NA.

34. GO 1, January 1, GO 2, January 3, 1867, ibid. The Black Codes were canceled seven months later. See GO 25, August 3, 1867, DT, RG 94, NA. See also G. W. Chilton and A. W. Branch to AAG, January 10, 1867, LR, FB, RG 105, NA.

35. SO 19, January 28, 1867, DT, RG 94, NA; Sinclair, "Freedmen's Bureau in Texas," pp. 10–11.

36. *Galveston Daily News*, February 5, 1867.

37. *Dallas Herald*, March 3, 1867; GO 3, January 29, 1867, FB, RG 105, NA; Circ. 3, February 1, 1867, DT, RG 94, NA. Circ. 3 caused some complaint to headquarters that the work load was too great. See, for example, Capt. J. C. Connor to AAG, July 16, 1867, LR, FB, RG 105, NA.

38. Throckmorton to Griffin, December 11, 1866, Throckmorton to Heintzelman, December 3, 1866, Throckmorton to Griffin, January 30, 1867, Throckmorton Papers, UT. See also Throckmorton to R. W. Black, December 6, 1866, Black Papers, UT.

39. Throckmorton to Sheridan, December 11, 1866, Throckmorton Papers, UT.

40. GO 177, Fourth Cavalry, December 1, 1866, Sheridan to Throckmorton, January 18, 1867, "Transcript of Records, 1838–1869," TAGO, UT.

41. AGO to Sheridan, January 21, 1867, Grant Papers, LC; Sheridan to Grant, January 25, April 5, 1867, *House Executive Documents*, 40th Cong., 2d sess., no. 57, pp. 34, 83–84.

42. Various letters in "Transcript of Records, 1838–1869," pp. 106, 107, 108, 116–21, 123, 125, 127–29, 134–39, 142, TAGO, UT; Throckmorton to Stanton, March 9, 1867, Throckmorton Papers, UT; Circ. 8, March 25, 1867, DT, RG 94, NA; [R. W. Black] to Throckmorton, January 6, 1867, Black Papers, UT.

43. Sheridan to Grant, March 14, April 12, 1867, Grant to Sheridan, March 15, 1867, Johnson Papers, LC.

44. AAG to Griffin, March 23, 1867, Sheridan Papers, LC; AGO to

AAG FMD, August 24, 1867, LR, FMD, RG 393, NA; Sheridan to Griffin, August 27, 1867, TS, FMD, RG 393, NA; SO 2, March 21, 1867, FMD, RG 94, NA; Griffin to Pease, September 12, 1867, LS, DT, RG 393, NA.

45. Throckmorton to Heintzelman, December 5, 1866, Throckmorton Papers, UT.

46. W. C. Philips to Throckmorton, December 14, 1866, Byron Porter to Bvt. Lt. Col. H. A. Ellis, December 18, 1866, Governor's Papers (Throckmorton), TSL; Throckmorton to Bvt. Maj. Gen. S. Sturgis, December 17, 1866, Throckmorton Papers, UT; Throckmorton to Griffin, February 7, 1867, RG 307, TSL.

47. Bvt. Maj. Gen. J. J. Reynolds to AAG, January 19, 1867, *House Executive Documents*, 40th Cong., 2d sess., no. 57, p. 34.

48. Griffin to Throckmorton, January 21, 1867, "Transcript of Records, 1838–1869," TAGO, UT; Throckmorton to Griffin, January 30, February 18, 1867, RG 307, TSL.

49. Bvt. Capt. C. F. Rand to AAG, February 11, 1867, "Transcript of Records, 1838–1869," TAGO, UT; Throckmorton to Griffin, March 4, 1867, Throckmorton Papers, UT; Throckmorton to Harrison County judge, March 4, 1867, RG 307, TSL.

50. Throckmorton to Harrison County judge, March 4, 1867, RG 307, TSL.

51. Throckmorton to chief justice, Panola County, February 8, 1867, Throckmorton to county attorney, Parker County, April 2, 1867, ibid.

52. A. F. Manning to Kiddoo, January 20, 1867, "Transcript of Records, 1838–1869," TAGO, UT; Griffin to Throckmorton, January 28, 1867, Governor's Papers (Throckmorton), TSL.

53. Lt. A. F. Manning to AAG, January 20, 1867, "Transcript of Records, 1838–1869," TAGO, UT.

54. Flint and Chamberlain to Throckmorton, January 22, 1867, ibid.

55. Throckmorton to Griffin, January 25, 1867, Throckmorton Papers, UT; Griffin to Throckmorton, January 28, 1867, Governor's Papers (Throckmorton), TSL.

56. Throckmorton to Griffin, January 31, 1867, Throckmorton Papers, UT; Throckmorton to Epperson, January 29, 1867, RG 307, TSL. This case alone seems to challenge the contention of one historian that there was very little trouble between the army and civilians in McLennan County during Reconstruction. See Tony E. Duty, "The Home Front—McLennan County in the Civil War," *Texana* 12 (1974): 197–238, especially pp. 221–23. Duty's Civil War era extends through Reconstruction. See also AAAG to Lt. A. F. Manning, February 7, 1867, LS, FB, RG 105, NA.

57. D. T. Allen to AAG, January 2, February 7, 1867, ——— McBryde to AAG, February 7, 1867, J. M. Avarne to AAG, January 5, 1867, LR, FB, RG 105, NA.

58. A. H. Meyer to AAG, January 2, 14, 1867, ibid.

59. Judge John Dix to AAG, March 27, 1867, ibid.

60. D. E. Hayne to AAG, December 29, 1866, ibid.

61. Lt. Col. W. H. Sinclair to AAG, February 26, 1867, ibid.

62. Such assaults strengthened the desire of Congress to authorize Military Reconstruction. See "Murder of Union Soldiers," *House Reports,* 39th Cong., 2d sess., no. 23, p. 5.

63. 1st Lt. William A. Sutherland to AAG, March 25, 1867, "Transcript of Records, 1838–1869," TAGO, UT. See also E. D. Johnson to Throckmorton, April 27, 1867, Governor's Papers (Throckmorton), TSL; AAG DT to AAG Texas FB, December 22, 1866, Lt. Col. W. H. Sinclair to AAG, February 27, 1867, LR, FB, RG 105, NA; Griffin to AAG, March 21, 1867, TR, FMD, RG 393, NA.

64. D. J. Baldwin to Henry Stanbery, U.S. attorney general, February 2, 1867, RG 21, FRC, FW.

65. *Statutes at Large,* XIV, 428–29, and XV, 2–4, 41. See also GO 10, March 11, GO 33, March 28, 1867, AGO, RG 94, NA. For an analysis of the possible inadequacies of the Reconstruction Acts, see Michael Les Benedict, "Preserving the Constitution: The Conservative Basis of Radical Reconstruction," *Journal of American History* 41 (1974): 65–90. Those who oppose Les Benedict's view are listed in ibid., p. 66 n. 3.

66. Sheridan to Grant, March 8, 1867, and endorsement, March 9, 1867, Grant to Sheridan, March 13, 1867, Johnson Papers, LC.

67. Grant to Sheridan, March 9, 1867, ibid.

68. GO 1, March 1, 1867, FMD, RG 94, NA.

69. GO 2, March 1, 1867, ibid.; Sheridan to Griffin, March 28, 1867, LS, FMD, RG 393, NA. The secretary of civil affairs had the responsibility for informing candidates of their appointment, receiving oaths of loyalty, paying registrars of voters, explaining the Reconstruction laws to local authorities, declaring election results, and supervising local government. The secretaries also assisted in the enforcement of law and order and in the conduct of military trials of civilians.

70. Throckmorton to Griffin, March 28, 1867, Throckmorton Papers, UT.

71. Throckmorton to Griffin, April 6, 1867, ibid.

72. Griffin to Throckmorton, April 23, 1867, "Transcript of Records, 1838–1869," TAGO, UT.

73. Griffin to SCA Forsyth, March 28, 1867, LS, CA, DT, RG 393, NA;

Sheridan to Throckmorton, March 29, 1867, Governor's Papers (Throckmorton), TSL.

74. Jesse A. Ashbury to AAG, April 10, 1867, LR, CA, DT, RG 393, NA; Citizens of Parker and Jack counties to Griffin, April 16, 1867, "Transcript of Records, 1838–1869," TAGO, UT; John Dix to AAAG, April 23, 1867, *House Executive Documents*, 40th Cong., 1st sess., no. 20, p. 90; S. M. Swenson to Pease, March 29, 1867, Pease Papers, APL; W. B. Moore to AAG, March 29, 1867, LR, CA, FMD, RG 393, NA; A. M. Boatwright to AAG, April 15, 1867, LR, CA, DT, RG 393, NA; A. H. Latimer to Pease, July 25, 1867, Pease Papers, APL; B. F. McFarland and others to AAG, March 20, 1867, John Plumer and others to AAG, April 16, 1867, LR, CA, FMD, RG 393, NA.

75. Griffin to Throckmorton, April 26, 1867, Governor's Papers (Throckmorton), TSL; William Alexander to Pease, April 12, 1867, Pease Papers, APL.

76. E. P. Hunt to Pease, March 25, 1867, Pease Papers, APL. According to John Reagan, Griffin had also contacted him and offered him the provisional governorship, but Reagan refused to serve unless first elected by the people (Reagan, *Memoirs*, p. 240).

77. W. C. Rives to Pease, November 13, 1866, Pease Papers, APL.

6: THE PYRRHIC VICTORY

1. C. Caldwell to Pease, September 3, 1867, Pease Papers, APL.

2. William Alexander to Pease, April 12, 1867, ibid.

3. Ibid. See also Petition from Tarrant County, April 6, 1867, B. F. Floydstin to AAG, August 10, 1867, LR, CA, FMD, RG 393, NA; W. B. Thompson to AAG, May 12, 1867, LR, CA, DT, RG 393, NA.

4. Patten to AAG, April 13, 1867, LR, CA, DT, RG 393, NA.

5. *San Antonio Express*, July 9, 11, 1867, Lt. Col. W. H. Sinclair to AAG, July 18, 1867, LR, CA, DT, RG 393, NA.

6. J. L. Haynes to Griffin, April 30, 1867, *House Executive Documents*, 40th Cong., 1st sess., no. 20, pp. 90–92.

7. Citizens of San Antonio to AAG, March 28, 1867, LR, CA, FMD, RG 393, NA; Lt. J. T. Kirkman to AAG, April 30, 1867, LR, CA, DT, RG 393, NA; J. L. Haynes to Griffin, April 30, 1867, *House Executive Documents*, 40th Cong., 1st sess., no. 20, pp. 90–92.

8. SO 65, June 10, 1867, CA, FMD, RG 94, NA.

9. Sheridan to Grant, June 20, 1867, Grant Papers, LC. Sheridan never did explain how a New Mexico Territory court could try a case arising under

Texas state law. See also Griffin to Sheridan, August 13, 1867, LS, DT, RG 393, NA. No letter or order in response was found.

10. Circ. 13, April 27, 1867, DT, RG 94, NA.

11. M. S. Huson to President Johnson, April 30, 1867, Johnson Papers, LC.

12. A. H. Shanks to Johnson, May 8, 1867, ibid.

13. G. B. Lipscomb and others to Johnson, May 9, 1867, ibid.; M. D. Ector to Throckmorton, May 10, 1867, Governor's Papers (Throckmorton), TSL; [torn] to A. J. Hamilton, May 29, 1867, Hamilton Papers, UT.

14. *Brownsville Daily Ranchero,* May 11, 1867, Griffin to Throckmorton, May 7, 1867, SCA to Judge William H. Burkhardt, April 29, 1867, LS, CA, DT, RG 393, NA; John E. George to AAG, May 8, 1867, LR, DT, RG 393, NA; Throckmorton to Griffin, May 14, 1867, Throckmorton Papers, UT.

15. Mary E. Wallis, "The Life of Alexander Watkins Terrell, 1829–1912" (M.A. thesis, University of Texas, 1937), pp. 70–71; H. S. Thomas to AAG, June 24, 1867, LR, DT, RG 393, NA.

16. Printed form addressed to all judges, May 2, 1867; Throckmorton to President Johnson, May 2, 1867, Throckmorton Papers, UT.

17. Griffin to Throckmorton, May 7, 1867, Griffin to Judge J. C. Watrous, May 16, 1867, LS, CA, DT, RG 393, NA. Throckmorton to Johnson, May 20, 1867, Throckmorton to Griffin, May 20, 1867, Johnson Papers, LC; Throckmorton to Epperson, May 4, 1867, Throckmorton Papers, UT.

18. Sheridan to Grant, May 22, 1867, Griffin to Sheridan, May 29, 1867, Sheridan Papers, LC.

19. Griffin to Forsyth, June 10, 1867, Griffin to Sheridan, May 29, 1867, ibid.

20. Sheridan, *Personal Memoirs,* II, 275; Sheridan to Griffin, May 25, 1867, *House Executive Documents,* 40th Cong., 1st sess., no. 20, p. 72; Bvt. Brig. Gen. F. T. Dent to AAG, August 8, 1867, LR, FMD, RG 393, NA.

21. Grant to Sheridan, August 15, 1867, Sheridan to Grant, August 15, 17, 1867, Grant Papers, LC; SO 151, September 28, SO 192, October 20, 1867, FMD, RG 94, NA.

22. For the procedural options, see GCMO 51, August 11, 1866, DT, RG 94, NA; or any GCMO; U.S. Judge Advocate General, *Digest of Opinions,* pp. 222–35.

23. Sheridan, *Personal Memoirs,* II, 260–61.

24. *Brownsville Daily Ranchero,* August 29, September 3, 1867.

25. Circ. 10, April 5, 1867, DT, RG 94, NA.

26. 1st Lt. S. C. Plumer to Judge John Ireland, May 14, 1867, Bvt. Brig.

Gen. James Oakes to district judge, 2d Judicial District, May 26, 1867, Governor's Papers (Throckmorton), TSL; J. L. Haynes to Griffin, April 30, 1867, *House Executive Documents*, 40th Cong., 1st sess., no. 20, pp. 90–91.

27. GO 71, April 20, 1867, DT, RG 94, NA.

28. SO 133, July 16, SO 155, August 20, 1867, ibid. Santos Benavides and his brothers were prominent tejanos (Mexican-Americans) who recruited Confederate troops near Laredo. The Benavides family fought Yankees and Mexican marauders and generally worked for law and order along the vast borderlands. See Jerry Don Thompson, *Vaqueros in Blue and Gray* (Austin: Presidial Press, 1976).

29. GO 51, April 10, 1867, AGO, RG 94, NA; Grant to Sheridan, April 13, 1867, AAG to Sheridan, May 11, 1867, *House Executive Documents*, 40th Cong., 1st sess., no. 20, pp. 11–12, 82; Maj. Gen. J. J. Reynolds to AG USA, December 29, 1869, ibid., 41st Cong., 2d sess., no. 59, pp. 1–2.

30. Circ. 15, May 12, 1867, as modified by Circ. 17, May 25, 1867, DT, RG 94, NA. See also SO 192, October 20, 1867, ibid.

31. See, for example, SO 81, May 4, 1867, ibid.; SCA to state comptroller, August 17, 1867, LS, CA, FMD, RG 393, NA; SO 3, January 4, GO 41, March 25, SO 55, March 5, 1869, SO 17, January 22, 1867, FMD, RG 94, NA; *Brownsville Daily Ranchero*, June 13, 1867; SO 97, Subdistrict of the Rio Grande, July 11, 1867, *House Executive Documents*, 40th Cong., 2d sess., no. 342, pp. 207–208; R. W. Lane to AAG, May 26, 1868, LR, DT, RG 393, NA; Bvt. Maj. Gen. James H. Carleton to AAG, March 15, 1869, LR, FMD, RG 393, NA; Betty Jeffus Sandlin, "The Texas Reconstruction Constitutional Convention of 1868–1869" (Ph.D. diss., Texas Tech University, 1970), pp. 182–84; SO 35, September 18, SO 64, October 22, 1868, FMD, RG 94, NA.

32. Griffin to Throckmorton, April 4, 8, 1867, "Transcript of Records, 1838–1869," TAGO, UT. The lists can be found in "Registration MSS," boxes 1 and 2, RG 393, NA.

33. E. P. Hunt to Pease, March 25, 1867; William Alexander to Pease, April 12, 1867; W. B. Moore to Pease, July 7, 1867, Pease Papers, APL.

34. See, for example, E. P. Hunt to Pease, March 25, 1867, ibid. The Loyal League was a Republican political front that organized the black vote in the South. See the printed form dated June 11, 1867, ibid., and Paul Casdorph, *A History of the Republican Party in Texas, 1865–1965* (Austin: Pemberton Press, 1965), 4–5.

35. Colored Republicans of Navasota to AAG, August 5, 1867, LR, FB, RG 94, NA; Pease to Carrie, July 11, 1867, Pease Papers, APL. For the early organization of the party, see James A. Baggett, "Origin of Early Texas Re-

publican Party Leadership," *Journal of Southern History* 40 (1974): 450–54; and his "Birth of the Texas Republican Party," 1–20; Griffin, "Pease," pp. 196–203.

36. Griffin to SCA, March 27, 1867, Griffin to Sheridan, March 30, 1867, LS, CA, DT, RG 393, NA; Sheridan to Grant, April 12, 1867, Grant Papers, LC; printed circular, April 8, 1867, Throckmorton to Griffin, May 3, 1867, Throckmorton Papers, UT; Sheridan to Grant, May 18, 1867, Johnson Papers, LC; Griffin to AAG, May 7, 8, 1867, TR, FMD, RG 393, NA.

37. Circ. 12, April 17, 1867, as modified by Circ. 16, May 16, 1867, DT, RG 94, NA.

38. Circ. 16, May 16, 1867, as modified by Circ. 19, June 1, 1867, ibid.

39. Circ. 12, April 17, 1867, ibid.

40. Circ. 12, April 17, 1867, as modified by Circ. 14, May 1, 1867, ibid.

41. SO 163, September 2, 1867, ibid.; Thomas Affleck to A. G. Powers, May 15, 1867, Affleck Papers, LSU.

42. Sheridan to Grant, April 1, 1867, Grant to Sheridan, April 7, 1867, Grant Papers, LC; Sheridan to Grant, April 6, 1867, Johnson Papers, LC; Grant to Sheridan, April 21, 1867, Sheridan Papers, LC; SO 15, April 10, 1867, FMD, RG 94, NA.

43. Sheridan, *Personal Memoirs*, II, 253, 270. The attitude of Grant and Sheridan on the attorney general's opinion about the registration question correlates well with the Republican party theory that the presidency and the executive branch should be a mere administrative agency subordinate to the dictates of Congress. This theory was based on old Whig ideas on the same topic. See Leonard D. White, *The Republican Era* (New York, 1958), pp. 20–21, 23–24, 46–48. Sefton details the situation in Washington (*Army and Reconstruction*, pp. 128–34) and also makes some telling criticism of Grant's attitude. The relationship between Johnson and Grant during this period is developed in Martin E. Mantell, *Johnson, Grant, and the Politics of Reconstruction* (New York: Columbia University Press, 1973).

44. The memorandum is reproduced in GO 3, January 11, 1868, FMD, RG 94, NA. See also AAG DT to AAG FMD, December 27, 1867, AGO file 57M1868, microcopy 619, roll 634, RG 94, NA; Carrier, "Texas during the Reconstruction," pp. 226–27. Sheridan was concerned less with disfranchising Conservatives than with denying "rebels" the vote, although the effect was similar. See further, *Statutes at Large*, XV, 14–16; Circ. 12, April 17, 1867, DT, RG 94, NA.

45. J. T. Allen to M. Evans, August 8, 1867, Registration MSS, box 1, RG 393, NA.

46. Circ. 12, April 17, 1867, reiterated in Circ. 16, May 16, 1867, DT, RG 94, NA.

47. John K. Connally to AAG, December 23, 1867, John M. Claiborne to Hancock, December 23, 1867, I. L. Irion to AAG, December 26, 1867, John W. Hood to Hancock, December 27, 1867, AGO, file 57M1868, microcopy 619, roll 634, NA. See also Brig. Gen. E. D. Townsend to AAG, October 29, 1867, LR, FMD, RG 393, NA; R. W. Davis to AAG, April 10, 1867, Stephen Southwick to AAG, December 24, 1867, LR, CA, FMD, RG 393, NA; Capt. N. H. Randlett to AAG, April 17, 1867, LR, FB, RG 105, NA. The men rejected and various letters and figures can be found in "Protests," box 1, RG 393, NA. See also C. G. Forshey to General Hancock, January 5, 1868, AAG to John Hancock, December 28, 1867, AGO, file 57M1868, microcopy 619, roll 634, RG 94, NA; Nat Benton and others to AAG, February 15, 1868 LR, CA, FMD, RG 393, NA.

48. W. H. Horton to AAG, April 10, 1867, LR, FB, RG 105, NA.

49. J. W. Wilbarger, *Indian Depredations in Texas* (Austin: Steck Co., 1935), p. 128.

50. J. T. Allen to Dr. Musgrove Evans, June 21, 1867, Registration MSS, box 1, RG 393, NA.

51. Capt. L. H. Sawyer to AAG, April 15, 1868, LR, DT, RG 393, NA; Griffin to Sheridan, July 15, 1867, Sheridan Papers, LC; John C. Brooke to AAG, April 9, 1867; Edward D. Jarrot to AAG, April 29, 1867, John Dix to AAG, April 29, 1867, LR, CA, FMD, RG 393, NA; Ange J. de Saint to AAG, May 27, 1867, LR, CA, DT, RG 393, NA. Dozens of registrations were received. See, for example, James Brown to AAG, September 28, 1867, LR, CA, DT, RG 393, NA. For the increase in salary requests, see Richard Allen to AAG, November 12, 1867, LR, DT, RG 393, NA.

52. William Alexander to Pease, April 12, 1867, Pease Papers, APL; AAG to all COs of MDs in the South, May 22, 1867, *House Executive Documents*, 40th Cong., 1st sess., no. 20, p. 12; Circ. 20, June 1, 1867, DT, RG 94, NA. For a description of a military escort, see John W. Speer, *A History of Blanco County* (Austin: Pemberton Press, 1965), p. 46.

53. William Alexander to Pease, April 12, 1867, Pease Papers, APL.

54. W. B. Thompson to AAG, August 12, 1867, LR, CA, DT, RG 393, NA.

55. Sheridan to Griffin, April 12, 1867, AGO, file 57M1868, microcopy 619, roll 634, RG 94, NA, GO 66, April 15, 1867, DT, RG 94, NA; Griffin to Throckmorton, May 4, 1867, Governor's Papers (Throckmorton), TSL. See also, Throckmorton to Uvalde County judge, May 7, 1867, RG 307, TSL.

56. For Throckmorton's policies, see Elliott, *Leathercoat*.

57. Griffin to SCA FMD, March 28, 1867, LS, CA, DT, RG 393, NA; Sheridan to Grant, April 2, 1867, Grant to Sheridan, April 3, 1867, Johnson Papers, LC.

58. Grant to Sheridan, April 5, 1867, Sheridan Papers, LC.

59. Grant to Sheridan, April 21, May 6, 1867, ibid.; Stanton to Sheridan, June 3, 1867, Grant to Sheridan, June 7, 1867, Grant Papers, LC; Sefton, *Army and Reconstruction,* p. 141.

60. William Alexander to Pease, April 12, 1867, Pease Papers, APL; W. B. Gray to AAG, July 25, 1867, LR, FB, RG 105, NA; Griffin to Sheridan, July 20, 1867, Sheridan Papers, LC.

61. Joseph Green Dawson III, "General Phil Sheridan and Military Reconstruction in Louisiana," *Civil War History* 24 (1978): 133–51.

62. Sheridan to ——— Newhall, November 20, 1866, Sheridan Papers, LC.

63. Griffin to Pease, August 15, 1867, Pease Papers, APL.

64. Pease to Carrie, July 11, 1867, ibid.; Griffin to Sheridan, July 15, 20, 1867, Sheridan Papers, LC.

65. SO 81, May 4, SO 90, May 20, SO 91, May 22, 1867, DT, RG 94, NA.

66. AAG to all COs of MDs of the South, May 22, 1867, LR, FMD, RG 393, NA; AAG to Griffin, May 21, 1867, LR, DT, RG 393, NA.

67. *Galveston Daily News,* June 11, 12, 1867; SO 109, June 11, 1867, DT, RG 94, NA.

68. Sheridan to Griffin, June 14, 1867, AGO, file 57M1868, microcopy 619, roll 634, RG 94, NA; Griffin to Sheridan, June 10, 1867, *House Executive Documents,* 40th Cong., 1st sess., no. 20, p. 86.

69. SCA to Livingston Lindsay, July 1, 1867, LS, CA, DT, RG 393, NA.

70. SO 110, June 12, SO 116, June 24, SO 128, July 10, SO 130, July 12, SO 136, July 20, SO 139, July 24, 1867, DT, RG 94, NA.

71. *Statutes at Large,* XV, 14–16.

72. Griffin to Sheridan, July 20, 1867, Sheridan Papers, LC; Sheridan to Grant, July 25, 1867, Grant Papers, LC.

73. Grant to Sheridan, July 30, 1867, Grant Papers, LC; *San Antonio Express,* August 13, 1867; SO 105, July 30, 1867, FMD, RG 94, NA.

74. Griffin to Throckmorton, August 2, 1867, Governor's Papers (Throckmorton), TSL; AAG FMD to Pease, August 2, 1867, Pease to Throckmorton, August 7, 1867, Throckmorton to Pease, August 7, 1867, Pease to Griffin, August 8, 1867, RG 307, TSL; W. B. Thompson to AAG, August 12, 1867, LR, CA, DT, RG 393, NA.

75. C. M. Nelson to Griffin, August 13, 1867, Governor's Papers (Pease), TSL.

76. SO 145, August 1, SO 150, August 10, 1867, DT, RG 94, NA.

77. Sheridan to Griffin, August 19, 1867, AGO, file 57M1868, microcopy 619, roll 634, RG 94, NA. For characterizations of the judges, see J. L. Haynes to Griffin, April 30, 1867, *House Executive Documents,* 40th

Cong., 1st sess., no. 20, pp. 90–92. See also SO 153, August 15, 1867, DT, RG 94, NA.

78. Griffin to Pease, August 15, 1867, Pease Papers, APL; Pease to AAG, August [?], 1867, LR, FMD, RG 393, NA.

79. SO 154, August 19, 1867, DT, RG 94, NA (original spelling retained). See also SO 111, August 8, 1867, FMD, RG 94, NA.

80. Sefton, *Army and Reconstruction,* pp. 153–56; Thomas and Hyman, *Stanton,* pp. 549–52.

81. Grant to Johnson, August 17, 1867, *House Executive Documents,* 40th Cong., 2d sess., no. 57, pp. 3–4.

82. Johnson to Grant, August 19, 1867, ibid, pp. 5–6; GO 77, August 18, 1867, AGO, RG 94, NA.

83. Johnson appointed Hancock on the advice of Lt. Gen. Richard Taylor, who had commanded the Confederate forces in Mississippi and Alabama in 1865. See Richard Taylor, *Destruction and Reconstruction: Personal Experiences of the Late War* (New York: D. Appleton & Co., 1879), p. 251.

84. See Sefton, *Army and Reconstruction,* pp. 156–57; GO 81, August 21, 1867, AGO, RG 94, NA.

85. See Johnson to Grant, August 20, 1867, *House Executive Documents,* 40th Cong., 2d sess., no. 57, pp. 6–7.

86. Grant to Sheridan, September 3, 1867, Grant Papers, LC. Sefton, *Army and Reconstruction,* pp. 162–63, errs here by ignoring Griffin's brief tenure before Mower assumed command.

87. 87. Sheridan to Griffin, August 27, 1867, AGO, file 57M1868, microcopy 619, roll 634, RG 94, NA; GO 30, September 3, FMD, RG 94, NA.

88. SO 160, August 27, 1867, FMD, RG 94, NA.

89. SO 169, September 10, SO 170, September 11, SO 171, September 12, 1867, ibid.

90. SO 169, September 10, 1867, ibid.; C. Caldwell to Pease, September 3, 1867, Pease Papers, APL.

91. Griffin's postwar career is detailed in Richter, "Tyrant and Reformer," pp. 225–41. For Griffin's death see unnumbered circular, September 15, 1867, DT, RG 94, NA. For the long-term effect of Griffin's demise on patronage, see Rush Plumbly to head of Internal Revenue, February 1, 1869, Assessors, box 33, RG 56, NA.

7: ANOTHER SETBACK

1. See Horace Porter to Grant, January 8, 1869, in Sefton, *Army and Reconstruction,* 190; *Brownsville Daily Ranchero,* January 15, 1870. For more on

Reynolds's character and flair for intrigue, see J. W. Vaughn, *The Reynolds' Campaign on Powder River* (Norman: University of Oklahoma Press, 1961), 25, 148–90; and Zenobia Self, "The Court Martial of J. J. Reynolds," *Military Affairs* 37 (1973): 52–56. For Reynolds's Reconstruction career, see William L. Richter, "'We must Rubb Out and Begin Anew': The Army and the Republican Party in Texas Reconstruction," *Civil War History* 19 (1973): 334–52.

2. For Reynolds's send-off from Brownsville, see *Brownsville Daily Ranchero*, September 29, 1867. See also A. J. Hamilton to M. C. Hamilton, September 22, 1867, Hamilton Papers, UT.

3. Heitman, *Historical Register* 1:825; Cullum, *Biographical Register*, II, 78; Warner, *Generals in Blue*, 397–98; Boatner, *Civil War Dictionary*, 649.

4. SO 141, September 17, 1867, FMD, RG 94, NA. GO 31, September 21; GO 36, October 14, 1867, DT, RG 94, NA. Bvt. Maj. Gen. J. J. Reynolds to AAG, October 4, 1867, TR, FMD, RG 393, NA. AAG to Reynolds, November 13, 1867, TS, FMD, RG 393, NA. E. Degener to Pease, September 24, 1867, Pease Papers, APL.

5. SCA to Pease, September 27, 1867, LS, DT, RG 393, NA.

6. Sandlin, "Texas Reconstruction Convention of 1868–1869," p. 50; Carrier, "Texas during the Reconstruction," p. 212.

7. Sheridan to Granger, June 13, 1865, *O.R.*, XLVIII, pt. 2, pp. 866–67; GO 5, June 30, 1865, MDSW, RG 94, NA; GO 4, June 19, 1865, DT, RG 94, NA; Proclamation to the people of Texas, July 24, 1865, RG 307, TSL; Carrier, "Texas during the Reconstruction," p. 212.

8. See Sandlin, "Texas Reconstruction Convention of 1868–1869," p. 50; James Alex Baggett, "The Rise and Fall of the Texas Radicals, 1867–1883" (Ph.D. diss., North Texas State University, 1972), pp. 76–77.

9. C. B. Sabin to Bvt. Maj. Gen. J. A. Mower, October 10, 1867, in *Flake's Daily Bulletin* (Galveston), October 10, 1867; A. J. Hamilton to Pease, October 28, 1867, Pease Papers, APL. An excellent discussion of the ab initio question is in Carrier, "Texas during the Reconstruction," pp. 217–21.

10. GO 192, October 20, SO 200, November 8, 1867, DT, RG 94, NA.

11. Proclamation of October 25, 1867, RG 307, TSL.

12. Republican leaders had suggested that Pease deliver such an "inaugural address." See, for example, C. Caldwell to Pease, September 3, 1867, Pease Papers, APL.

13. Alexander to Reynolds, October 27, 1867, in *San Antonio Express*, November 5, 1867.

14. M. C. Hamilton to Mower, October 29, 1867, in *Austin Weekly Republican*, November 13, 1867; Mower to Reynolds, November 23, 1867, Governor's Papers (Pease), TSL. This position was later assumed by the U.S.

Supreme Court in *Texas* v. *White*, 7 Wall. 700 (1869). See also William Whatley Pierson, Jr., "Texas versus White," *Southwest Historical Quarterly* 18 (1914–15): 341–67; 19 (1915–16): 1–36, 42–58; Charles Fairman, *Reconstruction and Reunion, 1864–1888* (New York, 1971, pp. 628–76, especially p. 646; Harold M. Hyman, *A More Perfect Union: The Impact of the Civil War and Reconstruction on the Constitution* (New York: Alfred A. Knopf, 1973), pp. 517–18; Scarborough, "George W. Paschal," pp. 95–136, especially pp. 111–14, 120.

15. Carrier, "Texas during the Reconstruction," pp. 214–17.

16. Grant to Mower, September 18, 21, 1867, Mower to Grant, September 16, 19, 1867, Grant Papers, LC.

17. Mower to Grant, September 18, 1867, Mower to C. B. Comstock, October 21, 1867, Grant to Mower, November 2, 1867, ibid. See also AAG to Reynolds, November 5, 8, 1867, TS, FMD, RG 393, NA; Reynolds to AAG, November 13, 1867, TR, FMD, RG 393, NA; SCA to Reynolds, November 15, 1867, AGO file 57M1868, microcopy 619, roll 634, RG 94, NA. It was not unusual for Texas and New Orleans to be out of touch. See, for example, Reynolds to AAG, February 18, 1868, LR, FMD, RG 393, NA; and AAG to Reynolds, February 24, 1868, LS, FMD, RG 393, NA. Mower rarely concerned himself as directly with Texas affairs as implied in Shook, "Federal Occupation," p. 336; see also Grant to Mower, November 22, 25, 1867, Mower to Grant, November 22, 1867, Grant Papers, LC. For Mower's tenure in Louisiana, see Joseph Green Dawson III, "Army Generals and Reconstruction: Mower and Hancock as Case Studies," *Southern Studies* 17 (1978): 255–72.

18. SO 192, October 20, SO 195, November 1, 1867, AGO, file 57M1868, microcopy 619, roll 634, RG 94, NA.

19. SO 197, November 4, SO 198, November 5, SO 199, November 7, SO 206, November 18, SO 207, November 19, SO 209, November 21, SO 210, November 22, 1867, DT, RG 94, NA. Ramsdell, *Reconstruction in Texas*, p. 181, misleadingly asserts that Mower followed a milder policy than Sheridan; Shook, "Federal Occupation," p. 336, is also in error when he maintains that Mower continued the "essential" policies of Sheridan and Griffin. In actuality, Reynolds swept the Democrat-Conservatives out of office more thoroughly than Sheridan had ever dreamed. Republicans defended themselves by understating the number of men removed by 50 percent and pointing out that Texas had 2,500 officials anyway. See Carrier, "Texas during the Reconstruction," p. 203. Counts of the officials appointed in army orders and of those recorded in state records often differ. Removals and appointments are listed by county in the ledgers marked "Election Register, 1866–1870," TSL; and "Civil Officers, Texas," RG 393, NA. For a

checkered account of this problem from Pease's point of view, see Griffin, "Pease," pp. 218–19.

20. Heitman, *Historical Register*, I, 496–97; Cullum, *Biographical Register*, II, 108–109; Warner, *Generals in Blue*, pp. 202–204.

21. Grant to Hancock, September 11, 15, November 29, December 3, 1867, Grant to Mower, November 27, 1867, Mower to Grant, November 27, 1867, Hancock to Grant, September 11, 14, 28, December 2, 1867, Grant Papers, LC. See also GO 40, November 29, 1867, FMD, RG 94, NA.

22. See, for example, George T. Todd to Hancock, December 9, 1867, M. H. Roysten to I. W. Harris, January 8, 1868, AGO, file 57M1868, microcopy 619, roll 634, RG 94, NA; T. T. Gammage to AAG, December 12, 1867, Pease Papers, APL; N. L. Hancock and others to General Hancock, January 1, 1868, Governor's Papers (Pease), TSL.

23. See Carrier, "Texas during the Reconstruction," p. 202. It is doubtful whether merely memorizing the law code could make Fayle as effective a judge as implied in Shook, "Federal Occupation," pp. 350–51. Even as loyal a man as Federal Judge John Watrous did not think Fayle qualified. See Walace Hawkins, *The Case of John C. Watrous, U.S. Judge of Texas: A Political Study of High Crimes and Misdemeanors* (Dallas: University Press, 1950), p. 58. Fayle was later fired from his post for failing to utilize black jurors. See SO 249, October 23, 1869, FMD, RG 94, NA. Judge Love's case is in A. N. Morrison and others to Hancock, December 4, 1867, William H. Crook and others to Hancock, November 27, 1867, Pease to Reynolds, December 27, 1867, Reynolds's endorsement of this last letter, AGO, file 57M1868, microcopy 619, roll 634, RG 94, NA.

24. For numerous letters to Reynolds and Pease recommending appointments of Republicans, see LR, CA, FMD, and LR, CA, DT, both in RG 393, NA; and Pease Papers, APL, throughout the winter of 1867–68.

25. SCA to Reynolds, December 4, 1867 (2 messages), TS, CA, FMD, RG 393, NA; Reynolds to Hamilton, December 30, 1867, Reynolds to AAG, December 31, 1867, AGO, file 57M1868, microcopy 619, roll 634, RG 94, NA.

26. Samuel L. Earle to Pease, January 29, 1868, citizens of Dallas to Pease, February 25, 1868, Governor's Papers (Pease), TSL; *Brownsville Daily Ranchero*, December 11, 1867.

27. Hancock to Brig. Gen. E. D. Townsend, January 11, 1868; Grant to Hancock, January 13, 1868, Grant Papers, LC.

28. SCA to T. T. Gammage, John Good, and James Love, January 2, 1868, SCA to T. J. Jennings and A. J. Stanley, January 6, 1868, LS, CA, FMD, RG 393, NA; "Election Register, 1868–1870" lists Hancock's appointees. See also SO 16, January 22, SO 18, January 25, SO 44, February

27, SO 48, March 3, SO 62, March 24, SO 89, April 25, 1868, FMD, RG 94, NA. Hancock's desire to stay out of local politics is expressed in SCA to Reynolds, January 30, 1868, LS, CA, FMD, RG 393, NA.

29. Hancock to Grant, January 27, 1868, Grant Papers, LC; A. R. Hancock, *Reminiscences of Winfield Scott Hancock by His Wife* (New York: Charles L. Webster, 1887), pp. 120–22.

30. Hancock, *Reminiscences*, p. 122.

31. GO 40, November 29, 1867, FMD, RG 94, NA.

32. *Brownsville Daily Ranchero,* December 11, 1867.

33. C. Caldwell to Pease, January 26, 1868, Pease Papers, APL.

34. See SCA to Pease, December 28, 1867, in *The Civil Record of Major General Winfield Scott Hancock, during His Administration in Louisiana and Texas* (N.p., 1871), pp. 18–21.

35. Ibid.

36. GO 1, January 11, 1868, FMD, RG 94, NA.

37. Pease to Hancock, January 17, 1868, *House Executive Documents,* 40th Cong., 3d sess., no. 1, pp. 268–71.

38. Ibid. (original spelling retained).

39. Pease to Carrie, January 25, 1868, C. Caldwell to Pease, January 26, 1868, Pease Papers, APL; Hancock to Grant, January 21, February 3, 1868, Grant Papers, LC.

40. Hancock to Maj. O. O. Howard, February 24, 1868, *Civil Record of Major General Hancock,* pp. 29–30.

41. See, for example, Andrew M. Moore to AAG, December 25, 1867, John R. Chite to AAG, January 7, 1868, anonymous to AAG, January 9, 1868, Margaret E. Love to AAG, January 27, 1868, S. J. Adams to AAG, February 19, 1868, LR, CA, FMD, RG 393, NA; AAG to Reynolds, December 23, 1867, LS, FMD, RG 393, NA; ASCA to AAG FB, February 4, 1868, LR, FB, RG 105, NA.

42. Bentley, *History of the Freedmen's Bureau,* p. 166.

43. A. H. Moore to AAG, January 25, 1868, LR, CA, FMD, RG 393, NA; Extract from Report of 1st Lt. H. E. Scott, March 31, 1866, 2nd Lt. C. G. Gordon to AAG, March 12, 1868, W. V. Tunstall to Reynolds, March 26, 1868, Governor's Papers (Pease), TSL.

44. See Consolidated Report of Registration, State of Texas, March 16, 1868, Registration MSS, box 1, RG 393, NA.

45. See Carrier, "Texas during the Reconstruction," pp. 229–30; Shook, "Federal Occupation," pp. 343–44.

46. Carrier, "Texas during the Reconstruction," pp. 230–32.

47. John Hancock to Gen. Hancock, December 23, 1867, AGO, file 57M1868, microcopy 619, roll 634, RG 94, NA.

48. GO 3, January 11, FMD, RG 94, NA. Hancock's orders really affected few persons, but again, his attitude was important. See Russ, "Radical Disfranchisement in Texas," p. 45 n. 22. Some of the boards perhaps ignored Hancock's orders and registered potential voters only if they favored a new constitution and Negro suffrage. See *Dallas Herald*, February 1, 1868, See also SO 61, April 11, 1868, DT, RG 94, NA.

49. SO 57, March 13, 1868, FMD, RG 94, NA; R. Anthony to AAG, February 19, 1868, LR, CA, FMD, RG 393, NA; Charles King to AAG, August 4, 1868, LR, FMD, RG 393, NA; Carrier, "Texas during the Reconstruction," pp. 225–26.

50. See printed form, AAAG to Nathan Patten, August 29, 1868, Johnson Papers, LC. See also SO 51, October 7, 1868, GO 78, April 20, 1869, FMD, RG 94, NA.

51. Sandlin, "Texas Reconstruction Convention of 1868–1869," p. 27.

52. Carrier, "Texas during the Reconstruction," pp. 228, 234–35, 246–47.

53. Grant to Mower, September 27, October 1, 1867, Mower to Grant, September 27, 1867, Hancock to Grant, December 8, 18, 1867, Grant Papers, LC; Hancock to Grant, December 17, 1867, TS, CA, FMD, RG 393, NA; SO 213, December 18, 1867, FMD, RG 94, NA.

54. Ramsdell, *Reconstruction in Texas*, pp. 194–99.

55. For a detailed discussion of Conservative strategy, see Carrier, "Texas during the Reconstruction," pp. 236–43; Baggett, "Texas Radicals," p. 81.

56. For the results of the election, see Capt. Daniel O. Drennan to SCA, March 16, 1868, Johnson Papers, LC; and SO 78, April 13, 1868, FMD, RG 94, NA. See also SCA to Reynolds, April 16, 1868, LS, FMD, RG 393, NA. Another election was held to fill the vacancies caused by the deaths of several delegates (SO 61, April 11, 1868, DT, RG 94, NA).

57. Hancock to Pease, March 9, 1868, *House Executive Documents*, 40th Cong., 3d sess., no. 1, pp. 262–67.

58. Hancock to Reynolds, January 30, February 12, 1868, TR, FMD, RG 393, NA.

59. Pease to Hancock, January 17, 1868, *House Executive Documents*, 40th Cong., 3d sess., no. 1, pp. 268–71.

60. Hancock to Pease, March 9, 1868, ibid., pp. 264–68.

61. Augustus T. Freed, *Hancock: The Life and Public Service of Winfield Scott Hancock* (Chicago: Henry A. Sumner & Co., 1880), pp. 84–85; John W. Forney, *The Life and Military Career of Winfield Scott Hancock . . .* (Rochester, N.Y.: H. B. Graves, 1880), pp. 233–35; Frederick O. Goodrich, *The Life and Public Services of Winfield Scott Hancock, Major General, U.S.A.* (Boston: Lee & Shepard, 1880), pp. 240–49, 285, 299, 301; "The Civil Record of Gen-

eral Winfield S. Hancock, during His Administration in Louisiana and Texas," *Southern Review* 9 (1871): 907–908, 912; Francis A. Walker, *General Hancock* (New York: D. Appleton & Co., 1894), pp. 299–302. Most of the above works were written when Hancock ran for president. The same theme, however, prevails in more modern studies. See Ulrich, "Northern Military Mind," pp. 48–49, 67, 75; and Glenn Tucker, *Hancock, the Superb* (Indianapolis: Bobbs, Merrill, 1960), pp. 279–80. Tucker (p. 337 n. 21) theorizes that Hancock's Reconstruction plans were influenced by discussions he may have had with Lincoln during the war. This hypothesis ignores Hancock's affiliation with the Democrats, which determined most of his political ideas.

62. James E. Merin to President Johnson, February 21, 1868, Johnson Papers, LC.

63. See Hancock to Grant, February 3, 6, 1868, Grant to Hancock, February 3, 1868, Grant Papers, LC, SO 27, February 26, 1868, FMD, RG 94, NA.

64. The troop movements are described in SO 37, February 27, SO 38, February 28, SO 39, March 3, SO 40, March 4, 1868, FMD, RG 94, NA. See also AAG to Reynolds, February 11, 1868, LS, FMD, RG 393, NA; Hancock to Reynolds, March 14, 1868, TS, FMD, RG 393, NA.

65. Fred Oklenburger to AAG, November 21, 1867, LR, DT, RG 393, NA.

66. Paris C. Looring to AAG, February 12, 1868, ibid.; *Brownsville Daily Ranchero*, March 4, 1868.

67. H. W. Branch to AAG, February 26, 1868, LR, FMD, RG 393, NA.

68. Reynolds to AAG, May 29, 1868, ibid.

69. Buchanan to Pease, June 5, 1868, Governor's Papers (Pease), TSL; GO 45, March 29, 1869, FMD, RG 94, NA.

70. 2d Lt. C. G. Gordon to AAG, March 9, 1868, LR, DT, RG 393, NA; AAAG to Capt. F. W. Bailey, September 25, 1868, LS, FMD, RG 393, NA; Capt. J. W. Bradford to AAG, November 27, 1867, LR, FMD, RG 393, NA; Maj. G. C. Cramm to AAG, August 1, 1868, LR, DT, RG 393, NA.

71. GO 14, October 7, 1868, GO 24, May 21, 1868, FMD, RG 94, NA.

72. *Army and Navy Journal,* 5 (May 16, 1868): 619; *Dallas Herald,* May 25, 1867.

73. Wallace, *Texas in Turmoil*, pp. 234–40; SO 13, January 16, 1869, FMD, RG 94, NA.

74. Hancock, *Reminiscences*, pp. 127–28; *Civil Record of Major Hancock*, pp. 30–31; *Congressional Globe*, 40th Cong., 2d sess., 1867–68, XXXIX, pt. 1 p. 491.

75. Thomas and Hyman, *Stanton*, pp. 553–80, especially p. 577.

76. Hancock to Grant, February 7, 9, 11, 27, March 15, 1868, Grant to

Hancock, February 8, 11, 24, 29, March 14, 15, 1868, Rawlins to Hancock, February 21, 28, 1868, Johnson Papers, LC; Hancock to AG USA, February 27, 1868, in *Civil Record of Major Hancock,* p. 31.

8: CONFUSION REIGNS SUPREME

1. See James Marshall-Cornwall, *Grant as Military Commander* (New York: Van Nostrand–Reinhold, 1970), p. 32; Heitman, *Historical Register,* II, 258; Warner, *Generals in Blue,* pp. 48–49; Boatner, *Civil War Dictionary,* p. 94.

2. See Hancock to Grant, March 15, 1868, Grant papers, LC; GO 14, March 16, GO 15, March 18, GO 16, March 28, 1868, FMD, RG 94, NA; Reynolds to AG USA, March 24, 1868, TS, FMD, RG 393, NA; Reynolds to AGO, March 30, 1868, LS, DT, RG 393, NA.

3. Reynolds made a total of 759 appointments, according to "Election Register, 1866–1870," TSL. "Civil Officers, Texas," RG 393, NA, lists 1,176 appointments by Reynolds during the same period, September 16, 1867, to November 4, 1868.

4. Buchanan to Grant, May 16, 1868, Grant to Buchanan, May 8, 1868, Grant Papers, LC; Buchanan to Rawlins, July 18, 1868, SCA to Pease, July 24, 1868, LS, CA, FMD, RG 393, NA. For Buchanan's removals and appointments, see SO 93, April 30, SO 95, May 2, SO 103, May 12, SO 120, June 1, SO 147, July 1, SO 148, July 3, SO 158, July 17, 1868, FMD, RG 94, NA. Buchanan made 171 appointments ("Election Register, 1866–1870," TSL). See also Griffin, "Pease," p. 222.

5. *Denton Monitor,* August 22, 1868.

6. Grant to Buchanan, June 26, 1868, Grant Papers, LC; GO 155, July 28, 1868, AGO, RG 94, NA; GO 1, August 10, SO 1, August 1, 1868, DT, RG 94, NA.

7. See Special Orders (1868), RG 94, NA. Nearly every other order refers to appointments.

8. L. L. Ward to CO Jacksboro, March 21, 1868, Registration MSS, box 1, RG 393, NA; SO 238, October 9, 1869, FMD, RG 94, NA.

9. Carrier, "Texas during the Reconstruction," pp. 249–50.

10. Ibid., pp. 254–57.

11. Sandlin, "Texas Reconstruction Convention of 1868–1869," pp. 36–41. Sandlin (p. 39) makes a good case for the delegates having more political experience than Carrier implies in "Texas during the Reconstruction," pp. 255, 257. See also Baggett, "Texas Radicals," pp. 81–88, and the tables

on pp. 8, 15, 26, 30, 35, 84, 86, 89. The best analysis of the convention blocs is in Carl H. Moneyhon, *Republicanism in Reconstruction Texas* (Austin: University of Texas Press, 1980), pp. 82–86.

12. Carrier, "Texas during the Reconstruction," pp. 250–52. For more on Evans, who ultimately served on the state supreme court, see Thomas Schoonover, "Documents concerning Lemuel Dale Evans' Plan to Keep Texas in the Union in 1861," *East Texas Historical Journal* 12 (Spring, 1974): 35–38; Waymon L. McClellan, "The Know Nothing Party and the Growth of Sectionalism in East Texas," ibid. 14 (Fall, 1976): 26–36; and his "1855: The Know Nothing Challenge in East Texas," ibid. 12 (Fall, 1974): 33–44; Randolph Campbell, "Political Conflict within the Southern Consensus: Harrison County, Texas, 1850–1880," *Civil War History* 26 (1980): 218–39.

13. For a good analysis of the Radical faction and its leader, E. J. Davis, see Gray, "Davis," pp. 111–49.

14. *Journal of the Reconstruction Convention . . . 1868*, 2 vols. (Austin: Tracy, Siemering Co., 1870), I, 9–10, 32.

15. Message to the state convention, June 3, 1868, RG 307, TSL.

16. Sandlin, "Texas Reconstruction Convention of 1868–1869," pp. 49–59, has an excellent discussion of ab initio.

17. Ibid., pp. 60–64. See also Moneyhon, *Republicanism in Reconstruction Texas*, pp. 72–75.

18. Ramsdell, *Reconstruction in Texas*, pp. 212–16. The best study of the division issue is Ernest Wallace, *The Howling of the Coyotes: Reconstruction Efforts to Divide Texas* (College Station: Texas A & M University Press, 1979).

19. Sandlin, "Texas Reconstruction Convention of 1868–1869," pp. 96–102; Carrier, "Texas during the Reconstruction," pp. 268–69; E. Degener to Pease, October 24, 1867, Pease Papers, APL. On the varied opinions held by Texans during the secession crisis, see Walter L. Buenger, *Secession and the Union in Texas* (Austin: University of Texas Press, 1984).

20. Carrier, "Texas during the Reconstruction," pp. 268–72. The various proposed states are described in Sandlin, "Texas Reconstruction Convention of 1868–1869," pp. 102–16. On Mills, see Alwyn Barr, "The Making of a Secessionist: The Antebellum Career of Roger Q. Mills," *Southwestern Historical Quarterly* 79 (1975–76): 129–44.

21. Carrier, "Texas during the Reconstruction," pp. 273–78 (quotation from p. 277).

22. Sandlin, "Texas Reconstruction Convention of 1868–1869," p. 70.

23. *Journal of the Reconstruction Convention 1868*, I, 12–13.

24. Susan Lawrence Davis, *Authentic History: Ku Klux Klan, 1865–1877* (New York: Privately printed, 1924), p. 254.

25. For Klan activity in Texas, see Stanley F. Horn, *Invisible Empire: The Story of the Ku Klux Klan, 1866–1871* (Boston: Houghton, Mifflin & Co., 1939), pp. 284–85; W. C. Nunn, *Texas under the Carpetbaggers* (Austin: University of Texas Press, 1962), pp. 247–49; William D. Wood, "The Ku Klux Klan," *Quarterly of the Texas State Historical Association* 9 (1905–1906): 262–68; Shook, "Federal Occupation," pp. 434–37; Allen W. Trelease, *White Terror: The Ku Klux Klan Conspiracy and Southern Reconstruction* (New York: Harper & Row, 1971), pp. 103–109, 137–48. See also Hodding Carter, *The Angry Scar: The Story of Reconstruction* (New York: Doubleday, 1959), pp. 197–229.

26. Charles H. Moore, "Anderson County during Reconstruction" (MS in Charles H. Moore Papers, UT), p. 6; Wood, "Ku Klux Klan," p. 266; Barbara Susan Overton Chandler, "A History of Bowie County" (M.A. thesis, University of Texas, 1937), p. 50; Sue Estella Moore, "Life of John Benjamin Long" (M.A. thesis, University of Texas, 1924), pp. 53–54.

27. Bryan to Hayes, August 29, 1871, in Winkler, "Bryan-Hayes Correspondence," pp. 60–62.

28. James Lee Martin, "History of Goliad, 1836–1880" (M.A. thesis, University of Texas, 1937), p. 134; Gladys Annelle St. Clair, "A History of Hopkins County, Texas" (M.A. thesis, University of Texas, 1940), p. 69.

29. Martin, "History of Goliad," p. 133; Bertha Atkinson, "The History of Bell County" (M.A. thesis, University of Texas, 1929), pp. 129–30, 142, 148; Marr, "History of Matagorda County," p. 165; George Louis Crockett, *Two Centuries in East Texas: A History of San Augustine County and the Surrounding Territory from 1685 to the Present Time* (Dallas: Southwest Press, 1932), pp. 347–49.

30. Flora G. Bowles, "The History of Trinity County" (M.A. thesis, University of Texas, 1928), p. 57.

31. Capt. E. C. Culver to AAG, October 11, 1867, LR, FB, RG 105, NA.

32. 2d Lt. J. H. Sands to AAG, October 3, 1868, LR, FMD, RG 393, NA.

33. See GO 15, October 12, 1868, FMD, RG 94, NA; B. W. Musgrove to AAG, July 20, 1868, LR, DT, RG 393, NA; Reynolds to AGO, October 22, November 4, 1868, LS, FMD, RG 393, NA.

34. See Ed Bartholomew's biography *Cullen Baker: Premier Texas Gunfighter* (Houston: Frontier Press, 1954). See also Boyd W. Johnson, "Cullen Montgomery Baker: The Arkansas-Texas Desperado," *Arkansas Historical Quarterly* 25 (1966): 229–39.

35. Bartholomew, *Cullen Baker*, pp. 26–27, 42, 43, 50–54, 61, 63, 76; Watlington, "Memoirs," pp. 72–73, 84–85. For the murder of Bvt. Capt. W. G. Kirkman, see *Denton Monitor*, November 7, 1868; and James Small-

wood, "The Freedmen's Bureau Reconsidered; Local Agents and the Black Community," *Texana* 11 (1975): 309–20, for the career of Kirkman.

36. When he died, Baker was armed with four revolvers, two double-barreled shotguns, three derringers, and six knives (Bartholomew, *Cullen Baker*, pp. 82–84, 130–32).

37. GO 195, November 5, 1869, FMD, RG 94, NA.

38. The activities of the Bickerstaff gang are described in the *Standard* (Clarksville), August 15, 1868; *Houston Weekly Times*, September 11, 1868; and *Austin Republican*, September 22, 1868. See also Capt. T. W. Tolman to AAG, August 31, 1868; Capt. A. R. Chaffee to AAG, September 21, 27, October 5, 30, 1868, LR, FMD, RG 393, NA; Reynolds to AGO, April 30, 1869; AAAG to Lt. Col. W. B. Pease, April 17, 1869, LS, FMD, RG 393, NA. Both Tolman and Chaffee had trouble with civilians in northern Texas who resisted to the death any effort to disarm them. The army was accused of several atrocities in this area. See H. H. McConnell, *Five Years a Cavalryman . . .* (Jacksboro: J. N. Rogers & Co., Tex., 1889), p. 192.

39. For the Bob Lee gang, see William H. Carter, "The Sixth Regiment of Cavalry," in *The Army of the United States*, ed. Theodore F. Rodenbough and William L. Haskin (New York: Maynard, Merrill & Co., 1896), p. 242; *Texas News* (Bonham), May 28, 1869; Lt. M. P. Eakin to AAG, February 8, 1869, Bvt. Col. R. M. Morris to AAG, June 8, 1869, LR, FMD, RG 393, NA; SCA to W. C. Phillips, July 14, 1869, LS, CA, FMD, RG 393, NA. A reward of one thousand dollars had been offered for Baker, Bickerstaff, and Lee; see the *Standard* (Clarksville), September 19, 1868. Lee may have been merely the local leader of the Democratic opposition, a victim of neighboring Radical Republicans. See G. B. Ray, *Murder at the Corners* (San Antonio: Naylor, 1957), pp. 7, 10–20, 25, 35, 40.

40. Chaffee to AAG, November 20, 1868, Bvt. Brig. Gen. George P. Buell to AAG, May 22, 1869, LR, FMD, RG 393, NA; S. L. Johnson to AAG, January [?], 1869, P. N. Yell to AAG, August 23, 1869, LR, CA, FMD, RG 393, NA.

41. AAAG to CO Galveston, June 16, 1868, AAG to CO Austin, January 20, 1869, LS, FMD, RG 393, NA; SCA to John B. Johnson, May 19, 1869, LS, CA, FMD, RG 393, NA; CO Austin to AAG, June 15, 1869, LR, CA, FMD, RG 393, NA.

42. *Journal of the Reconstruction Convention 1868*, I, 200–201.

43. CO Austin to AAG, July 5, 1869, Judge B. F. Barkley to AAG, September 5, 1869, April 27, 1870, LR, CA, FMD, RG 393, NA; SO 42, February 20, SO 256, November 1, 1869, FMD, RG 94, NA.

44. *Denton Monitor*, September 5, 26, 1868.

45. Wesley Ogden to Pease, August [?], 1868, Governor's Papers (Pease), TSL.

46. Lt. J. R. Fitch to AAG, February 7, 25, 1868, LR, FB, RG 105, NA; 2d Lt. James Davidson to AAG, June 21, 1869, LR, CA, FMD, RG 393, NA.

47. John W. Harris to AAG, March 23, 1868, LR, FMD, RG 393, NA; Reynolds to AAG, June 8, 1868, LS, DT, RG 393, NA; AAAG to Capt. T. M. Tolman, September 22, 1868, LS, CA, FMD, RG 393, NA.

48. Reynolds to AAAG FMD, July 4, 1868, Johnson Papers, LC; GO 41, November 22, 1867, DT, RG 94, NA; GO 3, August 29, 1868, FMD, RG 94, NA.

49. SO 142, September 18, 1867, CA, FMD, RG 94, NA; Pease to AAG, July 29, 1868, LR, DT, RG 393, NA; SO 2, August 11, SO 3, August 12, 1868, FMD, RG 94, NA; SO 93, October 30, 1868, SO 187, October 18, 1867, DT, RG 94, NA; GO 37, November 4, SO 192, November 21, 1867, CA, FMD, RG 94, NA; SO 36, September 19, GO 17, October 20, GO 19, October 24, GO 26, November 24, 1868, FMD, RG 94, NA.

50. Lt. Gregory Barrett to AAG, June 8, 1868, LR, FB, RG 105, NA; Reynolds to AAG, July 23, 1868, LS, FMD, RG 393, NA.

51. *Journal of the Reconstruction Convention 1868*, I, 193–96, 203, 262–63; Ramsdell, *Reconstruction in Texas*, pp. 217–24.

52. Carrier, "Texas during the Reconstruction," pp. 278–82; Sandlin, "Texas Reconstruction Convention of 1868–1869," pp. 65–77.

53. *Denton Monitor*, July 14, 1868.

54. "Register of Crimes Committed in Texas, 1866–1868," 3 vols. (listed by county), "Abstracts of Crimes Committed in Counties of Texas, 1869–1870," 3 vols. (listed by date), RG 393, NA.

55. Carrier, "Texas during the Reconstruction," pp. 282–83; Sandlin, "Texas Reconstruction Convention of 1868–1869," p. 79.

56. *Houston Telegraph*, July 14, 1868; Sandlin, "Reconstruction Convention of 1868–1869," pp. 77–79.

57. Carrier, "Texas during the Reconstruction," pp. 283–84.

58. Sandlin, "Texas Reconstruction Convention of 1868–1869," pp. 79–81. Sandlin accuses the convention of being unwilling to reveal the possibility that blacks caused the Millican incident.

59. AAAG to Lt. Charles A. Vernon, August 11, 1868, AAG to Brig. Gen. O. L. Shepard, August 18, 1868, LS, FMD, RG 393, NA; Reynolds to AAG, June 11, 1868, LR, FMD, RG 393, NA.

60. January, 1869, for example, has no records kept or reported; see "Abstracts of Crimes Committed in Counties of Texas, 1869–1870," RG 393, NA.

61. "Register of Crimes Committed in Texas, 1866–1868," "Abstracts of Crimes Committed in Counties of Texas, 1869–1870," ibid.

62. Kenneth W. Wheeler, *To Wear a City's Crown: The Beginnings of Urban Growth in Texas, 1836–1865* (Cambridge, Mass.: Harvard University Press, 1968), pp. 161–66, emphasizes the important role of Texas urban centers in stimulating nearby rural settlements.

63. Carrier, "Texas during the Reconstruction," pp. 263–64.

64. See Sandlin, "Texas Reconstruction Convention of 1868–1869," pp. 132–84, for a thorough discussion of these issues.

65. *Journal of the Reconstruction Convention 1868*, I, 779, 858–59, 1060.

66. Ramsdell, *Reconstruction in Texas*, pp. 235–36; Carrier, "Texas during the Reconstruction," pp. 290–93.

67. *Statutes at Large*, XV, 257.

68. SO 44, September 29, 1868, FMD, RG 94, NA; Ramsdell, *Reconstruction in Texas*, pp. 236–37.

69. Carrier, "Texas during the Reconstruction," p. 298.

70. Ibid., pp. 298–99.

71. GO 91, November 4, 1868, AGO, RG 94, NA.

72. For Canby's service in North and South Carolina, see J. G. de Roulhac Hamilton, *Reconstruction in North Carolina* (New York: Columbia University Press, 1914), pp. 232, 234–40; Francis R. Simkins and Robert H. Woody, *South Carolina during Reconstruction* (Chapel Hill: University of North Carolina Press, 1932), pp. 65–67, 107, 109–10, 175.

73. Carrier, "Texas during the Reconstruction," pp. 300–302.

74. *Austin Republican*, December 2, 1868. See also Baggett, "Birth of the Texas Republican Party," p. 20; Carrier, "Texas during the Reconstruction," p. 293.

9: THE ARMY WRITES A CONSTITUTION

1. *Denton Monitor*, November 21, 1868.

2. Carrier, "Texas during the Reconstruction," pp. 302, 309–10.

3. GO 91, November 4, 1868, FMD, RG 94, NA.

4. Heitman, *Historical Register*, I, 279; Cullum, *Biographical Register*, I, 590–91; Warner, *Generals in Blue*, pp. 67–68; Boatner, *Civil War Dictionary*, p. 118.

5. Boatner, *Civil War Dictionary*, p. 118; Max L. Heyman, Jr., *Prudent Soldier: A Biography of Major General E. R. S. Canby, 1817–1873* (Glendale, Calif.: Arthur H. Clark Company, 1959).

6. Heyman, *Prudent Soldier*, pp. 259–60, 268–69, 332–33, 383–84.

7. Ramsdell, *Reconstruction in Texas*, pp. 243–52.

8. Carrier, "Texas during the Reconstruction," p. 303.

9. Ibid., pp. 303–305.

10. Ibid., pp. 306–308.

11. Ramsdell, *Reconstruction in Texas*, pp. 243–52. For details on the parliamentary maneuvering, see Sandlin, "Texas Reconstruction Convention of 1868–1869," pp. 120–28.

12. Ramsdell, *Reconstruction in Texas*, pp. 240–41, 252–55; Waller, *Colossal Hamilton*, pp. 120–21; Adkins, "Hamilton," pp. 147–48.

13. Carrier, "Texas during the Reconstruction," pp. 312–13.

14. Sandlin, "Texas Reconstruction Convention of 1868–1869," pp. 191–92.

15. For an analysis of the final document, see ibid., pp. 198–214; Carrier, "Texas during the Reconstruction," pp. 317–26.

16. *Journal of the Reconstruction Convention 1868*, II, 518–20.

17. Canby to Davis, December 31, 1868, January 8, 1869, ibid., p. 243; Carrier, "Texas during the Reconstruction," p. 316.

18. Canby to Davis, February 5, 1869, Davis to Canby, February 5, 1869, *Journal of the Reconstruction Convention 1868*, II, 527, 529.

19. SO 30, February 7, 1869, FMD, RG 94, NA; B. Miller, "Pease," p. 135.

20. Canby to Rawlins, February 4, 1869, LS, FMD, RG 393, NA.

21. Heyman, *Prudent Soldier*, pp. 338–39.

22. Davis to Canby, January 14, 1869, *Journal of the Reconstruction Convention 1868*, II, 498.

23. Heyman, *Prudent Soldier*, pp. 338–39. Canby issued sixty orders making appointments. Typical examples are SO 15, January 19, SO 26, February 3, SO 40, February 18, SO 75, March 31, 1869, FMD, RG 94, NA. Canby is listed in "Civil Officers, Texas," RG 393, NA, as having made 203 appointments, and in "Election Register, 1866–1870," TSL, as having made 179. His removals are in "Civil Officers, Texas."

24. Carrier, "Texas during the Reconstruction," p. 307.

25. See reports in LR, CA, FMD, RG 393, NA.

26. GO 4, January 16, 1869, FMD, RG 94, NA.

27. Ibid.

28. AAAG to Capt. James Thompson, February 24, 1869, AAAG to Bvt. Brig. Gen. George Buell, February 26, 1869, AAAG to CO Camp Concordia, April 1, 1869, LS, FMD, RG 393, NA. See also SCA to CO Austin, June 2, 1869, SCA to CO San Antonio, June 8, 1869, SCA to CO Waco, June 17, 1869, LS, CA, FMD, RG 393, NA.

29. GO 5, January 20, 1869, FMD, RG 94, NA.

30. AAG to Judge G. T. Harris, May 26, 1869, LS, FMD, RG 393, NA;

Carleton to AAG, May 6, 1869, anonymous to AAG, May 3, 1869, LR, FMD, RG 393, NA.

31. The "bull pens" are described in T. B. Wheeler, "Reminiscences of Reconstruction in Texas," *Quarterly of the Texas State Historical Association* 11 (1907–1908): 62–64; Alexander White Neville, *A History of Lamar County, Texas* (Paris, Tex.: North Texas Publishing Co., 1937), p. 137; St. Clair, "History of Hopkins County," 65–66; Mary Starr Barkley, *History of Travis County and Austin* (Waco: Texian Press, 1964), p. 97.

32. The Bryan jail is mentioned in Joseph M. Nance, *Early History of Bryan and the Surrounding Area* (College Station, Tex.: Texas A & M University Press, 1962), p. 47. See also Elmer Grady Marshall, "The History of Brazos County, Texas" (M.A. thesis, University of Texas, 1937), p. 85c; SCA to Reynolds, May 12, 1868, LS, CA, FMD, RG 393, NA; prisoners of Brownsville to AAG, December 15, 1867, LR, CA, FMD, RG 393, NA.

33. Reynolds to AAG, May 12, 1868, LS, DT, RG 393, NA; Bvt. Col. James Biddle to AAG, June 28, 1869, LR, FMD, RG 393, NA; GO 15, October 12, 1868, FMD, RG 94, NA; Buell to AAG, May 16, 22, 23, 1869, LR, FMD, RG 393, NA.

34. GO 4, January 16, GO 5, January 20, GO 7, January 21, 1869, FMD, RG 94, NA.

35. SO 1, January 2, SO 36, February 13, SO 71, March 26, 1869, ibid. B. F. Barkley to Pease, March 9, 1869, LR, CA, FMD, RG 393, NA.

36. Carrier, "Texas during the Reconstruction," pp. 329, 331, 332.

37. For a detailed treatment of these petitions, see Sandlin, "Texas Reconstruction Convention of 1868–1869," pp. 220–25.

38. Some of these appointments are listed in Carrier, "Texas during the Reconstruction," p. 333. The pleading of both sides is apparent in files of the Internal Revenue, boxes 33 and 173, RG 56, NA. See also J. L. Haynes to W. W. Mills, April 9, 1869; A. J. Hamilton to Mills, June 1, 1869, W. W. Mills Papers, UT; Sandlin, "Texas Reconstruction Convention of 1868–1869," pp. 219–20.

39. *Journal of the Reconstruction Convention 1868*, II, 40–41, 171–73.

40. C. B. Sabin to Pease, November 14, 1868, Pease Papers, APL; GO 10, March 5, 1869, AGO, RG 94, NA. Canby was sent to Virginia (Heyman, *Prudent Soldier*, p. 339).

41. Carrier, "Texas during the Reconstruction," pp. 337–39.

42. A. J. Hamilton to W. W. Mills, June 1, 1869, Mills Papers, UT.

43. Carrier, "Texas during the Reconstruction," pp. 341, 352–61.

44. Pease to Reynolds, May 17, 1869, LR, FMD, RG 393, NA.

45. *Statutes at Large*, XVI, 40–41.

46. Reynolds to AGO, May 20, 1869, LS, FMD, RG 393, NA.

47. Carrier, "Texas during the Reconstruction," pp. 340, 342–51.

48. Ramsdell, *Reconstruction in Texas*, p. 271; Nunn, *Texas under the Carpetbaggers*, p. 14.

49. Carrier, "Texas during the Reconstruction," pp. 350–51; Baggett, "Texas Radicals," pp. 103–105.

50. Sandlin, "Texas Reconstruction Convention of 1868–1869," p. 226.

51. A. P. McCormick to [James H. Bell], April 20, 1869, Bell Papers, UT. See also J. G. Tracy to Pease, April 8, 1869, McCormick to Pease, April 28, 1869, Pease Papers, APL.

52. A. P. McCormick to [James H. Bell], April 28, 1869, Bell Papers, UT (original spelling retained).

53. SO 51, October 7, 1868, GO 78, April 20, 1869, FMD, RG 94, NA.

54. *Statutes at large*, XV, 344; GO 60, March 29, 1869, FMD, RG 94, NA; Judge W. A. C. Croghan to AAG, April 15, 1869, LR, FMD, RG 393, NA.

55. GO 74, April 12, 1869, RG 94, NA. Copies of these lists are in Registration MSS, box 2, RG 393, NA. See also A. P. McCormick to Pease, April 28, 1869, Pease Papers, APL.

56. Speech of February 4, 1867, Hamilton Papers, UT.

57. Ramsdell, *Reconstruction in Texas*, pp. 274–75; Reynolds to W. W. Mills, June 10, 1870, Mills Papers, UT.

58. This Radical ploy was mentioned in J. L. Haynes to Pease, June 15, 1869, Pease papers, APL.

59. E. J. Davis to J. P. Newcomb, September 22, 1869, James P. Newcomb Papers, UT.

60. William H. Fleming to Pease, July 8, 1869, Pease Papers, APL. For the election and issues from E. J. Davis's point of view, see Gray, "Davis," pp. 158–81.

10: THE ARMY INSTALLS A GOVERNMENT

1. Michael Hahn to Mrs. W. W. Mills, May 31, 1869, and enclosed clipping, Mills Papers, UT.

2. W. H. Fleming to Pease, April 20, July 8, 1869, Pease Papers, APL.

3. Carrier, "Texas during the Reconstruction," pp. 333–36, 365–66.

4. *American Annual Cyclopaedia* (1869), p. 674. See also William B. Hesseltine, *U. S. Grant: Politician* (New York: Dodd, Mead & Co., 1935), pp. 183–84; M. C. Hamilton and others to AAG, November 8, 1869; E. J. Davis to AAG, November 10, 1869, LR, CA, RG 393, NA. Moneyhon, *Republicanism in Reconstruction Texas*, pp. 115–16, 116 n. 33, asserts that

Reynolds's switch surprised everyone. The evidence shows that both sides maneuvered for his support. The only one genuinely surprised was A. J. Hamilton, whose adherents had worked behind his back.

5. A. P. McCormick to Pease, April 28, 1869, Pease Papers, APL.

6. ASCA to Charles Howard, August 6, 1869; ASCA to Allen L. Risk, August 25, 1869, LS, CA, FMD, RG 393, NA; M. C. Hamilton and others to AAG, November 8, 1869, LR, CA, FMD, RG 393, NA.

7. See printed orders, 1869 series, FMD, RG 94, NA. See also "Civil Officers, Texas," RG 393, NA, which lists 2,051 appointments, and "Election Register, 1866–1870," TSL, which lists 1,667 appointments. The oath requirement caused Reynolds to make only 139 removals. For the effect of Reynolds's manipulations on the local level, see Baggett, "Texas Radicals," pp. 108–109; and Marion Merseburger, "A Political History of Houston, Texas, during the Reconstruction Period as Recorded by the Press" (M.A. thesis, Rice University, 1950), pp. 44–45, 47–48, 78, 97. Whether there were 2,000 Radicals available and willing to hold office at this time is difficult to say. For preliminary work on producing names of such persons, see Robert W. Shook, "Toward a List of Reconstruction Loyalists," *Southwestern Historical Quarterly* 76 (1972–73): 315–20.

8. C. Caldwell to Pease, July 17, 1869, Pease Papers, APL.

9. Ramsdell, *Reconstruction in Texas*, pp. 276–77.

10. Reynolds to Grant, September 4, 1869, in *American Annual Cyclopaedia* (1869), pp. 674–75.

11. A. J. Hamilton had resigned his state supreme court position a week earlier; see SO 224, September 23, 1869, FMD, RG 94, NA; Pease to Carrie, August 3, 1867, March 21, 1868, Pease Papers, APL.

12. Pease to Reynolds, September 30, 1869, RG 307, TSL. For Reynolds's acceptance of Pease's resignation, see SO 232, October 2, 1869, FMD, RG 94, NA. Pease's most comprehensive biographer, Griffin ("Pease"), tells the story from the governor's point of view but is often vague as to Pease's political stance.

13. George C. Rives to James P. Newcomb, September 7, October 5, 1869, Newcomb Papers, UT.

14. M. C. Hamilton to James P. Newcomb, October 16, December 5, 1869, ibid.

15. Carrier, "Texas during the Reconstruction," pp. 358–61, 370–73.

16. The army did grant printing contracts to local editors to help them stay in business. See, for example, SCA to M. P. Barrett, February 16, 1870, LS, CA, FMD, RG 393, NA.

17. Sheridan to Wright, November 28, 1865, Sheridan Papers, LC; Sheridan to Grant, February 22, 1866, Grant Papers, LC.

18. GO 11, March 9, 1866, DT, RG 94, NA.

19. Unnumbered order, May 19, 1869, FMD, RG 94, NA. See also the broadside of the same date, RG 393, NA.

20. Broadside, May 19, 1869, RG 393, NA. The *Texas Republican* was not connected with the Republican party. It was named long before the Civil War and referred to the theory of government. For more on Loughery, see Campbell, "Political Conflict," pp. 18–39; Max S. Lale, "Robert W. Loughery: Rebel Editor," *East Texas Historical Journal* 21, no. 2 (1983): 3–15.

21. Sherman to AAG, March 31, 1869, LR, FMD, RG 393, NA.

22. Unnumbered order, May 19, 1869, FMD, RG 94, NA; *Standard* (Clarksville), July 10, 1869.

23. Reynolds to AGO, October 20, 1869, LS, FMD, RG 393, NA; GO 107, June 5, GO 127, July 7, GO 170, September 25, GO 175, October 13, GO 181, October 22, GO 202, November 12, GO 205, November 15, GO 211, November 20, GO 212, November 22, GO 234, December 20, all in 1869 series, FMD, RG 94, NA. For the 1870 trials, see GO 3, January 6, GO 8, January 18, GO 14, January 24, GO 26, February 10, GO 27, February 11, GO 33, February 26, GO 41, March 18, GO 53, April 6, GO 62, April 11, 1870, ibid. See also GO 12, February 13, GO 45, March 26, GO 67, April 1, GO 56, April 13, 1869, ibid.; AAAG to CO Ft. McKavett, March 15, 1869, AAG to CO Ft. Duncan, March 24, 1869, LS, FMD, RG 393, NA.

24. ASCA to CO Jefferson, August 9, 1869, LS, CA, FMD, RG 393, NA.

25. AAG to Jack Helm, June 14, 1869, ibid.; AAAG to CO Columbus, April 29, 1869, FMD, RG 393, NA; SCA to B. B. Hart, June 1, 1869, LS, CA, FMD, RG 393, NA; CO Jefferson to AAG, September 6, 1869, LR, CA, FMD, RG 393, NA; SCA to CO Corpus Christi, May 29, 1869, LS, CA, FMD, RG 393, NA; AAAG to Bvt. Maj. Gen. James H. Carleton, April 30, 1869, LS, FMD, RG 393, NA; SCA to CO Austin, June 29, 1869, ASCA to CO Jefferson, August 26, 1869, ASCA to CO Helena, September 11, 1869, ASCA to Messrs. McLemore and Hume, August 19, 1869, ASCA to CO Bryan, September 1, 1869, LS, CA, RG 393, NA.

26. Reynolds to AGO, October 20, 1869, LS, FMD, RG 393, NA.

27. *Standard* (Clarksville), July 31, August 7, 1869; GO 175, October 2, GO 192, November 21, 1869, FMD, RG 94, NA.

28. *Brownsville Daily Ranchero*, February 2, 1870; GO 4, January 16, 1869, FMD, RG 94, NA. Canby would doubtless disagree with Trelease's statement that the results of military commissions were "breathtaking by comparison with that of the civil courts" (*White Terror*, p. 147).

29. The changes can be found in Heitman, *Historical Register*, I, under the

regimental numbers. See also Rodenbough and Haskin, *Army of the United States,* again by regimental numbers.

30. The troop movements are described in Canby to AAG, March 4, 1869, Canby to Reynolds, March 10, 1869, Reynolds to AGO, May 26, 29, 1869, LS, FMD, RG 393, NA. See also GO 102, May 19, GO 133, July 30, GO 201, November 11, 1869, FMD, RG 94, NA.

31. *Dallas Herald,* May 29, 1869.

32. *Texas News* (Bonham), June 18, 1869.

33. Bvt. Maj. Lynde Catlin to AAG, September 16, 1869, LR, FMD, RG 393, NA.

34. Bvt. Col. S. H. Starr to AAG, November 18, 1869, ibid.

35. Bvt. Capt. J. Whitney to AAG, June 7, 1869, ibid.; CO Austin to AAG, July 5, 1869, LR, CA, FMD, RG 393, NA; SO 160, July 8, 1869, FMD, RG 94, NA.

36. Affidavit of F. R. Moun, January 18, 1870, LR, CA, FMD, RG 393, NA.

37. CO Jefferson to AAG, May 21, 1869, ibid.; 2d Lt. J. H. Jones to AAG, June 22, 1869, LR, FMD, RG 393, NA.

38. CO Austin to CO Waco, November 6, 1869, C. G. Napier to AAG, February 5, 1870, Lt. Col. George P. Buell to AAG, December 5, 1869, LR, FMD, RG 393, NA.

39. James Masterson to AAG, December 18, 1869, LR, CA, FMD, RG 393, NA; SO 29, February 27, SO 43, March 24, 1870, FMD, RG 94, NA.

40. SCA to Judge J. S. Goodrich, July 31, 1869, LS, CA, FMD, RG 393, NA.

41. A. G. Walker to AAG, March 7, 1870, LR, CA, FMD, RG 393, NA; GO 128, July 10, 1869, FMD, RG 94, NA.

42. GO 132, July 17, 1869, FMD, RG 94, NA; D. O. Norton to AAG, March 3, 1868, LR, CA, FMD, RG 393, NA; ASCA to CO Waco, September 27, 1869, LS, CA, FMD, RG 393, NA.

43. See J. L. Haynes to W. W. Mills, April 9, 1869, Mills Papers, UT.

44. GO 64, September 1, 1869, AGO, RG 94, NA; GO 174, October 1, 1869, FMD, RG 94, NA.

45. GO 174, October 1, GO 92, May 12, 1869, FMD, RG 94, NA.

46. GO 174, October 1, 1869, ibid.

47. GO 179, October 8; GO 185, October 18, 1869, ibid.; Bvt. Maj. S. M. Whitside to AAG, October 30, 1869, LR, FMD, RG 393, NA.

48. Ramsdell, *Reconstruction in Texas,* p. 281; Carrier, "Texas during the Reconstruction," pp. 389–91.

49. L. P. Harris to AAG, December 31, 1869, James E. Wood to AAG, December 31, 1869, LR, CA, FMD, RG 393, NA.

50. SCA to Thomas H. Brenard, July 5, 1870, LS, CA, FMD, RG 393, NA; E. Degener to AAG, February 7, 1870, LR, CA, FMD, RG 393, NA.

51. Carrier, "Texas during the Reconstruction," pp. 393–94. For the figures, see GO 18, February 1, GO 19, February 1, GO 73, April 16, 1870, FMD, RG 94, NA. See also *Texas Almanac* (1870), pp. 194–97. The manuscript records are missing, which has led to charges that Reynolds juggled the figures and destroyed the evidence or removed it from the state. See Wallace, *Texas in Turmoil,* p. 209.

52. M. C. Hamilton and others to Reynolds, December 20, 1869, *House Executive Documents,* 41st Cong., 2d sess., no. 60, pp. 1–2.

53. SO 6, January 8, GO 5, January 11, GO 21, February 5, 1870, FMD, RG 94, NA; Russ, "Radical Disfranchisement in Texas," p. 51.

54. CO Ft. Brown to AAG, January 31, 1870, J. B. Ferguson and others to AAG, February 18, 1870, LR, CA, FMD, RG 393, NA. See Special Orders, 1870 series, FMD, RG 94, NA. See also SCA to all COs, January 21, 1870, LS, CA, FMD, RG 393, NA.

55. These changes can be seen by comparing the Special Orders, 1870 series, FMD, RG 94, NA, with the election announcements in GO 18, February 18, 1870, ibid. See, for example, SO 72, April 2, 1870, which replaced the elected sheriff of Live Oak County with another man. The elected sheriff "failed to qualify" (i.e., take the oath properly).

56. See, for example, GO 24, February 9, GO 25, February 9, GO 28, February 14, GO 30, February 19, 1870, FMD, RG 94, NA.

57. Ramsdell, *Reconstruction in Texas,* p. 290.

58. *Brownsville Daily Ranchero,* March 1, 1870; Carrier, "Texas during the Reconstruction," p. 425; Shook, "Federal Occupation," pp. 416–18; Ramsdell, *Reconstruction in Texas,* p. 307; Self "Court Martial," pp. 52–56.

59. For details, see Carrier, "Texas during the Reconstruction," pp. 424–26.

60. The last special orders is appropriately a list of military appointments; see SO 84, April 16, 1870, FMD, RG 94, NA. For the termination of military rule, see GO 35, March 31, 1870, AGO, RG 94, NA. The office of civil affairs did not complete its work (e.g., paying election registrars and election supervisors) until August 31, 1870.

CONCLUSION

1. See, for example, *San Antonio Herald,* January 10, 1870.

2. Board of Registrars to AAG, December 4, 1869, LR, CA, FMD, RG 393, NA.

3. James L. McDonough, "John Schofield as Military Director of Reconstruction in Virginia," *Civil War History* 15 (1969): 237–56. See also Sefton, *Army and Reconstruction,* pp. 120–21; Sefton, "Aristotle in Blue and Braid: General John M. Schofield's Essay on Reconstruction," *Civil War History* 17 (1971): 45–57.

4. Frank L. Byrne, "'A Terrible Machine': General Neal Dow's Military Government on the Gulf Coast," *Civil War History* 12 (1966): 5–22, especially p. 22.

5. Thomas Affleck to O. Judd and Co., January 26, 1868, Affleck Papers, LSU.

6. Jeannie Chew Young to Louisa Wharton, January 16, 1866, Wharton Papers, LSU.

7. Most of these observations agree wih Sefton's analysis of army activity in the South. See Sefton, *Army and Reconstruction,* pp. 27–31, 37, 42–43, 127, 137, 147–48, 165, 157–68, 185, 193, 229, 233, 253–54, 257.

8. John Hope Franklin, *Reconstruction: After the Civil War* (Chicago: University of Chicago Press, 1961), pp. 35–36, 119–21.

9. Robert W. Shook, "Military Activities in Victoria, 1865–1866," *Texana* 3 (1965): 347–52; Shook, "Federal Military Activity in Texas, 1865–1870," *Texas Military History* 6 (1967): 44–45. A similar debate exists among historians of Florida Reconstruction. See Merlin E. Cox, "Military Reconstruction in Florida," *Florida Historical Quarterly* 46 (1967–68): 219–33, who argues that the influence of the army in Reconstruction was minimal; and Ralph L. Peek, "Military Reconstruction and the Growth of Anti-Negro Sentiment in Florida," ibid., 47 (1968–69): 380–400, who blames the army's actions for the poor showing and support of the state's Republican party.

10. Sefton, *Army and Reconstruction,* pp. vii–viii, 87, 183, 225, 226; William A. Dunning, *Reconstruction, Political and Economic, 1865–1877* (New York: Columbia University Press, 1907), p. 109.

11. See Brig. Gen. James Shaw to AAG, April 16, May 1, 1866, *House Executive Documents,* 40th Cong., 2d sess., no. 57, pp. 96–97; Jacob Weber to A. M. Bryant, May 31, 1868; D. Campbell to Pease, August 25, 1868, Governor's Papers (Pease), TAS; Crockett, *Two Centuries in East Texas,* pp. 348–49.

12. A. J. Hamilton to Sheridan, January 17, 1866; Sheridan to Grant, January 25, 1866, *House Executive Documents,* 40th Cong., 2d sess., no. 57, pp. 19–20, 34–35.

13. The political manipulation of various generals in Texas confirms Sefton's key contention, namely, that the scope of military power is often determined independently of the number of soldiers present. See, for example, Sefton, *Army and Reconstruction,* pp. 165–67. Houston politics offer

a good example of Sefton's thesis; see Merseburger, "Political History of Houston," pp. 1–7, 9, 11–12, 13, 18, 21–22, 28–29, 31, 44–48, 72–74, 78, 88, 97.

14. AAAG to CO Indianola, June 8, 1869, LS, FMD, RG 393, NA.

15. The position of sheriff was usually the most difficult to fill. See continuous correspondence in LS and LR, FMD, RG 393, NA. See also appointments made in Special Orders series, FMD, RG 94, NA.

16. ASCA to CO Jefferson, August 19, 1869, LS, CA, FMD, RG 393, NA; SO 84, April 16, 1870, FMD, RG 94, NA. See also Sefton, *Army and Reconstruction*, pp. 137–38, 140, 142–43.

17. Studies that state or imply that Texas suffered from negro rule include Harrell Budd, "The Negro in Politics in Texas, 1867–1898" (M.A. thesis, University of Texas, 1925); Seth Shepard McKay, "Texas under the Regime of E. J. Davis" (M.A. thesis, University of Texas, Austin, 1919); Bancroft, *North Mexican States and Texas*; Ramsdell, *Reconstruction in Texas*; Nunn, *Texas under the Carpetbaggers*.

18. Circ. 14, May 1, 1867, DT, RG 94, NA.

19. J. Mason Brewer, *Negro Legislators of Texas and Their Descendants: A History of the Negro in Texas Politics from Reconstruction to Disfranchisement* (Dallas: Mathis Publishing Co., 1935), pp. 18–19, 28–30, 47–51, 55–56, 58–59. See also Romey Fennell, Jr., "The Negro in Texas Politics, 1865–1874" (M.A. thesis, North Texas State University, 1963). For a list of black legislators and members of the state conventions during Reconstruction, see Brewer, *Negro Legislators*, pp. 125–28. The Negro vote probably had more impact on county and city levels than on state government. See Pauline Yelderman, "The Jaybird Democratic Association of Fort Bend County" (M.A. thesis, University of Texas, 1938), pp. 16–17; Frank MacD. Spindler, "Concerning Hempstead and Waller County," *Southwestern Historical Quarterly* 59 (1955–56): 455–58; Lawrence Ward St. Clair, "History of Robertson County" (M.A. thesis, University of Texas, 1931), p. 147; Tausch, "Southern Sentiment among Texas Germans," p. 80. Other historians think that blacks had little influence on local politics. See Dorman Hayward Winfrey, "A History of Rusk County, Texas" (M.A. thesis, University of Texas, 1951), pp. 85–86, who finds that local scalawags helped prevent the black vote from becoming "oppressive." Frank Edd White, "A History of the Territory That Now Constitutes Waller County, Texas, from 1821 to 1844" (M.A. thesis, University of Texas, 1936), pp. 114, 120, admits the black vote was a "problem" but finds that no effort was made to keep blacks from the polls. Instead, white factions clashed with each other over who should control the Negro ballots. Rogers, *Lusty Texans of Dallas*, p. 100, finds that Dallas never suffered from Negro rule, even though blacks allegedly outnumbered whites at the

polls. Baggett, "Early Texas Republican Leadership," p. 454, points out that blacks had little control over Republican party affairs.

20. Carrier, "Texas during the Reconstruction," pp. 167–97, 477–81; Alwyn Barr, *Reconstruction to Reform: Texas Politics, 1876–1906* (Austin, 1971), pp. 17–18, 23, 24–25, 192. See also Kenneth Ray Bain, "The Changing Basis of the Republican Party, 1865–1870" (M.A. thesis, North Texas State University, 1970); and Baggett, "Texas Radicals," pp. 123–24, 127, 153–54, 157–58, 175, 187–88, 191.

21. A good argument could be made that the Democratic-Conservative voters threw the 1869 election by refusing to vote for A. J. Hamilton, because they feared that a Davis victory was the only way to convince Congress to readmit Texas to statehood. Approximately twenty-two thousand registered voters failed to show up at the polls. See GO 73, April 16, 1870, FMD, RG 94, NA; and *Texas Almanac* (1870), p. 194, for the registration and voting figures. The assertion by Nunn, *Texas under the Carpetbaggers*, p. 16, that the regular Democratic candidate kept Hamilton from winning, seems to be in error, because he carried only 400 votes.

22. For a history of the Texas party, see Casdorph, *Republican Party in Texas.*

23. See the rosters listing the men at each installation, RG 94, NA.

24. Gammel, *Laws of Texas*, VI, 17–18; McKay, "Texas under Davis," pp. 118–19; Nunn, *Texas under the Carpetbaggers*, p. 27; Carrier, "Texas during the Reconstruction," pp. 405–67.

25. Carrier, "Texas during the Reconstruction," pp. 470–72; Nunn, *Texas under the Carpetbaggers*, p. 39–40. Moneyhon, *Republicanism in Reconstruction Texas*, p. 26 n. 51, states incorrectly that Reynolds stepped out of the Texas political picture when Reconstruction ended. In fact, he made continued (albeit unsuccessful) efforts to seek the senate seat.

26. William T. Field, "The Texas State Police, 1870–1873," *Texas Military History* 5 (1965): 131; Carrier, "Texas during the Reconstruction," pp. 428–30, 443–44.

27. Walter Prescott Webb, *The Texas Rangers: A Century of Frontier Defense* (Austin: University of Texas Press, 1965), p. 221; Nunn, *Texas under the Carpetbaggers*, p. 43. A good survey of the topic is Ann Patton Baenziger, "The Texas State Police during Reconstruction: A Reexamination," *Southwestern Historical Quarterly* 72 (1968–69): 470, 472–73, 476–77, 490–91; See also Field, "Texas State Police," pp. 136–38.

28. Ramsdell, *Reconstruction in Texas*, pp. 301–303; McKay, "Texas under Davis," pp. 120–21; Otis Singletary, "The Texas Militia during Reconstruction," *Southwestern Historical Quarterly* 60 (1956–57): 23–35; Carrier, "Texas during the Reconstruction," pp. 444–47.

29. See Rogers, *Lusty Texans of Dallas*, p. 100; Winfrey, "History of Rusk County," p. 84; *Memorial and Biographical History of Navarro, Henderson, Anderson, Limestone, Freestone, and Leon Counties* (Chicago: Lewis Publishing Co., 1893), pp. 206, 418; Yelderman, "Jaybird Association of Fort Bend," pp. 11–12, Atkinson, "History of Bell County," p. 131.

30. *Brownsville Daily Ranchero*, June 28, 1867.

31. Ibid., March 6, 1868. One of the myths of Reconstruction was that the South would have preferred military rule to readmission in 1868–70; see Dunning, *Civil War and Reconstruction*, p. 187; and Thomas Nelson Page, "The Southern People during Reconstruction," *Atlantic Monthly* 87 (1901): 293. This same fiction existed in Texas. See *Brownsville Daily Ranchero*, September 13, 1867, January 22, 1870; *Texas News* (Bonham), February 27, 1869; Wallace, *Texas in Turmoil*, p. 159. This rumor was merely a Conservative political maneuver to delay Davis's assent to power. The same sentiments had been voiced by Loyalists attempting to delay Throckmorton's takeover in 1866. See Judge John Dix to Pease, July 16, 1866, Pease Papers, APL.

32. James G. Randall, *Constitutional Problems under Lincoln* (Urbana: University of Illinois Press, 1964), pp. 218–19, 223–24, 234–35.

33. Ibid., pp. 234–35; William B. Hesseltine, *Lincoln's Plan of Reconstruction* (Tuscaloosa: University of Alabama Press, 1960); Eric L. McKitrick, *Andrew Johnson and Reconstruction* (Chicago: University of Chicago Press, 1960), pp. 103–108.

34. This general argument is presented in detail in McKitrick, *Andrew Johnson and Reconstruction*, pp. 97–98; and Dunning, *Civil War and Reconstruction*, pp. 102–103. For a contemporary version, see *Brownsville Daily Ranchero*, June 28, 1867. See also Hyman, *More Perfect Union*, pp. 268–70.

35. Sefton, *Army and Reconstruction*, p. 252; Randall, *Constitutional Problems under Lincoln*, pp. 219–21.

36. Sheridan, *Personal Memoirs*, II, 277–78.

37. Bancroft, *North Mexican States and Texas*, II, 488. For a fuller treatment of Southern attitudes, see Michael Perman, *Reunion without Compromise: The South in Reconstruction, 1865–1868* (New York: Cambridge University Press, 1973).

38. See Elliott, *Leathercoat*.

39. Carrier, "Texas during the Reconstruction," pp. 524–25.

40. For the Second Reconstruction, troop deployment, and its problems, see Woodward, "Equality"; Woodward, "Seeds of Failure"; and Robin D. S. Higham, ed., *Bayonets in the Streets: The Use of Troops in Civil Disturbances* (Manhattan, Kans.: Kansas State University Press, 1969).

Index

Harris County, 83, 110, 113
Harrison County, 44, 89
Hart, Hardin, 150–51
Haviland, J. E., 110–11
Hayes, Rutherford, 144
Haynes, John L., 61, 63, 110, 156, 166, 169, 191
Heintzelman, Samuel P., 21, 30, 63, 70–71, 73, 79–80, 137
Hempstead, 16, 19, 135, 151
Herron, Francis, 16
Hidalgo County, 108
Hoar, E. Rockwood, 172
Holt, J. J., 101, 110, 112, 115
Houston, Sam, 5, 21
Houston, Tex., 16, 18, 22, 27, 83, 99, 100, 135, 148–49, 151
Houston *Telegraph*, 151
Howard, Oliver Otis, 33, 35, 38, 40
Hunt County, 151
Huntsville, 59, 84

Indianola, 16, 17, 91, 187, 189
Indians: volunteers against, 69, 70, 74
Indian Territory (Oklahoma), 71, 107, 146
Ireland, John, 112
ironclad oath, 99, 100, 160, 186
Intolerable Acts, 4

Jacksboro, 67, 71
jails, 164
Jefferson, 27, 32, 101, 143, 164, 177–78, 179
Johnson, Andrew, 20, 31, 39, 49, 57, 66, 69, 72, 86, 99, 106, 113–14, 136, 137; appointments by, 126, 155–56; and 1866 state election, 51; ends rebellion in Texas, 47; and military authority, 47; removal of Reynolds by, 155
Johnston, Albert Sidney, 85
Jones, G. W., 95
Juárez, Benito, 24
juaristas, 24, 30
"Juneteenth," 14–16
jury order, 99–101

Kiddoo, Joseph Barr, 40–45, 58, 86–87
Kirby-Smith, Edmund, 4, 6, 7, 13, 18, 23
Ku Klux Klan: attacks by, on blacks, 32, 34, 37, 38, 43, 58–59, 81, 143–45, 165, 177–78; secret societies of, 34, 143–44; as self-defense units, 35

La Grange, 35, 111
Lamar County, 43
Lavaca County, 111
law and order. *See* crime and violence
Layton, C. R., 161
Lee, Bob, 145–47, 245
Liberty, 16, 91, 110
Lincoln, Abraham, 21
Lindley murder, 64
Lindsay, Livingston, 140
Lockhart, 99
Logawell incident, 90
Longworth, William, 58
Loughery, R. W., 178, 252
Love, James, 124
Loyalists. *See* Unionists
Lubbock, Francis R., 5

Mabry, H. P., 112
McCormick, A. P., 140, 169
McGray, D. L., 64–65
McLennan County, 89–90, 152, 227
McNeill, J. C., 144
Magruder, John Bankhead, 6, 7
Manning, A. T., 90
Marin, James, 133
Marshall, 5, 16, 18, 27, 89
Matagorda County, 13, 58, 111, 144
Maximilian I, 12, 17–18, 73
Merritt, Wesley, 18–19, 28
Milam County, 184
military government: Confederate, 3–8; Federal, 188, 192, 194–95, 216, 258
military misconduct, 29, 57–59, 63–66, 72, 80–81, 133–35, 180–81; Brenham fire, 64–65, 72–73; Lindley murder, 64; Walker murder, 63–64
military ranks, Civil War, xii
military trials of civilians, 44–45, 86, 101–102, 127, 131–32, 177–78
Millican, 16, 27, 151

The Army in Texas During Reconstruction was composed into type on a Linotron 202 phototypesetter in eleven point Goudy Old Style with one point of spacing between the lines. Goudy Old Style was also selected for display. The book was designed by Jim Billingsley, composed by G&S Typesetters, Inc., printed offset by Thomson-Shore Inc., and bound by John H. Dekker & Sons, Inc. The paper on which this book is printed bears acid-free characteristics, for an effective life of at least three hundred years.

TEXAS A&M UNIVERSITY PRESS : COLLEGE STATION